Impossible Jobs
in Public Management

STUDIES IN GOVERNMENT
AND PUBLIC POLICY

Impossible Jobs
in Public Management

Edited by
Erwin C. Hargrove and
John C. Glidewell

University Press of Kansas

© 1990 by the University Press of Kansas

Published by the University Press of Kansas (Lawrence, Kansas 66045), which was organized by the Kansas Board of Regents and is operated and funded by Emporia State University, Fort Hays State University, Kansas State University, Pittsburg State University, the University of Kansas, and Wichita State University

Library of Congress Cataloging-in-Publication Data

Impossible jobs in public management / edited by Erwin C. Hargrove and
John C. Glidewell.
    p. cm.
    Includes index.
    ISBN 0-7006-0427-8 (alk. paper) — ISBN 0-7006-0428-6 (pbk. : alk. paper)
    1. Government executives—Job stress.   2. Public officers—Job
stress.   I. Hargrove, Erwin C. II.Glidewell, John C.
JF 1655.I46   1990
350.007′4—dc20   90-36069
                                                                    CIP

British Library Cataloguing in Publication Data is available.

Printed in the United States of America
10   9   8   7   6   5   4   3   2   1

The paper used in this publication meets the minimum requirements of the American National Standard for Permanence of Paper for Printed Library Materials Z39.48–1984.

Contents

Tables

Preface

This book began with the idea that some tasks in public management were so difficult that they could be called "impossible jobs." It was literally impossible to achieve any of the manifest objectives of the ascribed mission. These jobs were conceived as a class apart from other public management positions. And yet, paradoxically, we thought it possible that these jobs could be performed in more or less effective ways while still falling short of manifest objectives. Perhaps there were coping strategies that would mitigate impossibility.

We were not sure whether we had set a semantic trap for ourselves. Arthur Singer, of the Sloan Foundation, was willing to help us find out, and we were able to interest six scholars who became intrigued with our paradox. It took two meetings of editors and authors and two drafts of the manuscript before we felt ourselves to be on solid conceptual ground. This was very much a dialogue between editors and authors as a collegial group.

We would like to thank Art Singer, who made the adventure possible. Donald Kettl read a first draft to our benefit. Richard Elmore was the perceptive reader of the second draft after Kettl became our Vanderbilt colleague. The Vanderbilt Institute for Public Policy Studies organized the authors' meetings and prepared the manuscript for publication. We would like to thank Clifford Russell, the director of VIPPS, and Lottie Strupp and Claudia McCauley, of the staff. Betty McKee and Melissa Wocher, of the Political Science Department, were helpful in many ways. Finally, we thank the staff of the University Press of Kansas.

Vanderbilt University   *Erwin C. Hargrove*
January 1990   *John C. Glidewell*

PART ONE
IMPOSSIBLE JOBS
IN GENERAL

*John C. Glidewell and
Erwin C. Hargrove*

1

Dimensions of Impossibility

All jobs vary along several dimensions of difficulty, but some jobs fall at the difficult extreme of so many dimensions that they can legitimately be called "impossible." For example, an experienced and knowledgeable commissioner of corrections undertakes both to incarcerate and to rehabilitate a group of convicted criminals, most of whom have long histories of incorrigible behavior. This formidable task is complicated by a militant public conflict. On one side, the commissioner finds strong support for his or her relaxed restrictions and rehabilitation program from a popular prisoners'-rights group demanding absolutely minimum restriction and extensive rehabilitation. On the other side, he or she finds equally strong resistance to those programs from a popular "law-and-order" group demanding Spartan prison security and punishment that will long remain in the prisoner's memory. These strong pressures are reinforced by similarly strident disagreements among members of the legislature. Previous experience with these conflicts assures the commissioner that public opinion will generally take a hard-line in favor of security and punishment.

Even so, at times, public concerns focus on hope. Citizens hope for relief from the cost of building new prisons, for reform of degrading prisons that succeed only in making inmates into more efficient criminals, and for rehabilitation to keep discharged prisoners from returning to crime and to prison. Such hopes may make it barely possible to introduce more effective sentencing laws and more promising rehabilitation programs. The commissioner learns to steer among these shoals without crashing on the rocks, but the mental chart she or he follows is more intuitive than reasoned and therefore not easily transmitted to lieutenants or successors.

One may discover many such dilemmas in this book. A welfare commissioner undertakes to induce the poor to work but finds that they are sadly deficient in even the limited skills required. A plan to allow pay for such work in order to reduce the level of welfare payments is effectively blocked, first by the legislature because of its concern that the commissioner may be wasting tax money on lazy and intractable welfare clients, and second by recalcitrant clients who discover that the wages they can command are less than their welfare entitlement, a strong disincentive to work. A courageous commissioner of public health appears on television to advocate the use of condoms to prevent AIDS and returns to his or her office to be confronted by an alliance of outraged Catholic priests and bishops. A psychiatrist in charge of a state mental health department struggles to avoid making patients passively dependent on the hospital at the same time that he or she negotiates with community groups who loudly oppose the location of halfway houses in their neighborhoods. A special master finds that it is easier to get the judge to set general standards for equity than it is to get agreement between prisoner and warden about the demonstration of equity in daily prison operations. Oil is poured on the fire by the finance committee of the legislature when it refuses to appropriate the funds required to implement even an interim agreement.

These few examples do not begin to illustrate the fullness of the dilemmas that people in such jobs must face every day. Are such dilemma-ridden jobs a class apart? Or are they typical of most, if not all, of public administration? We contend that the frequency, severity, and duration of such dilemmas vary from job to job along several dimensions of difficulty, but that some jobs are performed under so many extremely difficult conditions that they can legitimately be called "impossible."

In the following section we will specify four dimensions of difficulty and the extremes that we call "impossible." We will then explain the antecedents and consequences of the impossible poles of the four dimensions, and we will call attention to the manifestations of impossibility described in this book. Subsequently we will specify how incumbents may cope with their impossible jobs quite ingeniously and imaginatively and again point to the coping detailed in later chapters.

We will often use the term *commissioner* to identify the incumbents of the jobs we will discuss. This all-purpose title refers to the administrative director of a complex bureaucratic system, a department of either state government or city government, such as a police department. These are positions of considerable autonomy in which the incumbent has the latitude to define missions and methods despite strong political and organizational constraints. For each job, we analyze an institutional role and the resources and constraints present in that role for most incumbents.

In Part Two, the authors first set out the history of the institutional strengths and weaknesses of each role, specify the extremes of difficulty that make the job impossible, and then compare the skills and strategies that particular incumbents have brought to the role. Such a dual analysis enables us to generalize about the degree to which effective performance in a role depends on personal skill or institutionalized capacities—or about the fit between the two.

AN OVERVIEW OF THE DIMENSIONS OF DIFFICULTY

Jobs falling at the extreme end of several dimensions can legitimately be called "impossible." That is true, we maintain, because logically the difficulties are too extreme, and empirically the incumbents have uniformly been unable to perform the job to the constituents' or to their own satisfaction.

We shall specify four dimensions:

1. Legitimacy of the commissioner's clientele
2. Intensity of the conflict among the constituencies
3. Public confidence in the authority of the commissioner's profession
4. Strength of the agency myth

The Legitimacy of Clients

This dimension embraces two issues, the first of which is client responsibility. At the possible end of this dimension, the commissioner serves responsible, proso-cial, and diligent clients, such as veterans, farmers, protectors of the environment, or children. The commissioner must compete with other commissioners for public resources, but the competition is legitimate and institutionalized. Many conflict management techniques are available, such as forming flexible coalitions that change as issues change, taking turns at "winning," increasing the variety of the actions available, and expanding the pool of public resources.

The impossible pole of the dimension applies to commissioners who serve people who become clients because they are irresponsible, strange, lazy, or antisocial—such as criminals, potentially dangerous schizophrenics, welfare de-pendents, and drug users-pushers, all of whose claims on public resources are suspect. Such a commissioner will lose whether he or she serves the clientele well and demands many public resources or whether he or she does not serve the clientele well or returns them unreformed to society.

Between the two poles are commissioners whose clientele stimulates ambiva-lence in the public. For example, the working poor may or may not be malinger-ers; first-time offenders may or may not be deserving of help; AIDS victims may or may not be morally reprehensible; inner-city school children may or may not be educable.

A further issue is client tractability. At the easy end of the scale, tractable clients are responsive and therefore legitimate. Public administration clients usually respond to commission services: Social security eligibility is readily determined and checks are distributed; employers are capable of complying with commission regulations, even if they choose not to; veterans adapt to the demands of the commission; most middle-class mothers have their children immunized. At the midpoint, there are commissions with hard but manageable problems, such as the schooling of inner-city children, the immunization of infants in poor families, and the regulation of industrial wastes. At the difficult extreme, intractable clients are not responsive and therefore not legitimate. The clients of such commissioners have already been characterized as intractable: chronically unsocialized, antisocial, dependent, or crazy. These include habitual criminals who are not rehabilitated but return to crime; people on welfare who do not overcome their chronic dependency and indeed enjoy rewards for dependency; deep-seated schizophrenias that are not cured and deteriorate further. When the intractability of the condition of the clients is added to public perceptions of their irresponsibility, their illegitimacy becomes more nearly conclusive and the job of serving them more nearly impossible.

Intensity of Conflict among Constituencies

Commissioners cope with at least five kinds of constituencies: (1) political masters, such as governors and legislatures; (2) advocates for client groups; (3) opponents of client groups; (4) the agency bureaucracy; and (5) the client or regulated group central to the agency's mission. The simple fact of multiple constituencies does not make the job impossible, but the greater the number, the greater the likelihood that some constituencies will become antagonistic toward one another, the commissioner, or both. At the pole of impossible jobs, the conflict is intense; at the pole of possible jobs, the conflict is quite mild, often taking the form of legitimate competition with or among coalitions that regularly realign themselves as issues and political climates change.

When combined with client legitimacy, intensity of conflict does identify several forms of impossible jobs. First there is the "no-lose" position of those commissioners who serve a legitimate clientele (such as veterans) with general public-interest constituencies, who are involved in mild conflicts about the allocation of public funds. Next there are those who serve legitimate clients (such as middle-class school children) with multiple special-interest constituencies (such as parents, churches, employers, and teachers' unions), all in mild conflict and often allied in frequently changing coalitions. The job can be done well as long as the conflict is mild and the commissioner forms, supports, or joins strategically powerful coalitions. In a balance of power, the commissioner either remains aloof or tips the balance in accord with current commission policy. Finally, there are commissioners serving illegitimate clients (such as chronic welfare dependents) with multiple constituencies (such as human resource advocates, taxpayers, legislatures, and prospective low-wage employers), all in intensely polarized conflict about the most effective means of mitigating the dependency on public funds. Even though a combination of factors makes a commissioner's job impossible, other forces can make it worse.

When the conflict among constituencies is moralistic or ideological, beliefs and values, more than interests, are at stake. The conflicts are intensified and adversaries polarized, as the pro-life and pro-abortion constituencies have become. Any action by the commissioner antagonizes one side or the other, while no action antagonizes everyone. The commissioner's vulnerability is produced by his or her most conflict-ridden constituencies and least legitimate clients. Table 1.1 classifies examples of serving-regulating agencies by the two dimensions and illustrates the association between illegitimate clients, conflicting constituencies, and impossible jobs.

Respect for Professional Authority

The third dimension is the public respect for the authority of the commissioner's profession. At one extreme are the agencies linked to the solid authority of scientifically based professions such as medicine and engineering. At the opposite end are professions, such as education, social service, mental health, corrections, and police, that are less respected and hence more impossible. Thus, commissioners are arrayed along the dimension by the degree of public respect for their professional authority. Fully respected professional authority sometimes mitigates the public doubts raised by the questionable legitimacy and tractability of the clients; less than fully respected professional authority intensifies the public doubts about legitimacy and tractability—and increases the impossibility of the commissioner's job.

Strength of the Agency Myth

Along this fourth dimension, the possible pole is the condition in which strong and stable myths define altruistic, impossible goals. The goals are maintained as reassuring and sustaining guides, but no one expects actual attainment and anyone who demanded it would have little public support. Commissioners at this pole

Table 1.1 Examples of Agencies Classified by the First Two Dimensions

	Legitimacy High	Legitimacy Mixed	Legitimacy Low
	(Possible)	(Possible)	(Impossible)
Intense Conflict (Polarized)	Null	Null	Welfare Corrections Police Mental health Special master
	(Possible)	(Possible)	(Difficult)
Mild Conflict	Public schools Environmental protection	Unemployment insurance Medicaid	Null
	(Possible)	(Possible)	(Possible)
Low Conflict	Veterans admin. Hospitals Medicare	Null	Null

have goals that are such altruistic public goods that all constituencies fully understand actual attainment is not expected. Public education, for example, is universal and compulsory, but "everybody" understands that there will be chronic truants whose parents doubt the value of attending school. Health officers are committed to humane and continuing nursing-home care for indigent, chronically ill, or aging people, but "everybody" understands that the resources required, both material and human, are scarce and very hard to marshal.

The impossible, opposite pole of the fourth dimension is the condition in which the agency myth is weak, unstable, and controversial. We contend that commissioners with impossible jobs are sustained by myths that shift in the public mind from guiding ideals well worth pursuing to convenient fabrications to cover operational failures. When the myths command no sustained commitment to an ideal worth pursuing, the shift from idealism to cynicism is easily stimulated by either ineffectiveness of the commission's actions (however diligent) or a single unexpected discrediting event. The affective intensity of the experienced disillusion feeds the conflicts among constituencies, especially conflicts between the moral idealism of some constituencies and the worldly pragmatism of others. Commissioners are quite vulnerable to the shifts in power from idealistic constituencies to pragmatic ones, vulnerable in that they are easily sacrificed by elected politicians, who prudently seek to avoid the fervor directed at the commissioner by either idealists or pragmatists.

SUMMARY

Using these four dimensions the jobs of commissioners can be differentiated. The possible jobs are those with one legitimate clientele and with few constituencies in only mild conflict, those enjoying great public respect for professional or scientific authority, and those guided by strong, well-understood myths that sustain policy continuity and feasible goals. In contrast, commissioners holding impossible jobs must serve irresponsible and intractable clients in intense conflicts with more legitimate clients for public resources; must satisfy multiple and intensely polarized, active constituencies; possess professional, scientific authority that commands little public respect; and are guided by weak, controversial myths that cannot sustain policy continuity, so that the commissioner is vulnerable to swings of public opinion and to political scapegoating.

Table 1.2 classifies a number of jobs and clients along the four critical dimensions of difficulty that differentiate possible from impossible jobs. The core position is that impossible jobs have illegitimate clients and multiple, intensely conflicting constituencies; enjoy little public confidence in the professional expertise available; and are guided by weak myths that do not sustain policy continuity. The following chapters use theories and empirical findings from political science and social psychology to help explain how these conditions develop and how the consequences of that development contribute to the impossibility of the job.

Table 1.2 Possible and Impossible Jobs

	High	*Medium*	*Low*
		Clients	
Legitimacy of clients	Veterans Farmers Environment Business customers Middle-class school children Federal courts Harmless mentally ill Mature pregnant women	Low-income workers AIDS victims	Truants Welfare dependents* Criminals* Prisoners* Inner-city school children* Chronically mentally ill* Pregnant teenagers*
		Commissioners	
Intensity of conflict among the commissioner's constituencies	Public health commissioners Welfare commissioners* Corrections commissioners* Inner-city school superintendents* Mental health commissioners* Special masters*	Environment control agents Suburban school superintentents	Business managers Veterans administrators Agricultural agents Maternal and child health officers
Public confidence in professional authority	Medical officers Agricultural agents Special masters* Maternal and child health officers Environment agents	Business managers Truant officers	School superintendents Mental health commissioners* Police commisioners* Welfare commissioners*
		Agency	
Strength of agency myth	Agricultural agents Business managers Maternal and child health officers Special masters* Truant officers Veterans administrators	Environmental protection agencies	Mental health commissioners* Welfare commissioners* Corrections commissioners* Police commissioners* School superintendents

*Designates impossible jobs

2

An Analysis of Impossible Jobs

Having described the spectrum of possibility-impossibility along which all jobs vary, we turn now to analyze the characteristics of impossible jobs. We will give special attention to the antecedents and consequences of the impossible end of each dimension, taking the last dimension first because its antecedents involve some concepts whose early definition will facilitate the entire analysis.

THE STRENGTH OF THE AGENCY MYTH

The basic issue is the degree of strength and stability of the myth that guides the actions of the commissioner. Popular myths of the viability of altruistic goals serve important functions in guiding the directions of the commissioner's programs and in sustaining the public faith that the commission is moving in the right direction, even when it cannot move very far. The envisioned public goods that form the goals of many commissions are such guiding myths. Hence the concept of public goods is one key to understanding impossible jobs.

P. A. Samuelson defined public goods as those that "are enjoyed in common in the sense that each individual's consumption of a good leads to no subtraction of any other individual's consumption of that good."[1] Public goods must be equally available to everyone. For our purposes, public goods include such widely shared resources as a noninfectious and safe environment, the education of self-reliant citizens, the protection of civil rights by the courts, the security of prisons, the rehabilitation of criminals, and the achievement of self-sufficiency by the poor and disabled—all of which enhance the lives of all citizens. Public goods are distinct from private goods in that private goods are restricted in their distribution to those who have a right to them. Such rights derive from investments in the development of the goods, the purchase of them, or the intensity of needs, as in emergency surgery. In this study, money, jobs, property, medical treatment, information, and recognition are examples of private goods, as distinct from public ones.

Commissioners distribute private as well as public goods. In a very influential work, Mancur Olson argued that public goods are inadequate for marshaling support for collective actions.[2] Olson maintained that because public goods are equally available to all without regard to contribution, the individual would maximize his or her benefits by withholding support from the collectivity, that is, by freeloading. Thus, when all tried to maximize their individual benefits, no collective action could be taken. In order to be viable, such a commission as we are studying must, in Olson's view, provide some private benefits to supplement the disincentives of public goods.

A number of scholars have subjected Olson's theory to empirical test.[3] Generally, their findings oppose Olson. They found that the distribution of private goods is not essential to the viability of collective action and that a commitment to the provision of public goods is commonly necessary for individual support of a collective action as a legitimate effort in the public interest. Private goods may also be supplied as egoistic incentives to support the collective action. Accordingly, commissioners work to provide public goods in order to establish the legitimacy of the prime public mission. Simultaneously, they work to provide private goods as incentives to cooperation.

One of the commissioner's guides to effective public service is the myth that the commissioner makes public goods equally available to all. There is always a gap between the myth and reality, but that gap is trivial if the myth is strong and very important if the myth is weak.

A strong myth develops when the public good is equally accessible but access requires some effort, as in universal public education, a healthful environment, or a stable food supply. A strong myth also develops when the recipients of public goods are responsible and tractable, especially when they are persons who have already exerted great efforts or been subject to great risks in the public interest, such as veterans subject to the perils of combat or farmers facing droughts and floods.

Because efforts at self-help, sometimes extraordinary efforts, are demanded as the equity invested for the benefits received, the public perceives that both the self-help ethic and the equity norm of justice are being realized. As a result, the myth is consensual and stable rather than controversial and unstable. The inevitable gap between myth and reality is blamed on lack of client effort and not the negligence or incompetence of the commissioner. Therefore, a strong myth sustains policy continuity.

A weak myth develops when the public good is accessible with little or no individual effort and indeed is sometimes "delivered" by outreach to those who make no effort at all, as in welfare and preventive public health. A weak myth also develops when the recipients are irresponsible and intractable and have exerted no special efforts or made any sacrifices in the public interest. Thus both the self-help ethic and the equity norm of justice are violated. The myth and consequently the efforts of the commissioner are controversial, unstable, and subject to sudden swings of public opinion. The inevitable gap between the myth and reality is attributed to both the ill-advised actions of the commissioner and the irresponsible lack of effort by the recipients. The myth does not sustain policy continuity. Weak myths do stir the public's hope, but the hope wavers and shifts to despair very quickly.

The public goods ostensibly provided in possible jobs are generally perceived to create widely shared benefits. The politics and policy of scientific research, national defense, public works, and public education are "distributive" rather than "redistributive." Of course, resources are still preferentially allocated in distributive policy and possible jobs, but the common perception is that all benefit. On the other hand, the public goods ostensibly provided in impossible jobs are commonly regarded as redistributive, i.e., robbing Peter to pay Paul. Redistributive politics and policy are much more controversial in the American polity than are distributive. And redistributive programs are more difficult to administer either because the eligibility to receive benefits is subject to very complicated and arbitrary means tests or because the clients are segregated as unworthy by some other judgments.

Commissioners also distribute egoistic private goods to those who have a right to them because they earned the goods by contributions to the commission. Such goods provide incentives for staff, suppliers, and citizens to contribute to the work of the commission and are important supplements to the legitimating public goods.

In summary, commissioners in impossible jobs find themselves guided by weak myths that they are contributing to the very long-term development of such idealistic public goods as a healthy, self-sufficient, responsible citizenry. They also find themselves faced with the fact that, as a short-term means to that end, they are administering a law that takes private goods from some responsible citizens and redistributes them to some free-loaders. As public attention shifts from the long-term ideals to the short-term redistribution and back again, the commissioner becomes vulnerable to sacrifice on the altar of a public disillusion not created by him or her.[4]

THE LEGITIMACY OF CLIENTS

The legitimacy of clients depends upon their responsibility and tractability, both in fact and as perceived by the commissioner's constituencies. Such social perceptions have their roots in the inferences of citizens as to the causes of the clients' plight. Consider first the roots of perceived irresponsibility.

The Irresponsibility of Clients

Throughout this study, a strong theme is vividly manifested in the impossible jobs: the tension between dependence and independence in client groups. It is very difficult for many members of the client population to make the transition from dependence to independence, a matter closely related to the state's perennial lack of sufficient funds to implement programs effective in accomplishing the transition from dependence to independence. Further, the public is angered by client populations who are persistently unwilling to help themselves or to respond to the helping attempts of others. Attribution theory, sketched in the following paragraphs, provides a convincing portrait of the antecedents of this theme.

Current explanations of the findings of such students of social cognition as Susan Fiske maintain that all members of a society fit the social roles of the society to commonplace cognitive models.[5] Like all cognitive models, the boundaries are not sharp, and the linkages of the components range from strong to weak.[6] Each cognitive model, however, often has a central prototype that is surrounded by more or less similar variations. Social psychologists have discovered the importance of the attribution of causes of behavior in the cognitive models of the plight of people.[7] The distinction between the attribution to causes *internal* to the person and causes *external* to the person has been especially important. Such causal attributions have been shown to precede and underlie feelings of pity, anger and guilt.[8] Another analysis holds that two of the components of the commonplace cognitive model are, first, the attribution to internal or external causes of the clients' problems and, second, the assignment of internal or external responsibility for solving or managing those problems.[9]

To the public, then, some clients did not cause their problems and cannot solve or manage them without help from the society. Examples include farmers in flood or drought, the genetically handicapped, victims of epidemics, veterans of wars, especially traumatized veterans, and people who have been clearly unjustly oppressed or neglected in the past. The causes stem primarily from the environment, and in the eyes of the public, the responsibility for remediation is primarily the society's. Such clients are seen as legitimately in need of help, and the use of public funds to help them is popular. Commissioners charged with serving such clients find their jobs very possible.

Some clients are close to the foregoing prototype but may not always fit it. They may or may not have caused their own problems, and they may or may not be able to solve or manage them without help from the society. Families dependent on welfare, AIDS victims, truants, habitual criminals, alcoholics, the harmless mentally ill—all these are examples of clients in this ambiguous category. Their legitimacy as public charges is sometimes in doubt to the public, and because of that doubt, the use of public funds to help them is acceptable when money is plentiful and unacceptable when money is scarce. Commissioners who serve such clients find their jobs quite possible in good times and in periods of reform; quite impossible in bad times and periods of stabilization.

Apart from the question of whether the locus of an attributed cause is perceived as internal or external, B. A. Weiner has considered the stability and controllability of the attributed cause and found them to be powerful additional components of the commonplace cognitive model of a client's plight.[10] In his experiments on pity, anger, and guilt, he showed that uncontrollable causes of negative events gave rise to pity, whether the cause was in the self or in others. On the other hand, the causes of some troubles were indeed internal but also stable and controllable. Those gave rise to anger. Problems caused by laziness, lying, impulsiveness, and persistent dependency in spite of ability—all causes perceived to be clearly internal, stable, and controllable but not controlled—are fitted to a model of moral irresponsibility and seen as illegitimate. Persistence over time and situation in spite of social pressures to change has been shown to be a very important basis for attributing behavior to stable, internal causes. Clients of commissioners in impossible jobs often become clients because their problems persist over time and situation despite social pressures to change. The use of public funds to solve or manage such problems is very unpopular.

Not only do the commissioners face the social-psychological attribution of internal, stable, controllable-but-not-controlled causes of the plights of the irresponsible, they also face a special political-economic conflict. The commission must follow redistributive policies, yet American society has a profound and painful ambivalence about programs that redistribute resources from one group to another. The redistribution may be politically mandated, because the transfer appears to benefit all—as in public works, research and development, or protective tariffs. But the redistribution is unacceptable when commissions reach down the social ladder to help those who are perceived as persistently bringing on their own problems and persistently failing to responsibly develop the resources they do receive. The American self-help ethic is affronted. Welfare policies of all kinds are often seen as burdens on the community, thus the programs are underfunded, unpopular, and exceedingly difficult to administer.[11]

The Tractability of Clients

Attribution theory also applies to the intractability of clients. Irresponsibility was the label given to attributions to internal, stable, controllable causes of the conditions of the clients, especially when the attribution was clearly accurate. The issue of controllability is critical here. When a client *could* control impulsiveness, criminal acts, or promiscuity but does not, the client is irresponsible. But what if a cause is in fact internal, stable, but *not controllable*? Is there any hope for change?

A brain injury may be internal, permanent, and uncontrollable, but sometimes people with brain injuries can regain control of their muscles and their actions. A schizophrenic may have an internal, permanent, uncontrollable propensity to the illness, but sometimes chronic schizophrenics can gain sufficient control of themselves to maintain group homes in which they live quite independently and productively. Criminals may have internalized a very perverse socialization to their criminality that cannot be excised, and their crimes may thus have internal, stable, uncontrollable causes. But sometimes perversely socialized criminals can be rehabilitated. Welfare dependents may sometimes be unable to imagine a self-sufficient way of life, but some can be trained to become independent and to take great pride in their self-sufficiency.

In the cognitive models of one another that people carry in their minds, even strong evidence of intractable human nature is tempered by hope. Commissioners who are charged with the realization of that hope despite evidence of patent intractability live in a fragile professional existence. They try to change people who have been referred to them because the people have uniformly resisted all prior attempts to change them. They must keep some hope of reformation alive in the face of frequent frustration. As Gary Miller and Ira Iscoe point out in Chapter 6, on the mental health commissioner, the reinforcement of the hope is intermittent. A few successes appear—not regularly or predictably, but they do appear. As psychologists know well, such intermittent reinforcement eventually establishes a behavior that is hard to extinguish once it takes hold. "Commissioners of the intractable" experience these intermittent successes and so persist in attempting to change the intractable. Most important, however, once the pattern is established, the commissioner will continue in the face of failures for a very long time.

This dedication, this persistent effort, bolsters the public *hope* that the intractable can be changed, that learning never stops, that no person is completely and forever intractable. That hope must be kept alive despite the sober reality that many criminals are unable to give up a life of crime; that many welfare dependents cannot even imagine self-sufficiency and ridicule any honest effort as foolish and naive; and that some schizophrenics are unable to stop acting crazy. While attributing patently uncontrollable, internal, permanent causes to the plight of such clients, the public also keeps alive a very human hope of tractability. The hope backs and fills, but it does not die.

That hope, however, is frustrated by another social force. Processes as well as clients can be intractable. In Fritz Byers's words, "Litigation over prison conditions is almost by definition intractable" (Chapter 9). Further, Laurence Lynn, Jr., in his chapter on welfare, argues that the community and the welfare client are engaged in a kind of "prisoner's dilemma." Both community and client would be better off if the community ensured ready access to benefits and the clients represented their eligibility honestly. The dilemma lies in the fact that deceit by the client yields greater returns to the client. For the community, demanding rigorous proof of eligibility is necessary to avoid fraudulent claims, but that rigor makes benefits less accessible. The community, then, believes it must make access very difficult, and the client believes he or she must make dishonest claims. Both lose.

Commissioners charged with serving such clients often find themselves constrained to custodial or other kinds of dependency-maintaining care. Moreover, they are often vulnerable to charges that the custodial care itself is intractable because it trains the clients to be less self-sufficient, more irresponsible, and increasingly an illegitimate burden to society. Indeed, the custody may reinforce the belief in internal, stable, uncontrollable causes, controllable by neither the client nor the commissioner's custody. The commissioners are vulnerable to sanction if they serve their clients conscientiously and thereby take limited public funds from more deserving clients; they are equally vulnerable if they serve their clients poorly and make them more burdensome to society than before.

On a broader scale, American society is in an intractable double-bind about commissions that serve these clients. Because the possibility of eliminating or mitigating the problems seems so remote and unlikely, citizens are reluctant to spend or be taxed for great sums of money to put toward such service. Yet the concerned and involved citizens rail at inadequate custodial programs that seem to encourage the clients to persist in what is regarded as irresponsible behavior. Schemes of reform are almost always afoot, but in due time, they run into the stone wall of public skepticism about the possibility of making any improvement.

In summary, clients whose plight is perceived to be caused by their own internal, stable flaws, controllable but not controlled, are fitted to a cognitive model of irresponsible, overdependent people, to whom redistribution of society's resources is a wasteful burden to responsible citizens. Commissioners who serve such clients are damned if they serve their clients well and waste society's resources and damned if they serve their clients poorly and return them to society more irresponsible than they were before they were "served." If the cause of the clients' plight is attributed to internal, stable, uncontrollable causes, the clients are intractable. The existence of hope provides a guiding, altruistic goal and sustains the constituencies over long periods of frustration. The job becomes impossible when intractable clients are served by intractable processes, maintained by intermittent successes but doomed to failure in the long run.

INTENSITY OF CONFLICT AMONG CONSTITUENCIES

Constituencies, in this analysis, are groups of people who patronize and support the commission and act as advocates for it before the government. They have some stake in the way in which the commissioner goes about providing services to clients. Constituencies also include bodies that are involved in or served by the commission—sometimes even clients when they become their own advocates, which causes confusion between clients and constituents. Some client groups are latent and even reluctant constituencies, preferring to handle their own problems or avoiding the stigma of public identification, as Edward Lawlor points out in his examination of the AIDS controversy. Constituencies often include providers who serve or supply client groups. Two very salient constituencies are organized advocates for clients or for the general mission of the commissioner's organization, and opponents of the client advocacy groups. Public officials who authorize, oversee, and appropriate funds for the commission are almost always a powerful, albeit often indifferent, constituency that also responds to its own constituencies. A commissioner's employees in the bureaucracy beneath him or her are certainly a constituency that makes demands on the commissioner and requires persuasion and other inducements to comply with policy as set by the commissioner and public officials. Perhaps most deceptive is the case of the special master, whose dominant constituent seems manifestly single: the federal judge who appointed him or her. Yet, as Byers shows compellingly in Chapter 9, hidden constituencies (often themselves subdivided) exercise exceedingly strong influence on the actions of the special master.

The fortunate welfare commissioner may have only a single dominant constituency of public officials who act in concert as advocates for the clients of the welfare commissioner. However, such elected advocates are almost always opposed by another group of elected officials. When a community develops an organization of welfare advocates, whether composed of the clients or their friends, another constituency is formed that must be addressed. For instance, the mental health commissioner does not typically have a single dominant constituency of the families of the mentally ill. Rather, the variety of interests involved may cause constituencies to proliferate: The community may develop an organization of advocates for the mentally ill, or the families of the mentally ill may come into conflict with another community group, such as one seeking a site for a halfway house.

Advocacy groups often ally themselves with public officials. Whenever they take an interest in a commission, elected public officials are always a very powerful constituency. When advocacy organizations are also strong, a dynamic triad develops. The advocates address the commissioner as long as he or she responds to their satisfaction; when they are not satisfied, they turn to the public officials to whom the commissioner is responsible. The commissioner can form a coalition either with the advocacy group in order to influence (or oppose) the public officials or with the public officials in order to influence (or oppose) the advocacy group. The commissioner is acutely vulnerable to the joint demands of a coalition of the advocacy group and the public officials. One function of multiple constituencies is to provide the commissioner with a variety of options in forming coalitions, but this also exposes the commissioner to control (and opposition) by coalitions of constituencies.

The personnel of the commission, acting in concert as a constituency, add yet another factor. The interests of the employees in their employment gives them common cause with the clients, but in other respects, the two groups may conflict. For example, the staff's concern with controlling the clients puts them at odds with the clients' interests in minimum restriction.

In contrast to government authority in most other democracies, constituencies in American public administration are strong while the authority of the commissioner is weak. This characteristic of the American polity is the result of the constant counterforce of the checks and balances in the structure of government; of opposing political parties who can neither easily unify government structure nor mobilize the public against interest groups; of the strong ambivalence in American political culture about the powers of bureaucracy and about leadership. That ambivalence induces the citizens to demand decisive actions by their leaders to solve their social-political problems—but only in the desired direction and not at the sacrifice of individual privacy or freedom.

As a result, when constituencies are multiple, public executives often find themselves entangled in a web of no-win contests. Any action will be too little for some people and too much for others. The very structure of the situation is against the public executive. Bargaining may eliminate conflicts in the short run, but long-term resolution requires that the relationships must somehow be recast in order to overcome the deadlock of the no-win situation.

The genesis of such conflicts among constituencies is interdependent with focal concerns. In this context, the concept of "focal concern," as defined by John Glidewell, means the focus of the concerns of a particular constituency about the plight of the clients of the commissioner.[12] The development of a focal concern begins with the communication of individual hopes and fears, often stimulated by a dramatic, visible incident. A murder committed by a prisoner on furlough always concentrates attention on crowded prisons and on the furlough policies of the corrections commissioner. The calculation of prospective costs and benefits of applying the commissioner's furlough policy to a group that included both re-cidivistic and law-abiding furloughed prisoners could show a balance in favor of benefits. Such a calculation, however, simply does not defuse the strong, popular emotions surrounding the murder committed by one prisoner while on furlough. Research has shown that a protest of a policy under such conditions is most often prompted by the recalled outcomes of vividly remembered events rather than by a careful consideration of all the possible outcomes of all the possible actions.[13] Moreover, given the current state of knowledge, the costs and benefits are only partly measurable and the probabilities of the outcomes of the choice between occasional furlough and sustained imprisonment are imprecise. The calculation would not satisfy even the most coldly dispassionate statistician.

The uncertainty of outcomes leads people to try to reduce the ambiguity of the real world by seeking some confirmation from others, which provides the reassurance of shared views. Opinions are usually sought from those most proximate, most visible, most respected, and on whom the person is most dependent. As shared concerns accumulate, their joint articulation becomes more focused, and as this happens, people find one concern more vivid, more salient, and more fixed in their mind. The collectivity and its individual members mutually influence one another in accelerating one focus on one overriding concern, usually for short periods of time. As several constituencies develop their own focal concerns, the sheer multiplicity increases the likelihood of conflict. Underlying the probable conflicts is the scarcity of resources. Focal concerns define missions, but the accomplishment of the missions means competition for scarce resources from the environment—in the case of commissioners, primarily from the polity.

Focal concerns and conflicts about them develop and change in cycles, partly because of the impact of vivid events in recent memory. John DiIulio, Jr., estimates in Chapter 4 that legislative attention to prisons has shifted every few years from one to the other of punishment, rehabilitation, deterrence, and security. The focus changes as dramatic, visible incidents throw doubt on prior policies or actions and imply the need to reallocate community resources to manage the perceived underlying causes of the dramatic incidents—often the policies or actions of the commissioner. Commissioners with multiple, conflicting constituencies are constantly vulnerable to a change of focal concern that draws the energy and resources of the coalitions of constituencies away from professional priorities—as in DiIulio's corrections commissioners and their external "coaches, customers, and critics."

Conflicting focal concerns can also stimulate the formation of coalitions.[14] New, temporary coalitions sometimes form with the single aim of acting on the focal concern. Sometimes already well-established groups—for example, legislatures—alter their focal concerns and therefore their coalitions. The new coalitions find themselves in contention with other groups, established and new, that have incompatible focal concerns. The very act of engaging the opposition and negotiating some resolution of the conflict intensifies the focal concern, clarifies the identity and the solidarity of the coalitions, sharpens their boundaries, and crystallizes their social norms. Rules (or norms) of cooperation within the coalition and rules of the tactics of opposing other groups become more clear and consensual and sometimes more savage. Thus groups may create issues and issues may create groups, but both the issue and the group strengthen in identity and focus during encounters with opposing groups.

Conflict can thereby stabilize the power structure of a commissioner's constituencies, or it can change that structure. This process is well illustrated by the history of farmers' groups in the United States from the period after the Civil War until the present. The lineage begins with the limited and unstable American Farmers' Alliance whose mission was to protect farmers from horse thieves and unscrupulous land speculators, and ends with the modern, very large and stable Department of Agriculture, which is now both a commission and an advocacy group.

The social power of any contending constituency is likely to be at least somewhat unstable and ambiguous, especially in domains guided by weak myths. Active contention with opposing constituencies provides an excellent assessment of the relative social power of the groups, which is another important function of conflict among constituencies. The newly formed patients' advocacy group may try to prevail in the belief that the trying will reveal how much power it has. That clarification and specification of relative social power permits, although it does not ensure, the realignment of coalitions toward a balance of power among the contending constituencies. The process also positions the commissioner, strong or weak, in the power structure of the constituencies. In Chapter 5, Mark Moore provides dramatic example: the test of the political power of Police Chief Kevin Tucker of Philadelphia when he opposed Frank Rizzo in his last race for mayor— and Rizzo lost.

The public and those who must allocate resources accept a greater level of intensity in the pursuit of suprapersonal, altruistic missions than in the pursuit of very egoistic or special interests. In temporary coalitions seeking special interests, the alliances shift readily as issues change, and the contention is a matter of competitive bargaining for pragmatic benefits, not a crusade for fundamental rights to scarce community resources. Accordingly, a commissioner finds that coping with such mild conflict and changing coalitions is altogether a possible job.

On the other hand, when the constituencies are well established, the coalitions long-standing, the guiding myths weak, and the mission altruistic, the conflicts become intense and polarized. Witness the ''right to life'' and ''women's choice'' groups, formed of constituencies with a deep emotional investment in their version of fundamental human rights. The commissioner is trapped among the intensely clashing demands so that almost any action will antagonize an established and powerful coalition of constituencies. The job becomes impossible.

As pointed out previously, the combination of the first two dimensions of difficulty defines impossibility more clearly than does either one alone. Some commissioners serve a legitimate clientele, such as farmers, with a few constituencies in mild conflict over egoistic special interests. Their jobs are quite possible. At the opposite pole, some commissioners serve an illegitimate clientele with multiple, conflicting constituencies, such as the seriously mentally ill. If the contention among constituencies produces a flexible pattern of coalitions, which changes readily to balance the power allocation, the commissioner has options. He or she can judiciously join or support coalitions acting in his or her interest, or stay aloof and tip the balance in his or her favor. If, however, the contention among constituencies is marked by conflicting, altruistic, human rights declarations and produces a rigidly polarized, moralistic fight, the commissioner is trapped. To satisfy one constituency is to frustrate another. To take no action is to frustrate all of them. The conflict is a no-win situation.

In summary, the legitimacy of the clients and the polarization of the struggle among constituencies are dimensions of difficulty that, taken in combination, create some conditions, such as deserving clients and constituencies in mild egoistic conflict, that make a commissioner's job quite possible. These dimensions also characterize some conditions, such as illegitimate clients and polarized constituencies, that make the job quite impossible.

EXPERTISE, ENTERPRENEURSHIP, AND SOCIAL POWER

Thirty years ago John R. P. French, Jr., and Bertram Raven created a taxonomy of the bases of social power that is still used very widely and profitably.[15] They differentiated five such bases: expertise, socially established authority, ability to reward, ability to punish, and control of affiliation with an attractive person or group (called referent power, a classification not used here).

Professional Expertise. We argue that the power of the expert professional offers a great resource for public administration, despite two indications to the contrary. First, professional education and socialization do not prepare people to function in political arenas. Second, expert knowledge about attaining certain goals is often incomplete and limited. Even so, professional training and status offer resources for credibility. Professional expertise keeps the spotlight on the public good as it treats the ills and relieves the fears of individual clients—private goods for which the clients are grateful and often willing to pay. As a case in point, the medical profession may not know how to cure AIDS, but its research efforts have great credibility and sustain a real, important, and essential hope that guides the support of constituents. An announcement in a University of Southern California bulletin provides an excellent illustration of soothing fears by prestigious association.

> Initial toxicity testing of an experimental agent, intended to immunize individuals already infected with the AIDS virus to prevent development of the clinical disease, has shown that it is safe and that further studies are warranted, according to data presented by USC researchers at the International Conference on AIDS held in Stockholm in June. The research is being conducted by the School of Medicine . . . in collaboration with Jonas Salk, founding director of the Salk Institute in La Jolla.[16]

Commissioners whose professions inspire great public confidence, such as medicine and engineering, repeatedly demonstrate that professional intervention into the plight of their clients brings the expected correction or the management of a previously uncorrectable problem. Their technology works. The high standing of commissioners holding possible (as distinct from impossible) jobs results from an attribution of value and efficacy to their work: Health is achieved through research, security through military technology, progress through invention. As long as the professional expertise of the commissioner commands the respect of the constituencies, the job is rendered less difficult.

Conversely, commissioners whose professional expertise and technology are much less respected include those in education, social service, mental health, corrections, and police. These professions tend to inspire confidence through attractive personal style, so that a practitioner-commissioner becomes known for her or his style and the loyalty of his or her staff and clientele rather than for a communicable technology. Often such commissioners seem heroic: "Nobody can do it like he can!" "I don't know just how she does it, but ask her clients. She does it." As long as the reputation for heroic personal effectiveness is intact, the job can be done well—as demonstrated by the work of the three police commissioners whom Moore analyzes in Chapter 5. The fact is, however, that these professions lack a dependable technology. Although an individual commissioner can lean on his or her personal reputation, as a group such commissioners cannot. Commissioners in impossible jobs need a high level of expertise, but it is often simply not available. This means that they find close limits on the development over time of their ability to shape both policy and administration by virtue of professional expertise—close limits on what Theda Skocpol has called "state capacity."[17]

Administrative Expertise. Power may be based on a qualitatively different kind of expertise, that is, the mastery of the technology of policy implementation. The professional positions of most commissioners developed from the Progressive movement of the early years of this century. Educated, middle-class Progressive reformers hoped to take administration out of politics and establish it on a scientific basis. Good government was to be achieved not by filling jobs through the patronage of machine politicians, but by placing qualified professionals in them. Public administration itself was to be a science of policy implementation separated from politics and policymaking and neutral toward any political conflicts involved. The discipline of public administration developed around axioms of efficient government, many of them borrowed from the organizational archetype of the day, the modern business corporation.

Government organization was to be hierarchical, with all functions specialized but under one coordinating, accountability-ensuring umbrella. Efficient managers would use tools of budgeting, personnel development, measurement, and statistical analysis to bring light and order to messy government. It was easy to attach the concept of expertise-based administration to this ideal type of organization. Administration by engineers, geologists, physicians, and educators was to match the nonpolitical model of the technologically inventive, effective, profit-making business. The idea of "neutral competence" in public management emerged.[18] The public administrator was to assist the policymaker by providing neutral competence in the form of institutional memory and knowledge of an effective professional technology of policy implementation.

A large number of civil servants in American government at all levels embody this dual ideal. They are both expert public administrators and experts in their particular area of service. Such consultative expertise-based power is consistent with the democratic ethic because the expert is "on tap but not on top." Even so, political scientists have long since demonstrated that the idea of policy-implementing neutral competence is not realistic.[19]

Policy is made in the act of implementation, and civil servants are, in this sense, policymakers. The legislative process produces statutes that are often written in broad or even ambiguous language, sometimes stating contradictory goals. Legislative language must not be so specific as to prevent adaptation to unforeseen circumstances, and therefore administrative latitude is virtually inherent in lawmaking. Neutral competence, defined as institutional memory and understanding of both implementation pitfalls and specific professional knowledge, is certainly valuable. But the task of management includes the responsibility of interpreting policy as it is implemented.

Entrepreneurship. Such policy interpretation, however, is not sufficient for good administration. Professional expertise, institutional memory, and administrative technology must be supplemened by entrepreneurship. It is ironic that the efforts of the Progressive reformers to take administration out of party politics brought another kind of politics in through the back door. In a government of weak parties and divided authority, the phenomenon of interest-group politics developed, a politics in which organized interests used the many open windows in government to represent their claims. Nonpartisan civil servants have little protection against the organized constituencies with claims on the programs of the administrator. One outcome of fragmented government in a pluralistic society is the cooptation of administrators, such that government agencies represent constituent interests more than they represent the neutral authority of government. In such a system, majoritarian politics is weak.

By adding entrepreneurship to professional and administrative power (based on expertise), a commissioner can recruit the special interests with a stake in his or her work. At the same time, entrepreneurship is the key to securing some independence for the commissioner from such interests. The proliferation of social programs since the 1960s has generated a number of competing constituencies for most major programs. We maintain that this pattern of multiple, conflicting constituencies gives public administrators better opportunities to be selective in the formation of coalitions and in the balancing of the power of competing claims.[20] Commissioners studied here found that they must simultaneously create support for the interests they represent and harness those interests in working coalitions. Recognizing and using the patterns of coalitions among constituencies is, we maintain, political entrepreneurship. It is also the pragmatic, if unstable, supplement to the commissioner's expertise-based social power.

Social-Norm-based, Legitimate Power. Since he or she is legally commissioned by a collectivity, a commissioner of public goods is vested with legal authority, or legitimate power, as defined by French and Raven and elaborated by R. M. Emerson.[21] Such a collectivity, however, seldom acts explicitly. A dominant coalition of powerful groups actually authorizes the commissioner. For almost all commissioners, that dominant coalition includes the legislature, the executive, and, less formally but not less powerfully, the active special-interest groups with a stake in the work of the commission. The dominant coalition may be rigid and stable but more often is quite flexible, changing as focal concerns change. Moore believes that police commissioners usually must make their actions conform to the expectations of the currently dominant coalition of constituencies. Sometimes, however, they propose an action that has wide appeal, thus creating public support that they may use as a base of socially legitimate power to change their organization.

The dominant coalition arranged that the commissioner be legally authorized in the interest of providing some needed public goods and some deserved private goods. The commissioner, by personal and professional commitment, aspires to provide those goods but is dependent on the concerted action of the coalition of constituencies to do so. Therefore, he or she is subject to influence by the joint actions of the ascendant coalition. Thus, the commissioner has a domain-limited legitimate power over members of the collectivity, a power that was derived from, and can be withdrawn by, an often shifting ruling coalition of the collectivity. For that reason, political entrepreneurship in forming and joining coalitions not only supplements expertise but also becomes the means of consolidating and stabilizing one's legal authority.

Reward-based Power. To the extent that the public and its dominant coalitions are dependent on the commissioner for rewards of public goods, they will comply with the commissioner's instructions. In addition, the commissioner can reward with private goods: money, prestige, privileges, and other perks. Some rewarding privileges are allocated to special, eligible clients; some prestige to certain employees of the commission; and some money to those who supply the commission. As long as those clients, employees, and suppliers are obliged to the commissioner for continuing eligibility, employment, and sales, they will conform to the instructions of the commissioner concerning the implementation of her or his policies.

The commissioner's reward power, like any reward power, is effective only as long as the rewards continue and the groups involved depend on the commissioner for the rewards. A limit is set when the rewards become institutionalized and are regarded as a right. Then the rewards no longer serve as a basis of power.

Punishment-based Power. The commissioner, as an officer of the state, has at his or her disposal a particularly important tool—the coercive power that is reserved by law exclusively to the state. Such coercive power is authorized to control felons, the infectiously ill, the mentally disabled, or others whose acts represent a danger to society at large.

Unlike reward power, which makes a relationship more attractive, coercive power makes it more unattractive. Inflicting punishment, even fully justified punishment, induces those who are punished to try to avoid the person who punishes. Further, the public is always uneasy about the exclusive delegation of the coercive power of the state, because there is always the potential for misuse. The public, and its agents in the news media, often perform ''watchdog'' functions to make sure that coercive power is not abused. Moreover, as Lawlor shows in his chapter on public health commissioners who must cope with AIDS, the coercive power of the commissioner is often based on statutes that were written long ago and have not been amended as the concepts of freedom and privacy have developed. Generally, the tendency to be cautious about the exercise of coercive power is also justified by the outdatedness of many statutes.

Coercive power is the power to punish and is thus a private harm rather than a private good; watchdogs are supposed to ensure that such harms are distributed only to those who deserve them, according to some social norm of justice. But social norms in general are often vague. The boundaries of acceptable private harms are frequently ambiguous and differ according to the watchdog. Moore shows this ambiguity of the norms of justice quite eloquently in his analyses of ''like cases treated alike'' by police in Chapter 5.

Limits on Expertise, Entrepreneurship, and Social Power. The commissioner has many bases of social power, but all of them are narrowly limited in one way or another. Professional expertise, including policy-implementation expertise, is limited by the degree of public respect for the expertise of the profession and by the lack of a sound base in science or doctrine. Additionally, the power of special-interest coalitions requires that expertise be supplemented by entrepreneurship. Authority or legitimate power is limited by its base in the shifting coalitions with a stake in the programs of the commission. Reward power is limited by the changing availability of rewards from sources other than the commissioner and by a tendency toward institutionalization, transforming rewards to rights. Coercive power, the power to punish, is limited by its aversiveness and the watchdog functions of constituents and the news media.

The reward, coercive, and expert powers of a commissioner are also significantly restricted by the distance between them and their first-line subordinates. The "street-level" agents of many commissioners—agents such as prison guards, public health nurses, welfare workers, hospital attendants, and police patrolmen —operate far from the surveillance of the commissioner. It is impossible to directly control the discretionary routines practiced at the street level, revealing another intractable agency process. In Eugene Bardach's terms, our commissioners face social entropy in their control of street-level bureaucrats.[22] They must rely on the respect of such agents for the legitimate power of the commission and on their respect for the standards of their professions—kinds of respect often undermined by the shifting dominant coalitions that must legitimize the comissioner's power and the tenuous bases of professional standards. Paradoxically, commissioners must also rely on the capacity of street-level bureaucrats for adaptive innovations that transcend, and sometimes circumvent, the legitimate and expert power available.[23]

SUMMARY

In impossible jobs, commissioners are vulnerable to sanction when they are sustained by a weak myth that gives unstable guidance to controversial services and causes sharp swings in policy. Moreover, commissioners in those jobs are charged by law to supply public goods that are mythically idealistic, and they are therefore vulnerable to political scapegoating. A commissioner also provides private goods and can use them as incentives for contributing to the work of the agency.

Commissioners who serve illegitimate, intractable clients, who have many polarized constituencies, and who have very limited professional, legal, reward, or coercive powers are simply in impossible jobs. Their only hope lies in combining professional, expert power with political entrepreneurship and reward power. They thereby have a chance to recruit the legitimation and support of the dominant coalition that appointed them, a coalition that tends to be unstable and changing as focal concerns change. Responding to intermittent successes that keep their hope and commitment alive and resistant to extinction, commissioners cope with such impossible jobs. Often, their tenure is short and their accomplishments are limited, but they persist in pursuing the impossible goals until they burn out or are fired. In the next chapter we will analyze the approaches to coping that present themselves under these conditions.

NOTES

1. P. A. Samuelson, "The Pure Theory of Public Expenditure," *Review of Economics and Statistics* 36 (1954): 387.

2. Mancur Olson, Jr., *The Logic of Collective Action* (Cambridge, Mass.: Harvard University Press, 1965).

3. R. K. Goodwin and R. C. Mitchell, "Rational Models, Collective Goods and Nonelectoral Political Behavior," *Western Political Quarterly* 35 (1982): 161–81; D. Knoke, "Incentives in Collective Action Organizations," *American Sociological Review* 53 (1988): 311–29; D. Marsh, "On Joining Interest Groups: An Empirical Consideration of the Works of Mancur Olson, Jr.," *British Journal of Sociology* 6 (1976): 257–72; Terry M. Moe, *The Organization of Interests: Incentive and the Internal Dynamics of Political Interest Groups* (Chicago: University of Chicago Press, 1980); H. Tillock and D. E. Morrison, "Group Size and Contribution in Collective Action: A Test of Mancur Olson's Theory on Zero Population Growth, Inc.," *Research in Social Movements, Conflict, and Change* 2 (1979): 131–58; James Q. Wilson, *Political Organizations* (New York: Basic Books, 1973).

4. John W. Meyer and Brian Rowan, "Institutional Organizations: Formal Structure as Myth and Ceremony," *American Journal of Sociology* 83 (Sept. 1977): 340–63.

5. S. T. Fiske and L. M. Dyer, "Structure and Development of Social Schemata: Evidence from Positive and Negative Transfer Effects," *Journal of Personality and Social Psychology* 48 (1985): 839–52; S. T. Fiske and S. E. Taylor, *Social Cognition* (New York: Random House, 1984).

6. B. Hayes-Roth, "Evolution of Cognitive Structure and Process," *Psychological Review* 84 (1977): 260–78; G. Lakoff, *Women, Fire and Dangerous Things* (Chicago: University of Chicago Press, 1987).

7. F. Heider, *The Psychology of Interpersonal Relations* (New York: Wiley, 1958); E. E. Jones and K. E. Davis, "From Acts to Dispositions," in *Advances in Experimental Social Psychology,* vol. 2, ed. L. Berkowitz (New York: Academic Press, 1965); H. H. Kelley and J. L. Michela, "Attribution Theory and Research," in *Annual Review of Psychology,* vol. 31, ed. M. R. Rosenzweig and L. W. Porter (Palo Alto, Calif.: Annual Reviews, 1980).

8. B. A. Weiner, "Pity, Anger and Guilt: An Attributional Analysis," *Personality and Social Psychology Bulletin* 8 (1982): 226–32.

9. P. Brickman, V. C. Rabinowitz, J. Karuza, D. Coates, E. Cohn, and L. Kidder, "Models of Helping and Coping," *American Psychologist* 37 (1982): 368–84.

10. B. A. Wiener, "A Cognitive (Attribution)-Emotion-Action Model of Motivated Behavior: An Analysis of Judgments of Help-Giving," *Journal of Personality and Social Psychology* 39 (1980): 186–200.

11. Erwin C. Hargrove, "The Search for Implementation Theory," in *What Role for Government? Lessons from Policy Research,* ed. R. J. Zeckhauser and K. Leebaert (Durham, N.C.: Duke University Press, 1983).

12. J. C. Glidewell, *Chief Executive Officer: Studies of the Exercise of Social Power* (In press).

13. A. Tversky and D. Kahneman, "Judgment Under Uncertainty: Heuristics and Biases," *Science* 185 (1974): 1124–31.

14. L. Coser, *The Functions of Social Conflict* (New York: Free Press, 1956); G. Simel, *Conflict,* trans. K. H. Wolff (Glencoe, Ill.: Free Press, 1955).

15. J. R. P. French, Jr., and B. Raven, "The Bases of Social Power," in *Studies in Social Power,* ed. D. Cartwright (Ann Arbor: Institute for Social Research, University of Michigan, 1959).

16. University of Southern California, *USC Trojan Family* 20, 6 (July 1988): 6 (published by the USC Division of University Relations).

17. Theda Skocpol, Chapter 1, in *Bringing the State Back In,* ed. Peter B. Evans, Dietrich Rueshcemeyer, and Theda Skocpol (Cambridge: Cambridge University Press, 1985)

18. Herbert K. Kaufman, "Emerging Conflicts in the Doctrine of Public Administration," *American Political Science Review* 50, 4 (1956): 1059.

19. Paul Appleby, *Policy and Administration* (University: University of Alabama Press, 1949)

20. Hugh Heclo, *A Government of Strangers* (Washington, D.C.: Brookings Institution, 1977)

21. French and Raven, "Bases of Social Power," pp. 158–61; R. M. Emerson, "Power-Dependence Relations," *American Sociological Review* 27 (1962): 38–39.

22. Eugene Bardach, *The Implementation Game* (Cambridge, Mass.: MIT Press, 1984)

23. Michael Lipsky, *Street-Level Bureaucracy, Dilemmas of the Individual in Public Services* (New York: Russell Sage Foundation, 1980)

3

Coping with Impossible Jobs

Commissioners in impossible jobs must cope. To discuss how they do so, we will use the same dimensions of difficulty that were set out before, concentrating on the impossible poles. We will draw from both the chapters that follow and prior work on the exercise of social power under conditions of guiding myths, diminished and neglected clients, multiple and conflicting pressures, and incentives for political entrepreneurship.

COPING WITH A WEAK MYTH

Myths are not fictions. They are statements of ideals and aspirations, of fond dreams. Myths clarify the goals that guide action, and they provide assurance that the commission is really worth the extraordinary efforts and sacrifices that it demands from both its staff and its constituents. Myths furnish orientation for the public and a sense of worthy mission for those in the organization. The farseeing, intuitive political entrepreneur reinforces and perpetuates those practical, short-term actions that move the agency and its constituents toward the long-term, idealistic goals. Perhaps the most crucial coping strategies mentioned in this volume entail some form of balance between mythical long-term goals (e.g., a safe city) and pragmatic reality (people attack one another). In Chapter 5, Mark Moore provides a particularly cogent example of this in his analysis of the roles of the police chiefs Darryl Gates of Los Angeles, Lee Brown of Houston, and Kevin Tucker of Philadelphia. All of them mounted action agendas that articulated and symbolized both the ideal goals of the community and the efficacy of their programs.

People must maintain some myths, and they must act realistically. All people *could be* educated, all diseases *could be* prevented, all criminals *could be* apprehended, all prisoners *could be* rehabilitated. Limited resources must be used to prevent diseases when that is possible, but some resources must be reserved to manage diseases, such as schizophrenia and AIDS, that no one knows how to cure. Trying to apprehend as many criminals as possible in high-crime areas is necessary, but so is reserving some resources for prevention in low-crime areas.

Myths, to be sure, are sometimes misused in symbolic exercises that are designed to put an attractive facade on burdensome actions and to prevent any influence on operations. Or a myth may be a fine cover for doing nothing. The myth of universal compulsory education has long been a cover for strategic inaction in apprehending truants, a myth that relieves the school from having to teach children who are, in fact, very hard to teach and relieves those parents who do not want their children in school. Myths can also mislead people into believing that the commission is providing public goods, when it is actually providing private goods for those supplying and conducting the operations of the commission. Note how some physicians, pledged to the Hippocratic oath, profit from unnecessary surgery or from overhasty discharge when insurance no longer covers the costs. Note also how some hospitals, pledged to restore the health of the patient, are built for the convenience of physicians, not of patients.

The dramatic impact of symbolic actions may outweigh the dangers of their theatrics. Edward Lawlor, in Chapter 8, provides an excellent example of the use of symbols to support both worthy and very pragmatic ends. When a chef of the Bon Appétit restaurant in San Francisco died of AIDS, Dr. Ken Kizer, the California health commissioner, took the opportunity to eat a much-publicized meal in the restaurant, showing his confidence in his beliefs about the lack of danger of being infected. "It was a symbolic thing," said Dr. Kizer, "but . . . I think it turned a lot of people around."

In order to effectively maintain myths of idealistic goals (the unlikely cure of AIDS) while acting realistically on short-term projects (relieving the fear of AIDS infection from food), one must choose actions that have at least four properties: The actions can be done; they relieve focal concerns; they partly confirm the myth; and they require minimum and clearly justified restrictions on other ideals, such as safety, freedom, justice, and privacy. Some people can be educated without undue coercion; therefore, all people *could* be. Some diseases can be prevented without undue compulsion; therefore, all diseases *could* be. Some criminals can be caught without undue force; therefore, all criminals *could* be. Some prisons are both secure and humane; therefore, all prisons *could* be. These statements may indeed seem like non sequiturs; logic was never the main rigging for either the focal concerns or the cherished ideals of human societies. Moore demonstrates that the police commissioners whose coping he analyzed fitted their strategy to the historical context, to the focal concerns and current expectations of powerful constituencies, and to the capabilities of their organization. Moore believes that what is important is for the manager to find not only a successful strategy but a value-creating (or a value-affirming) strategy.

Although the myths guiding impossible jobs are extremely weak (as we maintain), they are used often in appeals to idealism. The utopian impulse never dies and is regularly expressed in writing and advocacy about crime, corrections, health, and welfare. The persistence of idealism makes it possible to marry the utopian aspects of myth to emerging, favorable political conditions on behalf of reform. Latent hope is again aroused. Such processes, nevertheless, are brief, because the perceptions concerning the irresponsibility and intractability of the clients will reassert themselves in due course.

As idealistic and formidable as the goals are, commitments to such impossibilities as the abolition of disease or crime need not be doomed to failure. J. D. Thompson's discerning analyses of evaluation processes shows that the very ambiguity and remoteness of the idealistic goals and the very weakness of the expertise mean that progress will be judged, not against compelling evidence of goal attainment, but by some social or historical comparison.[1] Current, very limited success stories will be linked to past, complete success stories (e.g., the University of Southern California research on AIDS immunization in collaboration with Jonas Salk, the hero of research on polio immunization), or to stories from neighboring jurisdictions.[2] The effective use of comparisons of processes that are instrumental means to the goals but not actual goal-attainment is demonstrated in the following statements: "Our achievement test scores are still below the national median, but they are rising faster than those of any district in this state." "Our crime rates are still rising, but more slowly than those of any other city this size." The oldest assurance is still viable, if issued in a context of vigorous goal-directed activity: "We are fully committed; we are doing everything humanly possible."

Weak myths, then, both guide and make one vulnerable. To reduce the vulnerability, a commissioner may choose strategic actions that have four properties.

COPING WITH IRRESPONSIBLE
AND INTRACTABLE CLIENTS

People are indeed overly inclined to attribute the plight of clients to unchanging, internal, controllable but not controlled causes. People are also, however, disposed to have some compassion for the plight of clients and to deeply respect the strength and courage needed to overcome such problems. Success stories, however few there may be, that demonstrate the accomplishments of persistent and extraordinary individual efforts are very popular. The persistence and effort may be both the client's and the commission's. The aim is simply to modify the attribution from "controllable but not controlled" to "controllable and controlled." Success stories are reassuring because each person is a possible future victim of externally caused, long-term illness and injury—or victims of just bad luck.

The success stories, however, have some negative side effects. They confirm that the attributed cause is in fact controllable, and they thereby reflect upon those clients who do not control and overcome the causes of their plight. Even so, they also provide real evidence that the attainment of altruistic goals is sometimes possible. Thus a concrete success story serves both to maintain the myth of the impossible goals and to partially protect the commissioner against sanction for not having achieved the impossible goals.

Fundraising among supportive constituents (whether lobbying for tax money or asking for private gifts) provides special opportunities to publicize success stories while simultaneously marshaling the power of multiple and conflicting constituencies. To be sure, once a constituency is polarized against the clients, fundraising achieves nothing. But there is almost always an opposite pole, a coalition of constituencies ready, willing, and capable of fundraising, both for the altruistic goals of the commission and for their own identification as generous, responsible, and leading citizens. Accordingly, coping with illegitimate and intractable clients has been made more feasible by regular and frequent attention to the communication of exceptional success stories and regular and frequent marshaling of supportive constituents for fundraising.

COPING WITH MULTIPLE, CONFLICTING CONSTITUENCIES

A commissioner's constituents are networks of collective-action organizations, taxpaying and otherwise. The commission, before and after the tenure of the commissioner, is inextricably linked to a web of shifting coalitions, composed of elected officials, colleagues, associations of clients and families, neighborhoods and communities where facilities are located, purveyors, customers, and friends. The various members are the nodes of the network, and they differ widely in their connection with, concessions to, and commitments to other members. The task of organizing these constituencies involves less rational analysis than intuitive recognition of patterns of changing concerns and changing power positions of constituencies.

Because few others will provide such leadership, commissioners discover that they must become advocates for the programs they have been commissioned to administer. The fragmented structure of American government not only permits but invites political entrepreneurship on behalf of both idealistic policy goals and realistic practical programs.[3] Governors pursue goals that cut across departments and focus their leadership on a few salient, politically popular issues. Only occasionally do the restrained objectives of a governor coincide with the few promising goals of his or her executive appointees. When that happens, as it sometimes may in education or environmental policy, the governor often provides the necessary political leadership. In most cases, however, governors would rather leave commissioners on their own. Legislators, like governors, promote specific, *ad hoc* interests but seldom give sustained policy leadership on behalf of particular programs. Governors and legislators sometimes actually undermine the efforts of a commissioner, as in Illinois, New York, and San Francisco when commissioners found themselves at odds with both the executive and the legislative branches in their attempts to cope with the threat of AIDS. (See Chapter 8.)

The jobs of commissioners become inherently political because they allocate scarce resources among conflicting policy demands from the constituents of the programs they administer. A passive stance that pushes the "policy buck" upstairs to elected officials ignores the need to prioritize conflicting demands in order to allocate resources. If programs are to do more than drift, an active stance is required—a stance in which policy goals are interpreted, articulated, and served by political priorities.

These conditions apply particularly to impossible jobs, because elected officials, whether executive or legislative, have few political incentives to grapple with the no-win dilemmas of commissioners who, with limited power, serve irresponsible, intractable clients and multiple polarized constituencies. Most of the time, the political benefit is too uncertain and contentious. Even the fortuitous movement toward one goal inevitably means moving away from another. Action stirs a hornet's nest, and the commissioners, not the politicians, are the ones who must gamble on getting stung. In fact, sometimes commissioners may be better able to help politicians than the politicians are able to help them.[4] Effective entrepreneurship by commissioners may increase the political credit of their elected bosses; it also may trigger political embarrassment. We maintain that for commissioners in impossible jobs the primary source of influence over elected officials is support they have from the actual or potential constituencies.[5]

The complex problems of impossible jobs, furthermore, readily admit of more than one coping strategy and style of leadership. Constituency concerns and policy goals that are idealistic, ambiguous, multiple, and conflicting may provide long-term guidance but can be interpreted in many ways in the short term. Strategies for coping with multiple conflicting constituencies vary in polarization. At the least polarized end, the coping strategy transforms the situation from incompatible demands to mutually tolerated competing demands. The balance of power shifts from one coalition of constituencies to the other, with each competitor having its own priorities. Each mutually tolerated, competing demand can be addressed by feasible short-term actions that yield some satisfaction to both sides, even if it is only the understanding that some demands get attention now, other demands, next time.

At the opposite extreme of the continuum, where impossible jobs lie, the strategy pits one altruistic, devoutly held demand against another—each one also with its own constituents and its own priorities, each side bent on discrediting the position and the proponents of the other. The controversy over abortion rights is a dramatic example, but the dispute over protection from AIDS is becoming equally intense and demanding.

No matter whether the issue is one of manageable egoistic competition or unmanageable moralistic conflict, each short-term action remains vulnerable to shifting concerns and to disastrous mishaps that appear to show neglect, even when the evidence reveals strong vigilance. In Chapter 6, Gary Miller and Ira Iscoe tell how a single tragic attack by one patient on another was used to claim a general excess of violence in all state hospitals. A class-action suit ended with a finding of excessive violence despite clear evidence of infrequent incidents of violence.

The rise and decline of focal concerns among multiple constituencies, in more or less polarized conflict, is the "tenor of the times" to which most public commissioners try to stay carefully attuned. Recognition, however tenuous, of shifting focal concerns allows the commissioner to choose salient, practical, visible programs to address a current focal concern and, with intuitively calculated risk, strategically bypass other concerns—to cope with the impossible.

PROFESSIONAL AND ENTREPRENEURIAL COPING

Even given the primacy of the constituencies, the authority of the expert professional offers a great resource for political entrepreneurship. As described previously, professional knowledge and status offer resources for credibility. Because it relieves the incapacities, pain, distress, and fears of clients, professional expertise serves a salient public good by enabling an active and productive citizenry. It simultaneously supplies immediate and appreciated private good; health, ability, and well-being.

Professional expertise can be sustaining under stress, even in the professions in which the public has less confidence. Studies have demonstrated that the professionalism of education is less established than that of medicine, but it too fosters essential hope.[6] Not all children have learned to read, but the credibility of the efforts of licensed teachers is remarkable, and it guides the support of parents for expert teachers. The familiar bumper sticker puts it succinctly: "If you can read this, thank a teacher."

The authority of professional knowledge and skill—part myth, part reality— becomes a valuable instrument for the commissioner as entrepreneur. That is evident from the studies in this volume. The professional expertise of policing, medicine, education and the law—all these have provided resources for imaginative leadership. Such professionalism creates commitment-building public goods and promises incentive-building private goods. Professional endorsement and accreditation help to mobilize constituent support for programs and to defend such programs from undue, nonprofessional attack. The political neutrality of professional expertise can be good politics. American science has used its apolitical character with great political skill to obtain millions of dollars from the government for scientific research. For all its utility, however, professionalism is far from sufficient for coping with impossible jobs.

The problems presented by conflicting goals and conflicting demands offer the professional commissioner the political challenge of inventing a way out. Standard solutions are not likely to be available. Successful strategies of the past are almost always inapplicable to present cases, because of new issues, personalities, and contingencies. More important, invention is a personal matter. The new situation requires the commissioner to reach into past experience and to draw on personal skills to find a strikingly novel way of coping with a problem of distributing both idealistic public goods and pragmatic private goods, a problem that may not in itself be new. Stock solutions lack not only luster but also the personal imprint so important to the heroic style of the entrepreneurial commissioner.

The commissioner tries to discern what threats and promises worry powerful groups the most, and he or she emphasizes actions that address those concerns. While the commissioner vigorously acts on the most salient focal concerns, he or she takes only limited or no action on other incompatible concerns, but neither credits nor discredits them. If the commissioner's actions credibly and energetically address (not necessarily relieve) what he or she has correctly sensed as the prevalent focal concerns of the society, the result will be only minimal concern about what has been neglected—and what concern there is will be confined to the less powerful or less concerned of the constituents. The commissioner must always be prepared, however, for a shift in focal concerns and be ready to respond by shifting resources to possible (or sometimes impossible) professional mitigation of the problems stressed by the new concerns. The commissioner gambles that he or she has correctly picked a focal concern that does not antagonize the most powerful constituents and that contributes at least some manifest progress to long-term, idealistic goals.

For example, Miller and Iscoe show how a program in which former mental patients maintain their own residences affects different constituencies. First, it mitigates the concern of constituents who are worried that their relatives will be trapped and forgotten in the custodial back wards of mental hospitals. At the same time, it stimulates and develops a focal concern among the former patients' neighbors, a concern about safety, maintenance, and value of their neighborhood. It also stimulates and develops a focal concern about indiscriminate discharge among families whose profoundly ill members do, in fact, require hospital care. And further, opening such residences also raises concerns of the communities in which mental hospitals are located: Will the hospital lay off workers?

Allowing furloughs to selected prisoners eases the focal concern of constituents about the isolation of prisoners from prosocial, cooperative community influences. The furloughs also intensify the worries of constituents about the dangers of additional criminal acts committed by convicted criminals on furlough from prison, as in the recent Massachusetts experience. However professionally adept, if a commissioner acts at all, he or she is likely to relieve the focal concern of some and increase the focal concern of others. When the constituencies with opposing concerns have about equal power to influence the allocation of resources to the agency, the commissioner is often wise to dilute each group's impact by spreading his or her resources among the several focal concerns. But how are the powers of the constituencies to be assessed?

PROFESSIONAL-POLITICAL ENTREPRENEURSHIP

At this point professional expertise and entrepreneurship merge with political expertise and entrepreneurship. Many commissioners are discerning political entrepreneurs. They quickly recognize emerging patterns of focal concerns and mount the programs that address the emerging concerns in the most visible way, for as long as the concern (or the commissioner) lasts. More police patrols are added, prison discipline is tightened, new welfare eligibility rules are announced, or a new and attractive "workfare" program is launched—all directed toward enhancing public goods and reallocating private goods. The focal concern may impose impossible demands on the commissioner—for example, to halt the spread of AIDS or to hide the homeless in mental hospitals. Impossible demands, however, also generate new resources. Lawlor notes in Chapter 8 that the shift of public health attention to the prevention of AIDS was important because it offered both promises of eventual success and the allocation of new resources to public health. One public health commissioner said: "The crucial thing is to see the popular and the possible, the noble goal and the likely action. Aye, there's the rub, the really likely action. To know what appealing thing you can really bring off, here and now, that's the political art of public health."[7] Professional-political entrepreneurship, then, is the most significant mode of coping with impossible jobs, and its many ramifications will be discussed in the following pages.

When constituents' focal concerns reach the level of emergency, more inroads on liberty are permissible as proper personal sacrifices in the interest of certain public goals. The commissioner may, therefore, gamble on curtailment of freedom in the interest of health and safety, even under close scrutiny by civil libertarians and the news media. Prisons can be locked down, curfews can be ordered, evacuations from dangerous areas can be required, medication can be increased, immunization can be made a condition of access to community schools and pools. Such emergencies, however, are usually temporary; the commissioner must be extremely sensitive to the diminishing sense of emergency and quickly match it by decreasing the restrictions on freedom of choice and action. Crisis conditions are an important prerequisite of restrictions that must be policed, such as lock-downs, curfews, and quarantines. Unless the danger is seen as real and pressing, enforcement usually requires more policing than scarce resources will allow and more staff commitment than the fading danger will support.

Sometimes emergencies provide opportunities for an imaginative commissioner. Research by a number of scholars demonstrates how a "foot in the door"—that is, a very limited action in accord with a public commitment—leads later to a more extensive action, consistent with the first small maneuver.[8] A crisis may require clients and constituents to make visible, small sacrifices, or slight extra efforts, that are manifestly directed toward exceptionally worthy public goods. Having publicly demonstrated their commitment once, albeit by a small step, the constituents often are willing at a later time to make greater, nonemergency sacrifices in the interest of progress toward those same goals.

Thereby, some proportion of clients and constituents may become new supporters of the commission and its idealistic goals. In the field experiments of Freedman and Fraser, 50 to 75 percent of those who first took modest actions showing a commitment to an altruistic goal were willing, when asked later, to take much more demanding actions to demonstrate that commitment—an astounding number when compared to controls.[9]

Although embarrassing, some low-frequency, high-cost, high-visibility, but inevitable tragic events may also provide opportunities for resource mobilization for reform. A publicized discovery that mental patients are being abused in a state mental health center could lead to the discrediting of the center and the commissioner responsible. However, the incident could also lead to new hiring practices and improved quality of care for patients. In the same way, welfare fraud could lead to allegations of neglect and theft by the commissioner, but it could just as easily lead to improved regulation and services, improvements that the commissioner had long been seeking.

If the incidents call attention to important but not focal concerns, the events can potentially redirect focal concerns. If the incidents mobilize support to push the commissioner to initiate some program that is really needed, they can also marshal the constituency support necessary to effect that program. If the commissioner can accept and be challenged by the criticism, adversity can be turned into opportunity. At such junctures, accepting responsibility and allowing constituents to influence the launching of new programs may be the commissioner's most powerful weapons in securing resources and allocating them to new, needed programs. Public involvement, of course, can be only a flash in the pan, if the concern shifts quickly to indifference again.

Again, the commissioner copes by recognizing political patterns, relying on intuition to assess the relative power position of the constituents and the direction in which the power relationships are changing. The astute commissioner has many options. A commissioner may choose to join or to form coalitions that offer the minimum necessary power at the lowest cost in concessions, very much as W. A. Gamson would have predicted.[10] On the other hand, the commissioner may act primarily to modify the power structure by bringing the least powerful groups together to oppose the more powerful. T. A. Caplow observed such power balancing in families, and R. M. Emerson proposed its presence in all social systems.[11] Conversely, both the "lowest cost" and structure-changing principles often give way to a power maintenance principle. The members of low-cost coalitions and power-balancing coalitions can often be enticed out of the coalitions by a desire to affiliate with more powerful figures. They then find themselves in a coalition that contains those groups currently highest in power and that acts to maintain the current power advantages of those groups.[12] What goals do these options fit?

When commissioners prefer the status quo, they promote coalitions that maintain the structure. When they wish to change the status quo, they back the coalitions that bring less powerful constituents together to increase their power so that it equals or exceeds that of the more powerful coalitions. In either case, they promote those coalitions that demand fewest concessions in return for their support. When they judge that the opposing coalitions have equal power, commissioners may foster or join no coalition at all and allow each to neutralize the others. A school superintendent, caught between powerful proponents of birth control instruction and equally powerful opponents, may stand aside. The stalemate maintains a desired status quo.

Partly because of uneasiness about the commissioner's use of the coercive power of the state and partly because the innovative actions of any political entrepreneur carry the entrepreneur's special stamp, any mistakes tend to be attributed to the commissioner personally. Commissioners are almost routinely accused of personal incompetence, neglect, deception, cover-ups, and even character flaws. Thus, one necessary condition to effective coping is a reserve of self-esteem that allows a commissioner to absorb considerable hostility without being baited into a public fight. Said one commissioner, "If you're right you don't need to get mad; if you're wrong you can't afford to get mad. I say that, and it's true, but I still get mad. I just try not to show it." It also helps to understand the dynamics of political entrepreneurship in impossible jobs and to recognize the *social* forces that stimulate personal accusations.

Many kinds of constructive responses are implied in the chapters that follow. One may simply invite public investigation by impartial agents, confident that they will find only understandable, honest mistakes. One may invoke the authority of the profession and invite professional review. Another option is to arrange reviews of the commission by conflicting constituencies and provide an orderly arena for their debate on the meaning of the findings. Or, the situation may be viewed as an opportunity for agency self-study and renegotiation of agency rules and procedures. When a commissioner is certain that the accusation is capricious or trivial, he or she may ignore it while asking influential outsiders to point out its caprice or triviality. If the commissioner's public esteem is robust enough, he or she may gently shift the responsibility to others, but such evasion usually takes more prestige than holders of impossible jobs can muster.

Some conditions are extraordinary, requiring more than an intuitive grasp of the current focal concerns and the interconnections of the many constituencies. They require changing those concerns and perhaps the linkages as well. For example, an irrational fear of AIDS must not be accepted or disparaged (which may cause it to intensify), but neither can it be ignored. It must be changed. An uninformed conviction that poor black children cannot learn in school must not be adopted or disregarded. It must be changed. Under such situations, commissioners must sometimes take actions intended to alter focal concerns and to shift power positions. The best opportunities arise when common, normative practices or ideas are in conflict with strongly held ideals and values, as is true currently with smoking and drunken driving but not quite yet with the practice of refusing any contact with AIDS victims. In conversations with *some* of the leaders of constituencies, the commissioner can often sense both the strongly felt need to change the doubtful practices and the pessimism about succeeding. Comments like the following are typical: "Nobody thinks crime is a good thing, but nobody knows how to stop the fast-spreading crime. Preaching doesn't do it, fines don't do it, jails don't do it, counseling doesn't do it. What does?"

To induce change, a commissioner may have to openly confront and contend with some constituencies, even those who appointed him. Given a base of power in professional expertise, consistency with cultural values, personal integrity, and articulated public support from some constituencies, a commissioner may accomplish more by confrontation than by trying to create consensus through accommodation. In Chapter 8, Lawlor points out that the commissioners who have been most successful in their efforts to limit the spread of AIDS (Surgeon General Koop being the most visible) have been those who publicly confronted their political resistance rather than those who searched for areas of compromise.

The studies presented in this book, along with the remarkably well-replicated research of Kurt Lewin,[13] indicate that the commissioner's chances for success are best when an attempt to change concerns and coalitions has these characteristics: (a) The attempt affirms a strongly held value, idealistic as it may be, such as the values of health, truth, justice, and freedom. (b) It is taken in concert with coalitions of constituents powerful enough to influence the actions of others (ideally the most powerful, but not necessarily), coalitions that have a strong commitment to the values being sacrificed and at least a little uneasiness about the value-sacrificing current practices. (c) The action requires a quite specific, readily observable change in current practices. (d) It encourages powerful-enough people to announce their public commitment to make the specific change. Such changes are usually *not* short-term shifts. The conflict between values and practices is, in time, resolved in favor of the values, and the change is stabilized over the long term, as has been true of buying seed in order to plant hybrid corn, careful use of antibiotics, and immunization of infants. Another example is prisons that cooperate with voluntary agencies to improve the health practices and vocational skills of inmates. Such prisons are tolerated, even though they might be suspected of coddling criminals. But if former prisoners get and hold jobs without much trouble to employers, and if they also commit no further crime, eventually the community may come to take such rehabilitation programs for granted, as they have hybrid corn. Drunk driving has been hard to change, as have smoking habits, but "No Smoking" areas in public places are now well supported. John Glidewell has reported the five-year course of some well-demonstrated induced changes, as citizens attempted to influence the decisions of a school board—changes that once established continued for at least two years.[14]

Again, the task requires recognition of shifting patterns of focal concerns and of changing coalitions. Moreover, if change is planned, the task requires astute alliance with, and concerted efforts by, powerful-*enough* coalitions to attempt to induce the intended changes in patterns of focal concerns. That knack for pattern recognition is difficult to pin down. Usually it is associated not only with years of experience but also with the ability to filter and organize current information as it relates to that experience. It seems to require a Winston Churchill-like mind that moves easily from logic and form to feeling and sensing, perhaps "sixth-sensing."

Herbert A. Simon has probably given more attention to this trait than anybody else.[15] He reported a comparison of the intuition of chess grand masters and novices. Both are first presented with a position from an actual but unfamiliar chess game with about twenty-five pieces on the board. After a few seconds, the board and pieces are removed. The grand master can usually reconstruct the whole setup, placing twenty-three or twenty-four pieces correctly. The novice can usually place only six pieces. The procedure is then repeated except that the twenty-five pieces are placed at random on the board. The novice again can locate six pieces correctly. And the chess master? Also about six. For the chess master, recall is dependent on whether the pieces form patterns incident to plausible games. The board is not a set of twenty-five pieces; it is an arrangement of familiar patterns with implications for actions.

Although chess masters are often highly analytical, taking as much as thirty minutes to decide upon a move, it is also true that some can successfully play as many as twenty opponents simultaneously, taking only a few seconds to size up the board and make a move. Simon has suggested that the intuition of business managers is similar to that of chess masters, both depending on the same sort of pattern recognition.[16] We suggest that the political intuition of public commissioners also hinges on the same kind of pattern recognition.

Note that we argue for quick, intuitive identification of patterns as a condition for coping with many opponents. The action of the chess master—"the move"—conforms to rigid and widely accepted rules of the game. On the contrary, the actions—"the moves"—of commissioners must conform to rules that are constantly changing; in fact, the "players" often disagree about what the rules are. The patterns to be recognized are patterns of power structures; the rules to be followed are primarily determined by those at the peak of the power structure—unless they become vulnerable to displacement themselves. As the power structure changes and others occupy the peak, the rules change.[17] Recognition of the pattern of changing power structures thus becomes recognition also of the pattern of the changing rules to be followed. The patterns appearing on the commissioner's "board" are always more varied—and the moves require much more flexibility—than those of the chess master.

It is important that "moves" is plural. An additional complication is that, unlike chess, the promise of favorable outcomes varies over time. An action taken today can have radically different prospects from the same action taken tomorrow. Analyses of dynamic decision making shows that, when all payoffs are at least somewhat uncertain, staking everything on the currently most promising action is likely to be unwise.[18] Commissioners, then, must take account of possible, not necessarily likely, changes in political power and salient focal concerns. They must also intuitively "compute" probabilities of unknown outcomes; that is, actions must be taken that currently hold high promise as well as low promise. The currently less promising options, however, will probably include some as yet unidentified projects that, after time and development, will trigger dramatic innovations. No one is sure which low-promise actions will break through current limits on the commission's effectiveness, but it is certain that one or two such projects will yield important new departures from the current practices of the commission. Time and conditional probability must be figured not only into the recognition of patterns from past experience but also into the targeting of patterns of possible, not yet identified, future outcomes.

How does a commissioner acquire such extraordinary talent for using information and experience? It may not be possible to acquire it systematically; it may not be possible to *acquire* it at all. Some maintain that it is genetic, some that it is a combination of being rewarded or punished, imitating models, and decoding ambiguous signals. There seems to be no clear evidence to explain the adult development involved, but pending refutation, we suggest that the development of such intuition is at least somewhat similar to the development of a chess master. The talent may be the outcome of the following sequence. Needed first is either a strong incentive (e.g., prospective status and pay), or a strong belief that the commission is worth the persistence and extraordinary effort demanded, or, more likely, both. Second, the person needs experiences in a wide variety of settings, such as that in which the commission operates. Third, the person must engage in an open-minded evaluation of his or her experiences in the interest of learning the myriad dynamic patterns and rules to be recognized. Fourth, the person must be attracted to experimentation with many strategies, even perhaps a playful interest in "seeing what happens" combined with a serious attention to acquiring dependable, practical knowledge. All those faculties must be coupled with a full understanding that "what happens" may be disastrous, as well as with the courage to take the risks necessary to cope with an impossible job.

In Chapter 7, Laurence Lynn, Jr., makes clear that commissioners do not have unlimited choices of strategies. The current focal concerns of the constituencies and the potential support or opposition from powerful groups (such as governors and legislators) represent the "demand side" of the rather vague social economics involved. Both the personal predispositions and the skills of the commissioner represent the "supply side" of this strategy choice. As Lynn shows so compellingly in his case studies of welfare commissioners, the political entrepreneur Gregory Coler simply could not have chosen Steven Minter's system-maintenance, risk-aversive approach. The personality, skills, and style of each commissioner had great impact on the strategies they chose. In those two cases, the predispositions of the person fitted the demands and the support available in the situations they faced, but the way commissioners are appointed does not always ensure a good match. A person will try to seek jobs that fit his or her nature, but that is not easy to determine when the job in question involves changing focal concerns and power relationships among constituencies—shifting demands which one must supply.

No one person can be broad enough to cope with all possible contingencies. It is therefore very important for commissioners to assess the fit between their skills, as they understand them, and the demands and support at hand. When the commissioner finds the fit shifting, he or she may seek help from associates who have the needed skills, if help-seeking is enabling and if such associates are available. It is likely that different people will read the same situation differently and therefore respond differently. It is also likely that more than one strategy will work in a single situation.

Personal skill must be empowered by politics, meaning that a lot of people will support the commissioner for reasons of their own.[19] The relationships between skill and empowerment can be depicted by a simple diagram, as in Table 3-1. In the first cell (the double positive), skill and strong support reinforce each other for empowerment; that is, personal skill adds to empowerment, but the commissioner receives vital help from many quarters. In the second cell, skill is limited, but the support is strong. The actions of others provide the motive force for success. In the third cell, the leader is skillful but the odds are against success, so a great premium is placed upon skill and personality. This is the most common situation facing the talented holder of impossible jobs. In the final, double-negative cell, low skill is further undermined by a formidable opposition.

The ability to analyze the political environment and identify the resources needed to complement and supplement one's skills is crucial for any public executive and vital for commissioners in impossible jobs. They must find a way to make an existing pattern of political support fit the predispositions and skills they supply—or they must change the pattern of political support to accomplish a fit.

Turning from the development of the entrepreneurial commissioner to the changing, patterned scene of the commission itself, a question arises: Is the environment of the commissioner always so unstable, impoverished, dispersed, and unpredictable? No, not always. After a period of desirable, dynamic but disrupting reform, both the support of the constituencies and the effectiveness of the commission's staff may depend upon increased stability. Then the emphasis turns to the efficient performance of the core mission: sanitation of the environment, immunization of children, discipline of prison inmates, justified distribution of benefits. Statistical reports of the scope of these activities are regularly issued, contrasted with past reports and with those of comparable jurisdictions, and celebrated in a lively fashion. The governor and the legislature may demand that the efficiency-oriented commissioner allocate his or her primary attention and

Table 3.1 Fit between Skill and Situation

	Strong Support +	Strong Opposition −
High applicable skills +	+ + 1	+ − 3
Low applicable skills −	− + 2	− − 4

energy to staying out of trouble or defusing embarrassing incidents, especially those compromising the governor and legislature. In Chapter 7, for example, Lynn analyzes the crisis-avoiding coping of several commissioners of welfare.

Moving down another path toward stabilization, commissioners may also concentrate on and frequently execute some striking procedural or technological innovations to increase the efficiency of the core mission. In Chapter 4, John DiIulio, Jr., observes that when stabilization is needed, such innovations have worked well in corrections. In addition, advisory and study groups can be appointed to analyze any conflicts and shortfalls and make public recommendations for remedial actions. The commission can then study the report carefully for quite some time. Any needed conflict resolution may be moved into traditional arenas of debate and negotiation in legislative committees, courts, and bargaining tables. The resolution process is then institutionalized and, to be sure, possibly stalemated. But change will be decelerated, and the commission stabilized.

In another scenario, the commissioner may excel at projecting his or her image as a figure of professional authority and as an expert problem-solver. Sometimes citation of professional authority is a good response to dramatic mishaps, particularly when responsible professional practice is at issue. Emphasizing politically neutral professional competence, after a period of change and disruption or after a tragic event, serves stabilization and consolidation quite well. It does not yield conflict management, program expansion, or creative provision of public and private goods.

Up to this point, we have given our attention to the interactions between the commission and its environment. Management, understood as the task of implementing programs through a bureaucracy buffered from the turbulence in its environment, receives less notice in this book than does entrepreneurship. To some extent, the public manager shares the preoccupation of elected politicians with the short-run political incentives arising from frequent elections. Issues of implementation often take a backseat when policy is developed, because the political credit is for invention, not follow-through. Reelection is the reward of having achieved good things for people *recently,* not of efficient administration of old, taken-for-granted programs.

Interest groups also often focus on the declaration of policy via the enactment of laws, in the effort to resolve long-standing policy debates in their favor by statute. If the statutory commitment of the state to a goal can be established in principle, implementation can come later. Commissioners get caught up in the game of policy innovation as a means of keeping abreast of changing demands and competing with their peers. Leadership in policy innovation outranks the straightforward tasks of managing the bureaucracy to achieve predictable outcomes: Leadership outside means influence inside. Entrepreneurs mobilize the constituents of programs as one method of galvanizing middle levels of the bureaucracy to be responsive to the top.

A more mundane kind of management is reflected in the way the best public managers understand the realities of the routine work of their fields. A police commissioner cannot be effective without personal knowledge of what police do to enforce the law and of what people expect them to do. A welfare commissioner must understand the tasks of caseworkers and the pressures in the lives of their clients. As DiIulio demonstrates, in order to meet minimum goals, a corrections commissioner must build an effective corps of prison guards with a sense of mission and a dedication to duty. Their dedication must hold fast despite great temptation to exploit their charges or to conspire with them. The development of such strong commitment counteracts a continuing external neglect and disparagement of the guards—a social force that undermines the very spirit essential for effective operation. This is management. The tools of budgeting, personnel records, and statistical analyses serve as instruments of efficiency, but they are no substitute for personal knowledge of the tasks of day-to-day work.

Those who staff the bureaucracy are very likely to be allied with internal coalitions that reflect the idealistic, multiple, and conflicting purposes of the outside world. Indeed, Lynn points out in his chapter on welfare that, given a crisis-avoiding, incident-defusing commissioner, subordinates seeking action often leak information to selected advocates in order to politicize an issue and create an exigency that demands response. Being able to cope successfully with the turbulent environment also requires successful coping with the in-house procedural systems, personal talents, conflicting coalitions, and internal symbols on purpose, commitment, and unity. One way to accomplish this is to take advantage of the hard boundaries around the components of bureaucracy and their limited communication and permit the various internal coalitions to go their own way, within tolerable limits. It may be possible for different constituencies to be linked to different internal coalitions and remain satisfied, so long as the implicit conflicts do not explode. A manufacturer may stabilize production by buffering the core technical factory from a changing environment, but a commissioner cannot: He or she must cope with strong linkage between internal workers and external constituents.

Another minimalist strategy is to seek marginal advances in output in order to claim that things are steadily improving. Commissioners may design improvements for their staffs that will motivate the employees to cooperate with one another and with the commissioner. Service to the underserved or success in attaining a particularly difficult objective can merit extra rewards. But carrots and sticks are not enough by themselves to create unity and coherence in a bureaucracy. There is also what Phillip Selznick called infusing the organization with value by articulating purpose and mission in a way that gives meaning to bureaucratic tasks performed throughout the organization.[20] Gary Miller revealed how rewarding organization members solely by their self-interest will not produce optimum effort on their part.[21] Further, as cited previously, a number of scholars have challenged Mancur Olson's view that only the allocation of private goods provides incentive for collective action. They have shown that organizational commitment to a public good is sometimes sufficient and often necessary to maintain member support. Although a commission is not the kind of collective-action organization those scholars had in mind, it requires the same type of contribution of time and effort from its members and supporting constituents. Both the commissioner and his or her followers must transcend self-interest to some extent, if long-term optimal goals are to be attained.

Accordingly, at some point, commissioners must shift from inducements aimed at short-term self-interest to appeals that develop commitment to the long-term good of the whole commission. One way to foster unity is to create an atmosphere of cooperation, dedication, and trust within the bureaucracy. Commissioners may keep alive a "community of memory" by stories of past group-sacrifices.[22] Cooperation requires that someone make an initial trial contribution and risk being exploited—if the contribution is used but not reciprocated, for example. Commitment is strengthened by clear evidence that co-workers freely choose to reciprocate and do their part, when they could have taken advantage of an opportunity to exploit the preferred contributions of others.[23] "Most people are willing to sacrifice as long as they are not the only ones sacrificing."[24] Repeated stories of such possible advantages foregone for the sake of organizational effectiveness builds dedication and strengthens trust.

There are many other ways in which a community of memory is articulated besides stories of reciprocated cooperation: for example, displayed records of the group successes of the commission; histories of the transcending of internal conflicts by allegiance to the superordinate goals of the commission; accounts of the actions of past heroes and heroines and their persistence, sacrifices, and extraordinary efforts in pursuing the ideals of the commission; elaborations of current awards to the commission; and celebrations of current successes. A focus on the ideals of public goods rather than on private accomplishments is particularly important to the inspiration of a community of memory. Individual effort is celebrated because the end is to provide valuable public goods equally available to all. Commitment of this sort also transcends short-term shifts in focal concerns and provides long-term resolve and persistent action congruent with the resolve. In accordance with P. Brickman's extended analysis, it is the very tension between the strength of the resolve and the inducements of short-term rewards that brings out a sense of integrity in the members of the commission.[25] As members forego exploitative, short-term rewards in the interest of their exceptionally worthy, long-term goals, their sense of integrity is affirmed. On the other hand, as the members grow rich on short-term rewards, their resolve erodes. Both phenomena are common enough.

SUMMARY

The commissioner in an impossible job may reduce his or her vulnerability by choosing actions that maintain the long-term guiding myths of the commission (even weak myths) and also address the ever-changing, short-term focal concerns of the constituencies. In the course of mobilizing constituents to raise funds, the commissioner may dramatize true success stories to stimulate compassion and respect for the courage and persistence of his or her clients in overcoming their plight, as well as to activate the eternal human hope that even irresponsible, intractable people can be changed and induced to take action to overcome their situation.

The commissioner must develop the intuition to recognize the mutable patterns of focal concerns and power relationships among the multiple conflicting constituencies. Recognition, however tenuous, of the shifting patterns allows the commissioner to choose salient, practical, visible programs to address a current focal concern and, with intuitively calculated risk, strategically bypass other concerns. The use of social and historical criteria in assessing the processes and potential of actions allows the commissioners to see progress toward ambiguous and idealistic goals. As undesirable as they are, low frequency, high cost, high visibility incidents can be useful as well as embarrassing, if the commissioner can accept responsibility and push for action that will mobilize support for a needed new program.

Sometimes the commissioner must undertake to change recognized focal concerns and networks of coalitions. The best chances come from actions have these properties: (a) They affirm a strongly held value, idealistic as it may be; (b) they are taken in concert with constituents who are powerful enough to influence others, who have a strong commitment to those values, and who are uneasy about the current practices; (c) they require a specific, easily observed, change in manifest current practices; and (d) they stimulate commitment to the specific change, commitment publicly announced by powerful-enough people.

In times of consolidation and stabilization, the commissioner's strategies are more likely to emphasize efficiency in performing the core tasks of the commission. Conflicting internal coalitions may be linked with conflicting external constituencies, each constituency having its own division pursuing its own goals—as long as the underlying tension does not stimulate mutually destructive actions. In addition to emphasizing internal efficiency and to knowing the ins and outs of the standard professional operations, the commissioner may emphasize and celebrate the ideals and traditions of unity and commitment that bind and drive the commission and those who work for it.

Each coping strategy is embedded in multiple, conflicting, and unrealistic concerns and constituencies. Each, therefore, is linked to forces that can lead to its own defeat. Commissioners cope with an impossible job; they never master or control it.

NOTES

1. J. D. Thompson, *Organizations in Action* (New York: McGraw-Hill, 1967), pp. 83–98.

2. University of Southern California, *USC Trojan Family* 20, 6 (July 1988): 6 (published by the USC Division of University of Relations).

3. Eugene Bardach, *The Skill Factor in Politics* (Berkeley and Los Angeles: University of California Press, 1972).

4. Jameson W. Doig and Erwin C. Hargrove, eds., *Leadership and Innovation: A Biographical Perspective on Entrepreneurs in Government* (Baltimore: Johns Hopkins University Press, 1987), p. 15.

5. Francis E. Rourke, *Bureaucracy, Politics and Public Policy* (Boston: Little, Brown, 1984), especially chapter 3.

6. A. Etzioni, ed., *The Semiprofessions and Their Organizations* (New York: Free Press, 1969); D. C. Lortie, *School Teacher: A Sociological Study* (Chicago: University of Chicago Press, 1975).

7. Personal communication in a confidential interview with J. C. Glidewell, January 1959.

8. R. B. Cialdini and K. Ascani, "Test of a Concession Procedure for Inducing Verbal, Behavioral, and Further Compliance with a Request to Give Blood," *Journal of Applied Social Psychology* 61 (1976): 295–300; J. L. Freedman and S. C. Fraser, "Compliance without Pressure: The Foot-in-the-Door Technique," *Journal of Personality and Social Psychology* 4 (1966): 195–203; F. Green, "The Foot-in-the-Door Technique," *American Salesman* 10 (1965): 14–16; H. A. Segal, "Initial Psychiatric Findings of Recently Repatriated Prisoners of War," *American Journal of Psychology* 111 (1954): 358–63.

9. Freeman and Fraser, "Compliance without Pressure," p. 198.

10. W. A. Gamson, "A Theory of Coalition Formation," *American Sociological Review* 26 (1961): 373–82.

11. T. A. Caplow, "A Theory of Coalitions in a Triad," *American Sociological Review* 21 (1956): 489–93; R. M. Emerson, "Power-Dependence Relations," *American Sociological Review* 27 (1962): 37.

12. P. Bonacich, O. Grasky, and M. Peyrot, "Family Coalitions: A New Approach and Method," *Social Psychology Quarterly* 48 (1985): 42–50.

13. K. Lewin, *Resolving Social Conflicts* (New York: Harper and Row, 1948).

14. J. C. Glidewell, "Induced Change and Stability in Psychological and Social Systems," *American Journal of Community Psychology* 6 (1987): 741–72.

15. For example Herbert A. Simon, *The Sciences of the Artificial*, 2d ed. (Cambridge, Mass.: MIT Press, 1979).

16. Herbert A. Simon, "Making Management Decisions: The Role of Intuition and Emotion," *Academy of Management Executive* 1 (1987): 57–64.

17. C. Perrow, *Complex Organizations*, 3d ed. (New York: Random House, 1986).

18. P. Whittle, *Optimization over Time* (New York: Wiley, 1982).

19. Doig and Hargrove, *Leadership and Innovation*, p. 14.

20. Phillip Selznick, *Leadership in Administration: A Sociological Interpretation* (New York: Harper and Row, 1957).

21. Gary J. Miller, *Administrative Dilemmas: The Role of Political Leadership*, Political Economy Working Paper (St. Louis, Mo.: Washington University, June 1987), pp. 1–20.

22. R. N. Bellah, R. Madsen, W. M. Sullivan, A. Swidler, and S. M. Tipton, *Habits of the Heart: Individualism and Commitment in American Life* (New York: Harper and Row, 1985).

23. P. Bonacich, "Norms and Cohesion as Adaptive Responses to Potential Conflict: An Experimental Study," *Sociometry* 35 (1972): 357–75.

24. R. B. Innes, Personal communication to John C. Glidewell, 1987.

25. P. Brickman, *Commitment, Conflict and Caring* (New York: Prentice-Hall, 1987).

PART TWO
IMPOSSIBLE JOBS
IN PARTICULAR

4

Managing a Barbed-Wire Bureaucracy: The Impossible Job of Corrections Commissioner

John J. DiIulio, Jr.

Unless there is a radical and unexpected change in both demographic trends and sentencing routines, by the year 2000 the total number of United States citizens in the charge of corrections officials will number over 4 million; the California Department of Corrections and the Federal Bureau of Prisons alone will be responsible for some two hundred thousand prisoners; and corrections will represent the largest single item in many state budgets.

In 1988 roughly one out of every fifty citizens of the United States was living under some form of correctional supervision—prison, jail, probation, parole, community treatment, house arrest, and so on. In prisons alone over six hundred thousand citizens spent their days under the direct control of state and federal government officials. These "barbed-wire bureaucrats"—corrections commissioners, wardens, uniformed officers, and others—were responsible for managing a diverse lot of people who had only one thing in common: Each had been found guilty of a crime and sentenced by a court of law.

It is somewhat surprising, therefore, that students of American politics and public management have paid so little attention to what corrections officials do and how they do it. Especially surprising is the almost complete neglect by scholars of the role played by the heads of corrections agencies. Where barbed-wire bureaucracy is concerned, the normal tendency to "view public administration from the top down" has been inverted.[1] Although an enormous amount has been written about convicted criminals and inmate leaders, and although there is a comparatively small but growing literature on line corrections workers (especially custodial staff), there have been few studies of middle- and upper-level corrections managers (wardens, deputy superintendents, parole supervisors, and so on) and virtually nothing has been written about the executives of penal bureaucracies.[2]

This chapter is about the role of the corrections commissioner. It is based on a detailed, first-hand examination of the tenures of some two dozen commissioners and a close familiarity with about two dozen more.[3] All told, this sample of commissioners represents experience at every level of government, in every region of the country, over the last six decades. A few of the commissioners (or directors) in the sample are famous (at least in corrections circles) and enjoyed exceptionally long tenures. Others are less well known and had much briefer terms. Several of them directed more than one agency, many worked at more than one level of government, and a dozen or so started out as uniformed corrections officers. After leaving their posts, a few went on to head corrections associations and research foundations, many became consultants and part-time professors, and at least one became active in private sector corrections. Finally, some have long since passed from the scene; others are just beginning their careers.

It is tempting to discuss the role of the corrections commissioner by focusing biographically on the often colorful personalities, professional histories, and leadership styles of those who have held the job, endeavoring to trace, on the one hand, the exceedingly complex interplay of their correctional philosophies and management practices and, on the other, the objective performance of their agencies (e.g., rates of prison violence, levels of inmate programming, cost-effectiveness, recidivism rates).[4] Such an approach would produce much that is worth knowing about the dynamics of correctional leadership, but it would reveal little that is general, meaningful, and true about the role of the corrections commissioner itself.

Of course, many of the commissioners I interviewed do not believe that there are any universal characteristics that define their job. Immersed in the particulars of "what it takes" to run a given agency and extremely well schooled in the differences between one jurisdiction and the next, most of them are suspicious (and in a few cases downright dismissive) of the proposition that by sifting through the experiences of corrections commissioners separated by time, place, professional background, inmate populations, political context, and countless other factors, one can discover common administrative patterns, problems, and coping strategies. They are, for example, quick to point out that in some jurisdictions corrections directors have been responsible only for incarcerated convicts, while in other places they have been responsible for both carceral institutions and "field services" (e.g., probation and parole).

At the same time, however, none of the commissioners I interviewed and (I suspect) none of those I studied from afar would disagree with the proposition that one can generalize intelligently about what the corrections commissioner does; indeed, commissioners themselves have written memoirs and "how-to" manuals that vent an implicit belief in the possibility of such generalizations.[5] I hope, therefore, that I can be given the academic's dispensation if I pitch my generalizations about the job a bit higher and faster than the commissioners themselves have, with no pretense to sage advice and minimal reliance on supporting anecdotes.

Understood theoretically, the role of the corrections commissioner differs little from that of any other executive, public or private. There is, for example, absolutely nothing about the functions of the corrections executive that make them unamenable to analysis in the terms laid down by the celebrated organization theorist Chester I. Barnard. In 1938 Barnard offered a seminal definition of formal organization as "a system of consciously coordinated activity or forces of two or more persons."[6] The difficulty of any executive management task varies directly with the complexity of the relationships among and between organizational inputs (such as people, money, or tools) and organizational outputs (such as public health or criminal victimization). Written in Barnardian shorthand, the role of the corrections commissioner is to consciously coordinate the management of often incorrigible adjudicated criminals subject to stated legal goals and public expectations that are multiple, vague, and contradictory, and in the absence of both proven technologies and adequate bureaucratic authority. It is an impossible job in which one neither clearly succeeds nor fails but more nearly (as one commissioner phrased it) "strategizes, copes, hangs on for a awhile, and then lets go."

That the executive management of a barbed-wire bureaucracy is an impossible job may be glimpsed from the fact that the average contemporary corrections commissioner "lets go" or gets fired within about three years of assuming his or her post. Between 1973 and 1987, fewer than one-third of all adult corrections agencies were headed by commissioners whose average tenure was five years or more; in more than one-third they held office for an average of three years or less (see Table 4.1).

Of course, tenures vary somewhat according to such factors as the commissioner's professional background and who made the appointment.[7] The commissioner may come from within or outside of the agency, may have plenty of previous experience in corrections or none at all, and may be formally appointed by the governor or a corrections policy board. It does not matter. A commissioner is beating the odds if he or she "hangs on" long enough to settle into office, break in the executive team, establish alliances with relevant outside actors (legislators, judges, activists, union leaders, community representatives, and so on), and orchestrate any significant changes. It is rare for anyone to be able to make changes either in corrections policies themselves or in how the policies inherited from predecessors are translated into administrative action in the cellblocks and on the streets.

Historically, and at each level of government, administrative instability at the top of a barbed-wire bureaucracy has been associated with corrections institutions and programs that are in disfavor and lack political support. Almost without exception, where directors have played musical chairs, corrections bureaucracies have been especially troubled. Yet some commissioners have mastered their impossible jobs. Even more remarkable is the fact that—regardless of place, time, ideological bent, and other fundamental differences—they have done so by employing strikingly similar coping strategies. Most commissioners, however, have been overwhelmed by their impossible jobs. They have worn the role of corrections commissioner like a straitjacket and appear to have drawn their coping strategies from the same poisoned well. But before examining how corrections commissioners have coped, we need to learn the basic elements of their impossible job.

Table 4.1 Number of Commissioners of Adult Corrections Agencies, 1973–87

Alabama	7	Missouri	7
Alaska	6	Montana	4
Arkansas	4	Nebraska	5
Arizona	4	Nevada	4
California	5	New Hampshire	4
Colorado	8	New Jersey	1
Connecticut	3	New Mexico	7
Delaware	3	New York	4
District of Columbia	4	New York City	5
Federal Bureau	2	North Carolina	4
Florida	2	North Dakota	4
Georgia	3	Ohio	3
Hawaii	4	Oklahoma	4
Idaho	4	Oregon	3
Illinois	4	Pennsylvania	5
Indiana	3	Rhode Island	4
Iowa	5	South Carolina	1
Kansas	6	South Dakota	4
Kentucky	3	Tennessee	7
Louisiana	4	Texas	5
Maine	4	Utah	5
Maryland	6	Vermont	6
Massachusetts	3	Virginia	7
Michigan	2	Washington	5
Minnesota	3	West Virginia	4
Mississippi	7	Wisconsin	6
		Wyoming	3

Source: Compiled from the directories of the American Correctional Association, College Park, Maryland. The compilation was completed in April 1987; hence, the numbers for some agencies may be higher than indicated.

PUNISH, DETER, INCAPACITATE, REHABILITATE: THE CORRECTIONS COMMISSIONER IN HISTORICAL PERSPECTIVE

At least since the Jacksonian era, most Americans have wanted a criminal justice system that, among other things, apprehends and visits harm upon the guilty; makes offenders more virtuous and law-abiding; protects the innocent from victimization; dissuades would-be offenders from criminal pursuits; invites most convicts to return to the bosom of the free community; and achieves these ends without violating the public conscience or emptying the public purse. For most of the last two centuries, Americans have wished to ride simultaneously upon the four horsemen of criminal corrections: retribution (or punishment); reformation (or rehabilitation); deterrence (individual and general); and public protection (or incapacitation). In addition, within the lesser constellation of penal goals, they have demanded jobs for prisoners without threats to free workers; more adequate inmate programs and living space without more taxes or sites for construction; stern treatment of offenders without damage to prisoners' rights; and so on.

The penitentiary was an American invention, created as a way of optimizing the disparate moral and practical aims of American criminal justice. In the preface to his translation of the 1833 study of American penal practices by Gustave de Beaumont and Alexis de Tocqueville, Francis Lieber wrote, "It ought always to be borne in mind, that a convict is neither a brute nor a saint, and to treat him as either, is equally injurious to himself and to society."[8] Lieber, however, was preaching to the already converted. In the United States, the Judeo-Christian ethic of justice tempered by mercy was well established; the bars of the penitentiary were forged by revenge and cooled by forgiveness. Religious idealism mixed with cultural pragmatism to create a public expectation that in this country if nowhere else, the criminally wayward could and should be reformed as well as punished.

The report by Beaumont and Tocqueville did much to heighten this expectation. For the apparent successes of the American penal system they credited the nation's prison superintendents—the administrative forerunners of the corrections commissioner. Though formally answerable to officials called inspectors, "the superintendent, whose written authority is not very great, is yet the soul of the administration." The Frenchmen continued:

> The most important place then in the prison, is without a doubt, that of the superintendent. Generally it is intrusted in the penitentiaries of the United States, to honorable men, entitled by their talents to functions of this nature. . . . To great probity and a deep sense of their duty they add much experience, and that perfect knowledge of men so necessary to their position.[9]

Beaumont and Tocqueville noticed that the superintendents welcomed the inspection and scrutiny of legislators and others.[10] "This general attention," they concluded, "a source of perpetual vigilance, produces within the officers of the prisons, an extraordinary zeal and extreme circumspection. . . . This surveillance of public opinion which constrains them in some respects, produces also its compensation, because it is this public opinion which elevates their functions, and makes them honorable, low and obscure as they formerly were."[11]

For most of the next century, prison superintendents continued to hold the central place noted by Beaumont and Tocqueville. Few, however, were the paragons of professional probity and openness to outsiders that so impressed the two Frenchmen. In the 1840s states began to turn convicts over to private contractors, a process that was accelerated after the Civil War. The inmate abuse and political corruption bred by the contract-lease system reached epic proportions.[12] Yet penal systems that remained in public hands were rarely better and often worse. For example, before the Federal Bureau of Prisons was established, there were seven federal prisons holding some twelve thousand inmates. Each prison was funded separately by Congress and run according to the whims of individual autocratic wardens. Disciplinary practices were harsh and arbitrary, meals were slop served from buckets, and educational, work, and recreational opportunities were nonexistent. In short, by 1930 American penal practices were a source of national disgrace instead of national pride, and the penitentiary was viewed far and wide as the American invention that failed.

The corrections commissioner was conceived in the administrative wake of an attempt to rescue the nation's prisons and jails from the wretched state into which they were believed to have fallen. The position was a belated offspring of the Progressive movement. A powerful and essentially accurate image of that movement as it related to public management practices was conveyed by Robert H. Wiebe in *The Search for Order, 1877–1920*. For the "personal, informal ways of community" the reformers substituted "rules with impersonal sanctions," "assigned far greater power to government," and "encouraged the centralization of authority."[13]

Consider, for example, the establishment of the California Department of Penology. In 1929 the agency was created to centralize administrative controls over the state's abuse- and corruption-ridden penal facilities, including San Quentin and Folsom prisons; however, the post of director of penology was statutorily weak.[14] After its first incumbent died in 1933, the office was left vacant for nearly seven years. In 1944 the Department of Penology was reorganized into the Department of Corrections. The most significant element of the reorganization was the creation of a salaried director of corrections position empowered by law to manage each and every facet of the organization and removable for cause by the governor following a hearing before the state's Board of Corrections. Governor Earl Warren selected the agency's first executive (Richard A. McGee) through a national competitive test conducted by the California State Personnel Board.

A year after the California Department of Penology was formed, President Hoover signed the act of Congress that created the Federal Bureau of Prisons. Again, a main rationale for the agency was to centralize administrative controls over problem-ridden penal facilities, and again, a major vehicle for accomplishing this end was the establishment of a directorship. Unlike in California, however, from the very beginning the federal director's position had real teeth. For example, the director was given complete authority to hire and fire wardens and division heads. The first director, Sanford Bates, was formally charged with managing the bureau in a way that subjected convicts to uniform care and custody while providing them with treatment based on their individual needs. Four years after the bureau was established, the latter goal was addressed through the creation of Federal Prison Industries, Inc. (known since 1978 as UNICOR).

Anyone who ventures through the little mountain of dusty tracts written by penal reformers, state officials, and others who spearheaded the development of the nation's barbed-wire bureaucracies is bound to be struck by how much they pinned their hopes on those who would direct the agencies. There was a faith, in many cases explicit, that the disparate ends of American corrections—punish, deter, incapacitate, rehabilitate, all without gross expenditures of human and financial resources—could be reconciled and achieved through the good office of the corrections commissioner. Not surprisingly, several of the early commissioners consciously shared that hope; some preached it till they died.[15]

It was believed that for the commissioner to be successful, no mere strokes of bureaucratic legerdemain would do. Instead, the requirements were historical vision; a zeal for helping society's asocial, antisocial, deviant, delinquent, and criminalistic members; a stomach for firm but fair discipline; and a bottomless capacity for hard work. Whether genetically given or forged by the fires of experience, if the commissioner had these traits and if he or she could reclaim "that perfect knowledge of men" possessed by the first prison superintendents who had so impressed Beaumont and Tocqueville, then he or she would be able to institutionalize measures that combined revenge and forgiveness, order and liberty, tender-loving care and hard-nosed custody. At the historical core of American thinking about criminal justice, the bountiful mercy of Saint Francis wrestled the retributive spirit of Draco. The corrections commissioner was not to declare a victor; rather, he or she was to somehow negotiate organizationally among the moral and practical ends of American corrections in a way that translated into simple bureaucratic routines.

Of course, that impossibly tall order was never filled, not during the 1930s or after; it was, however, approximated. Rather than fulfilling their impossible public commission, most of the nation's corrections directors became reluctant, de facto leaders in what one corrections textbook author has phrased the "parade of ideologies" about how to handle convicted criminals and manage penal bureaucracies.[16] Instead of trying to reconcile the irreconcilable, the commissioners embraced a single end or a subset of ends but declared that the remaining correctional goals were achievable as a by-product of a concentrated focus on the objectives they had adopted as primary.

For example, in the administration of prisons, most commissioners through the end of World War II clung to the goal of punishment defined in terms of a steady, stable, unbending, paramilitary routine of numbering, counting, checking, locking, contraband control, and so on. With a few notable exceptions, through the 1950s the nation's penal executives maintained that convicted criminals had gone astray because they had never been accustomed to a civilized, noncriminal way of life—working hard, being punctual, dressing neatly, respecting duly constituted authority and the life, liberty, and property of others. Corrections agencies, therefore, were to be organized and managed in ways that "rehabilitated" felons via enforced habituation to the laws and values of "straight" society.

Naturally, this approach frustrated the academics (mainly sociologists) who for at least thirty years had been stressing the goal of rehabilitation characterized as a demilitarized prison environment where custodial imperatives were relaxed to create a "treatment milieu." Nothing was more calculated to get academia's goat than the barbed-wire bureaucrats' repeated insistence that punishment qua strict custody could work as a genuine species of "rehabilitation."[17]

In the 1960s and early 1970s, however, the country's corrections chiefs began to experiment—a few on their own enthusiastic initiative, many in deference to political and judicial pressures, and at least one (as he reported) "just for the hell of it." They coordinated the design and implementation of a wide variety of rehabilitation programs ranging from daily inmate "rap sessions" and special education, to experiments in behavior modification, to work-release projects and various types of prisoner self-government. By the mid-1970s both intra- and extradepartmental researchers were discovering and broadcasting what most of the commissioners had expected; namely, that while the relationship between inmate participation in such programs and recidivism rates was ambiguous, negative, or nonexistent, the relaxed controls had led to serious institutional disorders.[18] Meanwhile, former champions of the programs complained that in the name of rehabilitation inmates were being coerced into treatment regimens, widening the already vast discretionary authority of corrections officials and leading to longer stretches for prisoners tagged "unrehabilitated."

In 1978 the California Department of Corrections, which had led the charge for rehabilitation, was given a new and simplified legal mandate by its state legislature: Punish offenders and protect the public. Other penal systems followed suit. Neither in California nor elsewhere, however, did barbed-wire bureaucrats respond by dismantling treatment programs; indeed, in dozens of jurisdictions these programs were expanded. From the mid-1970s through the early 1980s, noted academic penologists exhorted corrections directors to replace the "rehabilitation model" with the "punishment model," or what a practitioner-author described as the "justice model for corrections."[19] But as one commissioner recalled, he and several of his peers were neither willing nor able to shift administrative gears; in their view, such shifts were imprudent and unnecessary.

> This business about one corrections model replacing the next is not exactly false but it misses the fact that we've never been all about one thing or the other. Except maybe in a few places where you had strong public pressure on one side or the other, or visionaries in charge, we never treated convicts as fallen angels to be rehabilitated; we never treated them like trash to be stored or warehoused. . . . The commissioner of corrections who plays the avenging angel or the redeemer is cruising for big lumps.

As another commissioner explained:

> In corrections, you don't change the way you manage people just because some professor got a bright idea about what works and what doesn't. In the day-to-day of it, everything gets conserved—the things you do to deprive them, to help them help themselves, to make an example of them, to keep them from harming the public. No matter what anybody says, in corrections you try to do everything all the time or you are defeated quickly.

It is not too much to conclude that the core of the historic role of the corrections commissioner has been to rediscover, articulate, and administer the logic of the state-supervised deprivation of liberty as a criminal sanction. That mandate operates over and against the wishes and pressures of those who, at least in the abstract, would be satisfied with a criminal justice system that "only" punishes, or deters, or attempts to reform, or protects the public. A corrections commissioner who came to his post with experience as a parole-board member summarized the dilemma.

What's your job in corrections if you're the one in charge? What does the public really want from you? The polls and the budget, the academic fads don't say. But look at the job itself. What's its logic? If society wanted its pound of flesh, they could get it more simply and cheaply. You can deter crime by cutting off heads. You can incapacitate and keep him from preying on the public without the services of commissioners and parole agents and [the rest]. . . . The commissioner's true role must be as guardian of corrections, there because, despite the reactionary or radical whims of his own staff, or the legislature, or the board, or nowadays the judges . . . this society wants to keep at all four "R's"—reformation, retribution, reintegration, rehabilitation. . . . The commissioner's job is to steer towards them irrespective of the fact that nobody knows how and there are always the jokers who want to make a hard right or a hard left.

A fundamental and effective coping strategy employed by corrections commissioners (described in more detail later) has been to conceive of themselves less as the custodians of criminals and more as the custodians of an untidy bundle of public values, at least one of which is forever being sacrificed to assorted public frustrations, staff pressures, academic trends, and ideological currents. On the other hand, those commissioners who have coped by making some short-term accommodations have invariably been burned—been fired or moved to another agency, retired or adopted a new line of work, after having presided over poor correctional institutions and programs. Before considering strategy, however, it is necessary to highlight the political and bureaucratic elements of the corrections commissioner's impossible job.

COACHES, CUSTOMERS, AND CRITICS: THE CONTEMPORARY CORRECTIONS COMMISSIONER

Over the last two decades the difficulty of handling adjudicated offenders in the cellblocks and on the streets has increased steadily. The managers and line employees of barbed-wire bureaucracies have faced rising populations and caseloads; an increase in the percentages of young, hardcore, and "hard to handle" convicts; greater personal liability for job-related actions; and, least in their view, no commensurate increase either in salary or in public appreciation.

The executives of barbed-wire bureaucracies are confronted with all of these problems and many others as well: judicial intervention; the rise of correctional officer unionism and prisoners' rights organizations; challenges from the private sector; greater media scrutiny and political pressure; increases in public spending that lag behind both demographic and sentencing trends; and so on. Since around 1970, the political and legal constraints on corrections commissioners have increased while the bureaucratic authority vested in them has decreased. In the apt phrase of the late practitioner-penologist Richard A. McGee, contemporary commissioners face a formidable cadre of "coaches, customers, and critics."[20] Moreover, they face fundamental challenges to the moral and practical worth of their work.

Let me begin by understating the obvious: The clients of barbed-wire bureaucracies are nonvoluntary. The average police commissioner runs an agency that is visible to the general public, interacts largely with ordinary citizens, and spends much of its resources responding to the uncoerced and friendly requests of noncriminal persons. The average corrections commissioner, on the other hand, runs an agency that is out of the public eye and interacts mainly with prisoners who do not want to be in prison, jail detainees who wish to be released, parolees who have "done their time" and prefer to be unsupervised, and probationers who do not like to be "hassled" by their overseers. As one corrections commissioner observed:

> The cops get a very mixed bag—lost kids crying for their mommy, speeding businessmen, punks on corners, and now and then a real criminal or two. We [in corrections] get all of their hardest cases. We manage all of society's "bad asses"; that's pretty much what we do. . . . [I]n carrying out the will of the court, we force people with a history of beating the system and doing things their way to be places they don't want to be, do things they don't want to do, for longer than they want to, under conditions that are about a hundred times more restrictive and unpleasant than they'd like.

Sociologists have established *ad nauseam* that convicted criminals share an ethos that runs counter to the norms and values of "straight" or "middle-class" life and are prone to resist in subtle and overt ways the authority of their "keepers."[21] With respect to prisons and jails, the conventional view is that penal administrators once managed by entering into tacit, corrupt bargains with convicts in order to keep the peace, bending or breaking the official rules governing most aspects of inmate behavior in return for inmate compliance with major custodial goals (i.e., no escapes or riots). Of practical necessity, the government of keepers managed not "by the book" but in deference to the language, leaders, laws, rites, and rituals of the society of captives.

It is commonly believed that in the late 1960s such informal arrangements among inmates and between inmates and staff began to break down primarily as a result of two factors: First, there was the politicization of the inmates, especially acute among convicts from minority backgrounds; and second, there were deepening rifts and bloody battles among and within inmate gangs organized along racial and ethnic lines.[22] Meanwhile, there was a steady and unprecedented climb in the number of inmates and a simultaneous increase in the percentages of convicts who were violent offenders, repeat offenders, or violent repeat offenders; by the mid-1980s, nearly 95 percent of prisoners fell into one of these three categories. Beyond the walls, many adjudicated criminals on probation, parole, or under some other form of noncarceral supervision were people who, a few years earlier, probably would have been kept behind bars. Additionally, the rising number of convicts who are serious drug abusers has made the barbed-wire bureaucrats custodians of an ever more unpredictable and, many commissioners contend, unreformable population of offenders. In short, by every conceivable measure, today's adjudicated criminals—the nonvoluntary clients of corrections agencies —are the largest, most incorrigible, and hardest to handle lot in the history of American corrections.

Nevertheless, the contemporary corrections commissioner is expected to muster the human and financial resources necessary to manage these offenders. Although most studies suggest that commissioners have a good deal of latitude in shaping correctional policies, the task of translating those policies into administrative action requires them to harness the efforts of individuals and groups— legislators, activists, judges, union leaders, and others—whose interests and ideas may conflict sharply.[23] Consider, for example, the contemporary corrections commissioner's position vis-à-vis correctional officers and judges.

In 1954 a federal circuit court ruled that judges are "without power to direct prison administration or to interfere with ordinary prison rules and regulations."[24] Since 1970, however, the "hands-off" doctrine has been repealed as judges have intervened on a wide range of prison issues, including crowding, food services, sanitation, healthcare, due process protections for inmates, and the constitutionality of prison conditions. In 1986 some thirty corrections agencies were operating under conditions-of-confinement court orders; many had class-action suits in progress and population limits set by the courts; over a dozen state systems had court-appointed special masters, monitors, and compliance coordinators. In some jurisdictions, judges have become de facto commissioners of corrections.[25]

Some commissioners have tried to stay one step ahead of the courts, seeking accreditation for their facilities as a shield against unfavorable rulings and rushing their agencies into compliance with judicial decrees. Other commissioners have dragged their feet, with a few even rallying their rank-and-file workers to oppose the court's "interference." However, most of today's commissioners are cognizant of the bitter experiences of directors who have "argued with the umpires"; none of them came to office before the era of judicial involvement. They are inclined, therefore, to take the former approach. Yet in so doing, they risk weakening or destroying their often tenuous support within the department, especially among the uniformed custodial staff.

In 1967 the President's Commission on Law Enforcement and the Administration of Justice noted correctly that line corrections workers are "the most influential persons in institutions by virtue of their numbers and their daily intimate contact with offenders. They can, by their attitude and understanding, reinforce or destroy the effectiveness of almost any correctional program."[26] Those words are doubly true today, given the fact that over the last twenty years correctional officers in most jurisdictions have unionized. This development is partly a response to "pro-prisoner" court orders that in their judgment have gutted basic custodial controls and enhanced the physical dangers and emotional frustrations of their work.[27] As a result, the corrections commissioner has become the head of "management," the officers' union representatives the heads of "labor," and everything from changes in officer training to dental plans the objects of often complex, lengthy, and unfriendly negotiations.

The contemporary commissioner's delicate task of building among the officers a sense of mission, esprit de corps, and high morale is further complicated when, in response to a judicial decree, he or she must be the instrument of changes in agency policies and procedures, the real or perceived impact of which is to expose lowest-level employees to new and greater stresses and demands. The contemporary corrections commissioner is sometimes forced to choose between being held in contempt of court and being held in contempt by his or her subordinates.

Together with judges and union leaders, among the contemporary commissioner's most important "coaches and critics" are politicians and the members of the press. Even with the increases in public spending on corrections noted earlier, the work of barbed-wire bureaucracies remains low on the list of public priorities; by some measures it ranks dead last. Assignment to legislative committees that deal with corrections is no more prized by most politicians than assignment to the "prison beat" is coveted by most journalists. Both politicians and news pundits have strong incentives to emphasize what is wrong with corrections, stir controversies, oversimplify problems, and otherwise reinforce the impossible elements of the corrections commissioner's job.

Shifts in legislative sentiment about corrections have occurred every few years. A review of state and federal penal codes and the annual reports of corrections agencies suggests that between 1967 and 1987 the legal mandates of barbed-wire bureaucracies migrated from individualized treatment of adjudicated offenders to punishment. As should be obvious, it costs more to run meaningful inmate educational programs and the like than it does to merely "warehouse" offenders. To the extent that the aggregate data on corrections spending reveals anything, however, it appears that in most jurisdictions *more* money per inmate was being appropriated even as the lawmakers shifted the emphasis to "no-frills" custody. Thus, the politicians were inviting corrections commissioners to do less with more, while judges and activist organizations (e.g., the National Prisoners Project of the American Civil Liberties Union) were prodding them to expand their programs and to provide offenders with greater amenities and services.

Elected officials pay attention to what corrections agencies are doing mainly after some major prison disturbance has happened. Across the nation, more government hearings were held and reports issued in the two-year period following the 1971 uprising at New York's Attica Correctional Facility than in any two-year period since. There was a similar flurry of activity (at least in the southwest) following the bloody 1980 riot at New Mexico's Santa Fe Penitentiary. Governors are inclined to turn corrections departments into political footballs and to cashier directors at any major disturbance; new governors have been quick to replace incumbent commissioners.

Journalists who cover correctional issues can be great resources for the corrections commissioner, but more often they are great adversaries. Most corrections workers, including many commissioners, believe that members of the press are biased against them either because they have "watched too many Jimmy Cagney movies," or because they harbor ideological views that are antithetical to what penal administrators do, or both. However, some commissioners recognize that journalism has some occupational tendencies that work against accord regardless. Journalists prefer to embrace the "powder keg" theory of prison disturbances. Stories about unsafe, unclean, unproductive prisons that can blow any minute make excellent copy. As human interest material, the colorful and bitter book-length accounts of former convicts naturally garner more media attention than the dry and studied memoirs of former corrections officials.

There is a strong "no-win" element to the media's coverage of prison issues. For example, in reporting on escapes of short-term, nonviolent offenders from an experimental minimum-security work camp, the television cameras focus on the high walls of a maximum-security prison where no escapes have occurred for a generation. The next day the same station runs an editorial about how spending $70,000 per higher-custody prison cell is too much and more innovative ways of housing convicted criminals are needed. In one year, a leading state newspaper prints a series of articles criticizing corrections officials for doing too little to handle the prison crowding crisis and to cut costs. The next year the same paper runs a series denouncing the officials for experimenting broadly with tax-saving early-release programs. As one commissioner lamented, "No matter what you do or how you respond to public pressures, you're bound to play the goat or scapegoat."

In part as a response to the widespread public perception that corrections agencies have failed, by 1987 three states had enacted laws authorizing privately operated state correctional facilities, while more than a dozen states were actively considering the option. In 1985 the Corrections Corporation of America (CCA), a leader among the twenty or so firms that have entered the "prison market," made a bid to take over the entire Tennessee prison system. Though its bid was unsuccessful, CCA now operates several correctional facilities, among them a Federal

Bureau of Prisons halfway house, two Immigration and Naturalization Service facilities for the detention of illegal aliens, and a 370-bed maximum-security jail in Bay County, Florida. More than thirty-six states now contract for at least one correctional service or program.

The future of private sector corrections—and whether or not the market can provide more and better correctional services for less money—remains in grave doubt.[28] A majority of sitting corrections commissioners favor private involvement in such areas as medical and mental health services, community treatment centers, juvenile institutions, prison construction and financing, remedial education, drug treatment, college courses, vocational training, and counseling. Most, however, do not support the private management of adult prisons and jails.

The privatization movement is but the latest manifestation of the degree to which the moral and practical value of the corrections commissioner's work has been called into question. In the 1960s the commissioners heard shouts of "Tear down the walls!"; in the 1980s the shouts became "Sell them!" Over the last two decades, liberals have argued that correctional institutions and programs are unjust and inhumane; conservatives have claimed that they cost too much and punish too little. In the eyes of the former, commissioners who plead that corrections can be improved through better public management are guilty of arguing that the guillotine can work better if it is well oiled. To the latter, commissioners who operate programs designed to protect inmates and enhance their life prospects are guilty of displaying too much concern for remorseless criminals and too little for their innocent victims.

In this regard, perhaps the single best example of the impossible character of the corrections commissioner's job is the prison and jail furlough programs. A furlough is an officially sanctioned leave from confinement monitored by regular or random checks on the inmate's whereabouts and behavior. In most jurisdictions, furloughs of varied length are granted to inmates within months of their official release dates. They give the inmates a chance to reintegrate themselves back into the "free world," search for gainful postrelease employment, establish contacts with family members who will be vital to the inmate's successful return to the community, and so on.

In general, corrections officials are extremely careful in granting furloughs, and their carefulness pays off. In 1987, for example, over two hundred thousand furloughs were granted nationwide. Over 99.7 percent of them resulted in neither a technical violation of the terms of the furlough nor a new crime.[29] According to most of the existing research on the subject, and in the judgment of virtually every seasoned corrections administrator, inmates who receive furloughs have fewer behavioral problems behind bars, lower rates of recidivism, and a better postrelease employment record than comparable inmates who do not receive furloughs, or who receive them less frequently.[30]

As one corrections official stated: "What other government program do you know of that works over 99 percent of the time? . . . What other corrections program is there that comes after a long bout of punishment, clearly helps to rehabilitate some offenders, gives the inmates a real incentive to stay out of trouble inside and in the community, and poses very little risk to public safety?" He might have added "saves money" and "relieves institutional overcrowding" to this list: A day of furlough supervision costs a fraction of a day of confinement supervision, and furlough programs free up a little space in packed prisons and jails.

Nevertheless, corrections commissioners who tout their furlough program as an example of a cost-effective correctional management strategy with clear net benefits, both human and financial, are setting themselves up for a sure fall. This was illustrated clearly in the wake of the 1988 presidential race. Willie Horton, a Massachusetts inmate serving a sentence of life without the possibility of parole, was granted an unsupervised parole. While on furlough, Horton beat and raped a Maryland woman and assaulted her husband. In famous (or infamous) campaign ads, the Democratic presidential candidate, Massachusetts Governor Michael Dukakis, was blamed for the Horton incident and the "revolving-door justice" it supposedly exemplified. The Democrats struck back, albeit ineffectively, by publicizing the fact that during his tenure as governor of California, Ronald Reagan had "authorized" two furloughs that resulted in violent crimes, including one against a law enforcement officer.

Regardless of what effect the "furlough issue" had on the 1988 presidential race, its impact on furlough programs around the country was felt almost immediately: retrenchment in most jurisdictions, de facto abolition in others. North Carolina and Massachusetts were the only two states that granted furloughs to inmates serving sentences of life without possibility of parole; both states have removed those inmates' eligibility for furloughs. Despite their relatively liberal eligibility standards, Massachusetts and North Carolina had two of the nation's most successful furlough programs. But in Massachusetts, North Carolina, New Jersey, New Mexico, Maryland, California, Michigan, and many other states, the Horton incident had a chilling effect on prison and jail administration, and the percentage of furlough-eligible inmates granted furloughs declined from pre-1988 levels, in some cases to zero.

At the federal level, the Bureau of Prisons (BOP) boasted what was arguably the nation's most successful and tightly administered furlough program. To honor a Bush campaign promise, however, in August 1989 the BOP was formally directed by the attorney general to further tighten furlough eligibility requirements and to reduce the number of inmates being granted furloughs; in fact, well before this formal directive had been issued, the BOP had cut back on furloughs.

Upon hearing the news of the Bush administration's decision to curtail furloughs in the BOP, one former state corrections commissioner observed: "There it is, there's the impossible nature of this job. You run a program that's a success by any rational criterion. . . . Does a welfare director get pressured or axed if one AFDC [Aid to Families with Dependent Children] recipient fails to leave the welfare rolls after going through a welfare reform job-readiness program? Of course not. But in corrections, one Willie Horton can derail a good program nationally and ruin a career." In fact, Massachusetts Corrections Commissioner

Michael Fair resigned under pressure after the 1988 presidential election; by most accounts, Fair, who had served longer than his two immediate predecessors, was the state's best corrections commissioner since Sanford Bates.

Thus, surrounded and hounded by his or her agency's coaches, customers, and critics, the contemporary corrections commissioner manages a growing corner of the American criminal justice "nonsystem"—an exceedingly loose confederation of federal, state, and local courts, district attorneys' offices, police departments, and other bureaucracies, numbering in the thousands and operating under a mind-boggling array of administrative, legal, and political constraints. Like their cousins in policing, mental health, and certain other areas, executives of barbed-wire bureaucracies have ways of coping with the multiple, vague, and contradictory goals, with the fragmented and often fractured bureaucratic authority, with the uncertainty about how to achieve correctional ends, and with the nonvoluntary and often incorrigible character of their clients that define their impossible job.

THE COPING STRATEGIES
OF THE CORRECTIONS COMMISSIONER

The nucleus of any corrections commissioner's batch of coping strategies is his or her decision about what goals to emphasize and how to measure agency performance. The temptation to cater to one goal at the expense of others is great, especially if the favored goal is incapacitation (or public protection). Success can be measured with every count of the population; if every inmate is alive, present, and accounted for, and if every noncarceral charge reports when and where he or she is supposed to and is supervised intensively, then the agency is achieving its mission. It is equally tempting for the commissioner to proclaim that public expectations about corrections are unrealistic, highlighting (perhaps even whining about) the plethora of practical problems that beset the agency—dilapidated facilities, racially polarized inmates, insufficient funds, a rising probationer to probation officer ratio, demands to build new facilities but "not in my neighborhood," and so on. Yet another tempting approach is for the commissioner to "confess" that the agency provides at best some sort of socially necessary evil—an expensive, unavoidable, but essentially worthless public service. For example, one contemporary commissioner, invited by newspaper reporters to define the public value of his agency's work, responded with the rhetorical question, "What the hell good is a jail?"

Embrace less ambiguous and more easily achievable goals and downplay or sacrifice others; attempt to alter (usually lower) public expectations by rehearsing agency problems; express pessimism and resignation about the public value of the agency's work. Where the executive management of a barbed-wire bureaucracy is concerned, these three common responses to goal conflict and technological uncertainty represent three deadly sins. It is true that corrections commissioners who have responded in one or more of these three ways have won short-term benefits of various kinds. They have stimulated newspaper editorials about the commissioner's "new realism"; they have activated fresh or invigorated old internal and external allies from the ranks of those who support the goal (or subset of goals) the commissioner has embraced (or who favor shrinking the number of people under correctional supervision). Within a year or so, however, the latent costs of these responses invariably come home to roost. The commissioner confronts litigation and public criticism concerning inhumane warehousing conditions behind bars (where the commissioner's favored goals are punishment and incapacitation), or charges of coddling and "letting the inmates run the joint" (where the favored goal is rehabilitation); or a loss of public confidence and a fall from political and judicial grace for both the agency and its leader; or lower staff morale, higher turnover rates and, in many jurisdictions, an increase in the use of disability leaves and absenteeism by line employees.

There are, however, three coping strategies that appear to have served past and present corrections commissioners in good stead under all circumstances. The primary strategy has been to act as the even-handed custodian of all four vague, controversial, and self-contradictory purposes of corrections—punish, deter, incapacitate, rehabilitate—by translating them administratively into two or three operational goals. A good illustration is the Federal Bureau of Prisons.

As noted earlier, the BOP was created at a time when the nation's prisons were under severe criticism. The agency's first three directors gradually institutionalized a management system that stressed inmate discipline, work, and recreation. Between 1970 and 1987 the agency's fourth director, Norman A. Carlson, formally advanced an agency mission statement emphasizing three goals: safety, humanity, and opportunity. *Safety* meant the incidence of things that threaten the physical and emotional well-being of inmates and staff and place the public at direct risk—assault, homicide, suicide, escape, and so on. *Humanity* meant the incidence of things that might make for decent living conditions behind bars—good food, clean clothes, exercise opportunities. *Opportunity* meant the incidence of things that might improve the inmates' later life prospects—programs in remedial reading, job training, and so on.

In testimony before Congress, in dealing with the press, in response to court orders, and in virtually every aspect of its internal management, the director of the BOP kept himself and his staff focused on these three goals, forever implying, though rarely stating explicitly, that they were operational embodiments of the ultimate ends of corrections, or as near to such as one could get. Especially interesting in this regard was his blending of opportunity with rehabilitation in a way that held out the possibility, but not the promise, that offenders would return to the community as law-abiding citizens and that promoted the agency's public value as a facilitator rather than as guarantor of this outcome. In a typical bout of public questioning, the director once stated:

> Mr. Chairman, I must say that I have changed my attitude over the past few years, based upon [my reading of work by leading] scholars in this field. . . .

I still think, however, as I said in my testimony, that inmates can and do change. Why they change I don't know. I don't think anyone knows. But as I indicated, about half the inmates released from custody today stay out of trouble. The change has to come from within the inmate himself. . . . I think we can facilitate change, but we certainly cannot coerce it.[31]

This commissioner of corrections, building on the organizational themes and innovations of his predecessors, managed his agency around these three performance-based goals in a way that made it possible for him and his agency to absorb shifts in legislative sentiment, changes in public and "expert" opinion, new court decrees, and so on, without exposing his office to severe criticisms or exposing the agency to sudden, radical, and demoralizing upheavals. Corrections commissioners in several other agencies—from the Texas Department of Corrections to the Pennsylvania Bureau of Corrections—have also managed their agencies around a few such operational ends. Between 1962 and 1972 in Texas, Dr. George Beto dubbed the agency's aims as "obedience, labor, and self-improvement"; between 1953 and 1970 in Pennsylvania, that bureau's first commissioner, Arthur T. Prasse, styled their goals more loosely as "instructive labor, educational, and moral training."

Not suprisingly, there has been a cross-fertilization of administrative ideas among commissioners who have attempted to manage their barbed-wire bureaucracies around such operational goals.[32] Certain traits are common to penal executives who have taken this approach. Generally speaking, they are versed in the latest penological theories but profess to be swept away by none of them. They have strong, well-articulated personal views about corrections (usually traditional-punitive-custodial ideas mixed with progressive-reformist ones and weighted in favor of the former) which they advance in deference to their sense of professional mission as "the hands and feet" of important public values. Also, they are absolutely relentless in trying to interest important outside actors—judges, legislators, journalists, and others—in the workings of their agency. As one of the longest-reigning commissioners in the history of corrections observed:

You have to pursue all the goals all the time. People want retribution and rehabilitation. . . . Embodying all the goals in your institutional routine is difficult, but you get there by focusing on safety and programs. . . . The commissioner doesn't own the prisons, and so he must interest others in their quality of life.

There are at least two other coping strategies that have been employed successfully in the management of barbed-wire bureaucracies. First, commissioners have consciously sought to project an image of themselves that is appealing to a wide range of people both inside and outside of the organization. For example, Dr. George Beto of the Texas Department of Corrections earned the nickname "Walking George" for his practice of showing up at the prisons every day, usually unannounced. A tall, lean Lutheran minister and college-president-turned-prison-chief, Beto was as comfortable with a prison manual as he was with a Bible; he could quote the classics one minute and chew out a subordinate the next. Beto made himself popular with powerful state leaders, developed a reputation for omniscience among his subordinates, and retired while he was at the height of his powers and popularity. To inmates, Beto was "the preacher man with a baseball bat in one hand and a Bible in the other." To staff he was a bigger-than-life figure who would reward loyalty and good performance but be ruthless in punishing errors and insubordination. To state leaders he was an exceedingly talented, politically sensitive, tireless, and competent executive who could be relied upon to run the prisons well and cheaply.[33]

Second, commissioners have adopted technical and managerial innovations in order to create a sense of progress and generate favorable press: computerized cellblock-monitoring devices; sophisticated inmate-classification systems; reports by high-priced and credible outside management consultants; revamped staff recruitment and training programs; and so forth. Often, commissioners have made such innovations despite their belief that the results would be marginal at best. As one commissioner observed:

> Here's a field that's controversial. There's a sense in which, by definition, we can't make progress. It's stagnant. So every once in a while, you have to do something to stir the pot, motivate people, create some sense of visible, tangible progress—new hardware, new reports, new forms. None of it may amount to anything in the end, but you get inmates, your staff, the news people to recognize that you're alive, that you're trying. . . . In this business, all we can do is try, experiment, keep at it.

CONCLUSION

Historically, the impossible job of the corrections commissioner has had relatively few occupants with either the willingness or the ability to "try, experiment, keep at it." But it has had enough Betos, Bennetts, and Carlsons to suggest that creative coping strategies do exist and can make a difference. Although it is possible to make limited generalizations about the strategies themselves, it is not yet possible to generalize about the types of men and women who are likely to make good chief executives of barbed-wire bureaucracies. As tentative propositions, however, it would appear that some or all of the following general traits are necessary:

- an understanding of the multiple and conflicting nature of the agency's goals coupled with a genuine commitment to each of them
- a creative capacity to translate broad societal expectations and policy decrees into administrative action

- an energetic approach to the internal and external obstacles to mustering the human and financial resources necessary to make innovations
- a personality forceful and complex enough to become identified with the agency itself

In essense, my conclusion is that the best way for corrections commissioners to cope with their impossible job is for them to recognize it as such and to grapple with it accordingly. Those managers of barbed-wire bureaucracies who have been most successful have understood intuitively what I have discussed explicitly—that their agency's goals are many and in conflict; that the means to achieve these goals may not be at hand; that their authority is fragmented; and that their clients are a hard lot, usually uncooperative and generally unrepresentative of the better lights of human nature. Needless to say, corrections commissioners may succeed or fail for reasons (and from strategies) other than those highlighted in this chapter. Also, it is probably true that the effectiveness of corrections commissioners is more contingent upon broad contextual variables (e.g., economic conditions; whether the period is one of administrative expansion, consolidation, or contraction; the character of surrounding political structures) than the foregoing analysis suggests—anchored as it is in the skill and inventiveness (or lack thereof) of the jobs' incumbents. Still, it is fair to conclude that if our barbed-wire bureaucracies have failed more often than they have succeeded, it is largely because their leaders have more often been the unwitting victims than the dedicated masters of their impossible jobs.

NOTES

1. For a discussion of this tendency, see James Q. Wilson, *The Investigators: Managing FBI and Narcotics Agents* (New York: Basic Books, 1978), chapter 1.

2. See John J. DiIulio, Jr., *Governing Prisons: A Comparative Study of Correctional Management* (New York: Free Press, 1987), chapter 4.

3. Myrl Alexander; Sanford Bates; James V. Bennett; George Beto; Robert Britton; Robert Brown; George Camp; Norman Carlson; Benjamin Cooper; Roger Crist; Thomas Coughlin; George Denton; O. B. Ellis; J. J. Enomoto; W. J. Estelle; Michael Fair; William Fauver; Michael Franke; Frank Hall; Gus Harrison; William Hogan; T. Don Hutto; Glen Jeffes; Perry Johnson; Paul Keve; Richard Koehler; Anna Kross; William Leeke; Elaine Little; J. Lynaugh; Ellis MacDougal; Benjamin Malcom; Ronald Marks; Daniel McCarthy; O. L. McCotter; Richard McGee; D. V. McKaskle; Jacquelline McMickens; Larry Meachum; Arthur Prasse; Raymond Procunier; Orville Pung; Michael J. Quinlan; Joseph Ragen; Amos Reed; William Robinson; Ruth Rushen; Kenneth Schoen; Rick Seiter; George Sumner; Anthony Travisono; Louis Warnwright; Benjamin Ward. All quotations are anonymous.

4. This is the approach taken in DiIulio, *Governing Prisons*.

5. For examples, see Richard A. McGee, *Prisons and Politics* (Lexington, Mass.: Lexington Books, 1981); James V. Bennett, *I Chose Prison* (New York: Alfred A. Knopf, 1970); Joseph Ragen with Charles Finstone, *Inside the World's Toughest Prison* (Springfield, Ill.: Charles C. Thomas, 1962).

6. Chester I. Barnard, *The Functions of the Executive* (Cambridge, Mass.: Harvard University Press, 1968), p. 73.

7. For a nice overview, see Thomas N. Gilmore and Gary R. Carine, *Leadership Instability in a Domain: The Case of Corrections* (Philadelphia: Wharton Center for Applied Research, University of Pennsylvania, 1986).

8. Gustave de Beaumont and Alexis de Tocqueville, *On the Penitentiary System in the United States, and Its Application in France* (with an Appendix on Penal Colonies and Statistical Notes), trans. Francis Lieber (Philadelphia: Carey, Lea and Blanchard, 1833), p. xviii.

9. Ibid., p. 28.

10. Ibid., pp. 30–31.

11. Ibid.

12. For an overview, see John J. DiIulio, Jr., "What's Wrong with Private Prisons," *Public Interest* 92 (Summer 1988): 66–83.

13. Robert H. Wiebe, *The Search for Order, 1877–1920* (New York: Hill and Wang, 1967), p. xiv. Unlike their approach to other public organizations, however, the Progressive era reformers' approach to prisons was rather schizophrenic. On the one hand, they sought to encourage individualized treatment of offenders, more personal inmate-staff relations, and an end to the lock-step march, the rule of silence, and striped uniforms. On the other hand, they sought to bureaucratize the facilities by creating centralized departments of corrections headed by a commissioner or director who would enunciate uniform administrative standards and see to it that things were run accordingly. The reformers espoused an anti-institutional creed, yet they were institution-builders; they tried simultaneously to invest the wardens and officers with discretion and to place them under centralized leadership that would deprive them of any discretion; they sought to advance uniform procedures and to promote individualized treatment. The net result was hardly surprising: As it was pulled in opposite administrative directions, the prison stood still. For an excellent account of this era of penal reform, see David J. Rothman, *Conscience and Convenience: The Asylum and Its Alternatives in Progressive America* (Boston: Little, Brown, 1980).

14. As Lloyd L. Voight noted in his brief history of the agency, the statute made the director the nominal superior of five autonomous divisions. The director's formal powers went no further than calling a meeting of the division heads once each month. For an overview, see Voight, *History of California State Correctional Administration from 1930 to 1948* (San Francisco, Calif.: n.p., 1949), chapter 1.

15. See Bennett, *I Chose Prison*. Bennett wrote the 1928 report that led to the creation of the Federal Bureau of Prisons in 1930. He ran the agency from 1937 to 1964 and was "shadow director" from 1964 to 1970. His autobiography concludes with these words: "I believe there is a treasure in the heart of every man if we can find it—*if we can help him find it.*"

16. Clemens Bartollas, *Introduction to Corrections* (New York: Harper and Row, 1981).

17. For example, see Gresham M. Sykes, *The Society of Captives: A Study of a Maximum-Security Prison* (Princeton, N.J.: Princeton University Press, 1958). Sykes chided the officials of New Jersey State Prison as "indifferent to the task of reform, not in the sense that they reject reform out of hand . . . but in the sense that rehabilitation tends to be seen as a theoretical, distant, and somewhat irrelevant by-product of successful performance of the tasks of custody and internal order" (p. 38). Sykes and other analysts posited an unresolvable tension between the penal goals of treatment and custody. In the introduction to a landmark 1960 volume by leading sociologists of the prison, George H. Grosser noted that the book set forth a "pessimistic view": The prison cannot achieve both "the aims of custody, or punishment, on the one hand, and treatment and reform, on the other" (Grosser, introduction to Richard Cloward et al., *Theoretical Studies in Social Organiza-*

tion of Prison [New York: Social Service Research Council, 1960], p. 4). At least two recent studies have challenged this view; see DiIulio, *Go verning Prisons,* chapter 1, and Robert Johnson, *Hard Times: Understanding and Reforming the Prison* (Monterey, Calif.: Brooks/Cole, 1987). Among corrections workers, the tension between these goals is often acute. As one veteran correctional officer stated: "Think of a convicted criminal as a man who never learned to dance. Think of rehabilitation and treatment programs as his dance instruction. We can't teach a man to dance and tie his legs at the same time. But that's precisely what we're supposed to do" (DiIulio, *Governing Prisons,* p. 40).

18. Robert Martinson, "What Works?—Questions and Answers about Prison Reform," *Public Interest* 36 (Spring 1974): 22–54. A more detailed statement is Douglas Lipton et al., *The Effectiveness of Correctional Treatment: A Survey of Evaluation Studies* (New York: Praeger, 1975).

19. David Fogel, ". . . *We Are the Living Proof": The Justice Model for Corrections* (Cincinnati, Ohio: W. H. Anderson, 1979).

20. McGee, *Prisons and Politics.*

21. For a good overview of the sociological literature on prisoners, see Lee H. Bowker, *Prisoner Subcultures* (Lexington, Mass.: Lexington Books, 1977).

22. An excellent treatise on the subject is James B. Jacobs, *Stateville: The Penitentiary in Mass Society* (Chicago: University of Chicago Press, 1977). Also see his *New Perspectives on Prisons and Imprisonment* (New York: Cornell University Press, 1983).

23. See DiIulio, *Governing Prisons.*

24. *Banning v. Looney,* 213 F.2d 771, 348 U.S. 859 (1954).

25. For a discussion of one such judge, see John J. DiIulio, Jr., "Prison Discipline and Prison Reform," *Public Interest* 89 (Fall 1987): 71–90.

26. President's Commission on Law Enforcement and Administration of Justice, *Task Force Report: Corrections* (Washington, D.C.: Government Printing Office, 1967), p. 96.

27. John M. Wynne, Jr., *Prison Employee Unionism: The Impact on Correctional Administration and Programs* (Washington, D.C.: Government Printing Office, 1978).

28. See DiIulio, "What's Wrong with Private Prisons," and John J. DiIulio, Jr., "Private Prisons," in *Crime File,* ed. Michael Tonry (Washington, D.C.: National Institute of Justice, 1987).

29. John J. DiIulio, Jr., *No Escape: The Future of American Corrections* (New York: Basic Books, forthcoming), chapter 2.

30. Ibid.

31. Testimony of Norman A. Carlson, *Hearings before the Subcommittee on Courts, Civil Liberties, and the Administration of Justice of the Committee on the Judiciary of the House of Representatives* (July 28 and 30, 1975), pp. 113–14.

32. For example, Carlson admired Beto, Beto admired Prasse, and all three admired Carlson's predecessor James V. Bennett. William Leeke admired Ellis MacDougal.

33. For a detailed discussion of Beto's tenure as a corrections commissioner, see DiIulio, *Governing Prisons,* chapter 4. Beto, of course, represents just one variety of this strategy. Less charismatic penal executives have employed it to equally good effect. Anna Kross of the New York City system used a helicopter to swoop onto Rikers Island and make surprise visits. She posed as a tough administrator with a passion for reform. Norman A. Carlson of the Federal Bureau of Prisons, a hulking man with a crew cut, projected a spit-and-polish image, made a fetish of cleanliness and punctuality, was exceptionally soft-spoken and courteous to everyone from key congressmen to life-term inmates, and always gave credit for any publicized successes to his staff. As one long-time agency employee observed, "Carlson became the Bureau of Prisons to everyone on Capitol Hill and to everyone in the cellblocks." Yet another commissioner, Raymond Procunier, was bold, brash, controversial, and colorful, approaching inmates, staff, and outsiders like an old-time ward politician

seeking votes, and walking briskly into crisis situations in order to offer himself as a hostage or talk ''man-to-man'' with prison gang leaders. ''The Pro,'' as he was called, developed a reputation as a ''firm but fair'' (if often erratic and unpredictable) commissioner. By contrast, William Fauver of the New Jersey Department of Corrections (at this writing the nation's longest-reigning active corrections chief) has become known as a calm, quiet, and scrupulously honest executive who works methodically to form a consensus and to get things done.

5

Police Leadership:
The Impossible Dream?

Mark H. Moore

The field explored in this chapter is the management of large, urban police departments. These jobs are "impossible" for all the usual reasons. Their mandated policy goals are far too broad, internally inconsistent, imperfectly measurable, and fickle. Their operating capabilities are not equal to the tasks set for them—partly because the organizations lack the necessary resources, partly because their current operating programs do not work as well as one might hope, and partly because much that determines their performance lies outside their direct control.

My hypothesis is that what allows some police managers to "succeed" despite these impossible circumstances is their ability to manage the terms by which they will be held accountable. The key to their success is either making their operations conform to public expectations of what they should be doing, or changing public conceptions to make them consistent with their own ambitions for their enterprise.[1]

This assertion may seem tautological, or cynical, or both. The tautology lies in defining successful police managers as those who are perceived as being successful. The cynicism lies in suggesting that police managers should deal with public perceptions of success rather than concentrate on the material reality. However, I mean the statement to be neither tautological nor cynical. My argument is that successful police managers use the force of public expectations to guide the conduct of their organization. In some cases, they take existing concepts of policing and make their organizations conform to those expectations. In other cases, they propose an idea that commands public support and then use the support and the new conception to challenge their organization's current ways of doing business. In either case, what is important and interesting is that the successful police managers use the expectations and demands on their organizations not only to create perceptions of success but also to produce the reality.

WHY POLICING IS IMPOSSIBLE

Success in managing a public sector enterprise generally requires that the manager achieve mandated policy goals and objectives. In order for that to occur, two things must be true. First, the policy goals must be consistent and coherent rather than conflicting. If the goals are inconsistent, then at any given moment the organization is vulnerable. Even if the organization is maximizing its performance on one objective (say, crime control), it will be sacrificing performance on some other objective (such as the protection of civil liberties). This is not a problem if the public's attention remains focused on the first goal as the primary objective. But if the public suddenly elevates the secondary objective to first place, the organization will be perceived as failing. In this sense, inconsistent objectives, fitfully attended to, make it impossible to manage an organization successfully.

Second, the organization must have both sufficient resources and suitable operating programs to accomplish the desired results. If mandated purposes cannot be achieved, then the organization will have failed to produce the results that justify public backing. Support and legitimacy will wither; the organization will become "bankrupt."

Given that successful management requires coherent and operationally feasible policy mandates, a review of the mandates and capabilities of police departments will reveal why managing large urban police departments is, in principle, impossible.

INCONSISTENT POLICY OBJECTIVES

Impossibility begins with inconsistent objectives. Not every objective for which the police are held accountable can be maximized simultaneously.

The Tension between Cost and Output

Of course, every managerial job involves some conflict in objectives. For example, all managers are expected to deliver the maximum quantity and quality of services at the minimum cost. In principle, they cannot do this; something must give. Police managers confront this problem every time a city administration charges them to maintain response times to citizens' calls at current levels despite increasing demands and diminishing staff resources.

Ordinarily, this tension between maximizing performance and minimizing cost is resolved by holding managers accountable for maximizing the difference between costs and the value of the services they provide—what is measured by the private sector's "bottom line." In the public sector, it is usually called "efficiency" or "productivity." In effect, managers are held accountable for the net value of their organization's efforts.

"Net value maximization" provides a conceptual resolution of the intrinsic tension between maximizing output and minimizing cost in both private and public sectors. In the private sector, where the value of the organization's output can readily be measured, this conceptual solution has much practical bite. Unfortunately, it works less well in the public sector. The reason is simply that it is often hard even to define, much less measure, the value of public sector operations.[2] Indeed, managers find it difficult to calculate the quantity and quality of public sector activities, let alone the value of outcomes that occur much further down a chain of causation and that would serve ultimately to justify the public sector efforts. For example, the police can measure the speed of their response to calls for service but not the quality of the service rendered by the responding officer, and they have no way of knowing whether the fast responses succeed in controlling crime or stilling citizens' fears.

In the absence of good measurements of the value of organizational outputs, the efficiency of a public sector organization is often determined by performance standards or professionally agreed-upon rules about how an organization should be structured and operated. For example, a professional association might conclude that an excellent police department is one that can keep its response time under five minutes for priority-one calls; or, that an excellent police department is functionally organized, as a freestanding police academy and a forensic unit, and requires all its employees to have a college degree.[3] Such standards set useful benchmarks, but they are always susceptible to both criticism and change. Consequently, public sector managers are nearly always vulnerable to assertions that they are "inefficient" in the production of a given service.

The Proper Use of Authority

Even if this fundamental tension between costs and the value of the output could be resolved, there is a deeper problem. In pursuing their objectives, the police use two different kinds of resources. As a recent study of the Philadelphia police force explained:

> The police are entrusted with important public resources. The most obvious is money: $230 million a year flows through the Philadelphia Police Department. Far more important, the public grants another resource—the use of force and authority. These are deployed when a citizen is arrested or handcuffed, when an officer fires his weapon at a citizen, and when an officer claims exclusive use of the streets with his siren. This use (or misuse) of a public resource also occurs when an officer fails to make an arrest due to fear of or favor toward a suspect.[4]

Many scholars view the police use of legitimate force as the defining characteristic of police departments.

In a free society, there is at least as much concern about the proper use of "public force" as there is about the proper use of public funds. Consequently, the police are held strictly accountable for their exercise of authority and force. Unfortunately, the guiding principles for the use of force are far more complex than those for the use of public money. In both cases, there is a general expectation that the use will be economized. Hence force should not be used "excessively." Shooting a youth who is running to avoid an arrest for marijuana possession is excessive, as are blaring one's siren and driving fast through city streets to catch a speeder or expressing peremptory commands and racial insults while managing pedestrian traffic at sporting events.

In addition, there are clear boundaries—marked out by the constitutional rights of citizens—that must never be crossed despite the possibility that doing so may accomplish police purposes. Some uses of force are not only unwise or wasteful but inherently wrong. They cannot be justified even if they would allow the police to achieve other ends more "efficiently" (when calculated in terms of money) or more "effectively" (when calculated in terms of the value of the objective).

Finally, there is the expectation that force will be employed fairly as well as efficiently. Fairness seems straightforward, especially in its most intuitive form: the idea that like cases should be treated alike. But there is also a second principle that identifies fairness with being able to recognize relevant differences among the cases and treating different cases in an appropriately dissimilar manner. And there is a third principle that views private settlements and agreements as preferable to publicly enforced adjudications, so that if the parties can agree to some solution distinct from what would be imposed by the state, that is the preferable solution.

What is problematic about these principles for police managers is that they require, or make a virtue of, inconsistency—that is, acting on the basis of different ideas of fairness, depending on particular circumstances. Consider the issue of fairness in the way that the police respond to juveniles on the street late at night.

In such a situation, the principle of like cases treated alike would require the police to consider only the issue of whether an offense had been committed: whether children had violated a curfew. They would be discouraged from looking too closely at the circumstances surrounding the offense to decide if it was grave enough to justify an arrest. And they would be discouraged from thinking about the existence of private or non-criminal-justice-based solutions to the issues presented by the case. To ensure simple justice, they would respond only to those features of the situation that legally defined the offense and only in terms of applying or not applying the law.

The principle of treating different cases differently would require the police to investigate the circumstances of the crime to determine whether the situation was really as it appeared. Perhaps the child had left the house because he or she had been beaten by a parent. To the extent that the investigation revealed new, differentiating features of the situation, the police response might be modified to fit the case. Individualized justice would substitute for simple justice as a guide to police action. Also, the principle of preferring private settlements of disputes to public adjudications might influence the police response: If the parents of the child seemed capable of effective supervision, the police might simply return the child to the home.

In short, preferring one concept of "fairness" (or "justice") over another in the application of the law produces very different results in the handling of certain cases. These irregularities might well be inexplicable and therefore cast doubt on the fairness of the police operations, even though the police and many outside observers might agree that the police were being fair in a different sense than the crude notion of like cases treated alike.

To the extent that the principles governing the police use of force and authority are ambiguous and in conflict, and to the extent that the use of force has to be justified, the police mission is made "impossible." This conclusion is far more than a logical nicety. At their core, scandals focusing on police brutality and corruption reflect the public's concern that the police exercise the force and authority entrusted to them sparingly and fairly. More police departments and more police leaders have been skewered by such scandals than by concerns about their ability to handle public funds well. And police departments are often aggressively managed to ensure that corruption and brutality are minimized—frequently at the expense of other important police objectives such as controlling crime or keeping economic costs low.[5]

Uncertain Goals

A third inconsistency lies in the characterization of the police goals themselves. To most citizens, the purpose of the police department is axiomatic: to protect life and property from criminal attacks, and to enforce the criminal law.[6] The substantive value of protection against crime is what galvanizes political support. The commitment to enforcing the law fairly and effectively not only gives the police their most potent instrument in controlling crime but also legitimates their efforts in the eyes of both their working partners (i.e., prosecutors and judges) and those citizens who are (intermittently) fastidious about the use of public authority.

Which Crimes? The first problem with this characterization of police objectives arises in deciding which crimes should be controlled and which laws enforced. Police resources are not infinite; police skills are not entirely versatile. Thus, choices must be made about which crimes to tackle and what operational capabilities to develop. The police are currently organized to deal principally with what might be called "street crimes"—assaults, robberies, and burglaries that occur in public locations. That is the type of crime to which patrol operations, rapid response to calls for service, and retrospective investigations of crimes are particularly well suited.[7]

However, a great many other kinds of criminal activity are less suited to such operations. Organized crime, arson, terrorism, serial murderers, and electronic theft pose different kinds of challenges. To deal with these crimes, the police must be prepared not only to patrol the streets and respond to calls but also to develop intelligence networks, analyze crime patterns, conduct undercover operations, and form partnerships with business entities. In short, there is an enormous variety within the basic mission of crime control and law enforcement, and that variety prescribes a need to decide what kinds of crimes pose the greatest threats to community welfare.

Setting priorities on which crimes to control and investing in the complete range of operational capabilities the police need seem to be "impossible" tasks. Analytical methods for estimating the relative seriousness of different crimes are in their infancy.[8] Any implicit political agreement about which crimes to emphasize can come apart as a result of events in the world or changing political priorities. When such concurrence is not explicit, it can be disavowed, leaving the police vulnerable to anyone who believes their "favorite" crime is not being adequately addressed.

Law Enforcement or Peace-keeping? A second problem with the characterization of the police mission as crime control and law enforcement is a result of an important but subtle tension between the two concepts themselves. Most people, most of the time, see little incompatibility between these broad purposes: In their view, the best way to control crime is to enforce the criminal law. They are often right.

Sometimes, however, these different objectives come into conflict. For example, in riot situations, the police may often choose not to enforce the law in the interests of restoring order more quickly. They may allow some limited looting to occur, knowing that an aggressive, ill-considered response by the police might well inflame the crowd and lead to more widespread and destructive rioting. Or, the police may choose not to file charges against a teenager who is breaking school windows, turning the youth instead over to the justice meted out in the more intimate settings of family and school.

In these cases, the police face a conflict between enforcing the law or adjusting their response to one that they judge may be more effective in controlling future crime. They must decide which is their more fundamental purpose: law enforcement or order maintenance.[9] Whatever decision they make, they will be vulnerable. If they stand back in the riot, they can be sued by the owner of a looted store. If they return the juvenile to his or her parents, they can be attacked for their lenient or unequal response to juvenile crimes. On the other hand, if they step into the riot situation, arrest the looters, and fan the anger of the mob, they may well be criticized by a subsequent commission for failing to show "sensitivity" to the community's mood or for making a foolish tactical judgment. Or, if they bring a vandalism case against the youth, they may be criticized for branding a child as a criminal or for wasting the criminal justice system's time with trivial cases. In short, there are principled and pragmatic justifications for both purposes.

Crime Control or Crime Prevention? A third tension arises when there are actions the police could take to control crime that are not, strictly speaking, law enforcement. For example, a great deal of domestic violence might be prevented if the police mobilize social service agencies to assist struggling marriages at their first summons to noisy arguments—before the beating, stabbing, or shooting starts. Similarly, the police might help forestall burglaries by offering advice on security arrangements to residents and shop owners. Or, the police might be able to reduce juvenile delinquency by establishing after-hours recreational programs.

Although such activities are entirely consistent with their crime control responsibilities, they are inconsistent with an exclusive reliance on the enforcement of laws to accomplish police purposes. The activities fall into the domain of organizing or directly providing social services designed to prevent crime.

Reducing Victimization or Fear. A fourth difficulty for police priorities results from the fact that controlling crime is not quite the same as controlling fear. For many years, both police managers and those who reviewed their activities believed that the single most important problem to solve was actual criminal victimization. They judged fear to be a lesser concern, but they also assumed that the most direct, rational way to control fear was to reduce actual victimization.

However, recent research has shown that fear is a major problem in its own right.[10] For victims, it is one of the worst consequences of crime. Long after the bruises have faded, the memories and the anxieties they trigger remain. Moreover, fear is far more widespread than actual criminal victimization, since many more people are afraid of being victimized than actually are. Their anxiety must be counted as a loss to society. Finally, in many areas, the combined fears of those who have been victimized and those who dread the possibility have prompted citizens to take defensive actions which may enhance their own protection but also weaken the social bonds that in ideal circumstances help protect everyone. They stay inside and buy guard dogs, stronger locks, and guns. Such reactions turn communities that once had safe public spaces into isolated armed camps.

Studies have also shown that fear is surprisingly unrelated to real levels of victimization.[11] People who have been victimized are not necessarily more afraid of crime than people as yet untouched. Neighborhoods that are heavily hit by crime are not automatically more fearful than areas that are struck less often. Perhaps most unexpectedly, fear turns out to be associated more strongly with instances of disorder than with real victimization. It is noisy youth, graffiti, vandalism, and general rowdiness that creates fear in communities much more than serious crime.

Finally, it is now established that fear can be alleviated without necessarily reducing real victimization. When the police ring doorbells, walk foot patrols, and know the names of citizens, it controls fear but does not guarantee control of victimization.[12] Thus, fear reduction and order maintenance emerge as new police functions that are different from either crime control or law enforcement. Where fear reduction should fit in the overall scheme of police priorities is still uncertain.

Crime Control or Emergency Services? A fifth problem emerges when there are useful things the police could do that seem unrelated to both crime control and law enforcement. For example, the police are often involved in emergency medical services because they are typically the first at the scene of an auto accident, heart attack, or drowning. They are also often the first to encounter social emergencies.

They find the inebriates and the homeless who are about to freeze to death in a back alley. They are called to the scene of an ugly quarrel between two brothers. They see the child sitting in the bus terminal at 4:00 A.M., hoping to escape an abusive parent before the parent wakes up.

These actions occur not because the police take these tasks as important purposes; rather, they are largely by-products of police omnipresence and accessibility—characteristics that are crucial to their crime control role. Their twenty-four-hour duties, their proximity to the streets, their responsiveness to telephone calls, and their general value to citizens in trouble mean that they will be contacted by citizens for many reasons other than actual victimization. As a result, the police find themselves involved in these matters even though they and the general populace do not necessarily think they should be.[13] The issue is whether these activities should be considered valuable and thus incorporated into police operations, or whether they should be viewed as distractions from the basic police mission and their role in police operations minimized.

Summary

The police have a diverse and complicated mission that includes controlling street crime, equipping themselves to deal with sophisticated criminal organizations and special crime problems, deciding when crime control objectives are advanced more effectively by not enforcing the law, figuring out ways to prevent crime as well as control it, deciding whether and how to deal with the separate issue of fear in addition to criminal victimization, and judging whether their emergency service role is a valuable addition to or a distraction from their basic functions. In accomplishing these purposes, they are obligated to use the resources entrusted to them—money and authority—both economically and fairly.

On an analytic level, these different objectives need not be inconsistent. All the society has to do is write out an explicit function statement that defines the rates at which it is willing to grant money and authority to achieve the diverse objectives of controlling different kinds of crime, keeping the peace (rather than enforcing the law), preventing crime, reducing fear, and providing emergency medical and social services through police departments. As a practical matter, a coherent organization might be constructed that could produce fairly high levels of performance on all these different goals. In fact, most police departments do perform all these functions reasonably well.

Yet any political agreement that specifies the trade-offs among these competing objectives is by nature both general and fickle. As a result, for the most part, the police operate with diverse responsibilities whose relative importance is never clearly expressed. Moreover, an analytic solution does not abolish the sensation, keenly felt by those in the organization, that the police department is going in too many different directions. They experience the tension of unresolved priorities in at least three respects.

First, the different enterprises seem to vie for resources. When the police are pursuing one set of goals, there is the perception that resources are unavailable for other purposes. Second, the various goals compete for the soul of the organization. An organization devoted to law enforcement against violent offenders has a much different culture than an organization devoted to preventing crime, reducing fear, or providing emergency medical and social services. The inconsistencies show up, not in operating shortfalls in one function or another, but in the orientation, training, and psychological commitment of officers.

Third, the key measures of performance and success depend on mission focus. Some organizations stand or fall on arrests and levels of reported crime. Others are judged by the levels of victimization and the quality of the relationship between the police and the community. The volume of community services supplied is yet another criterion. Although it might be desirable to measure all of these things, the need to avoid complexity narrows the organization's attention to a few measurements, and it is in choosing ways of measuring success that the different goals prove inconsistent.

INADEQUATE OPERATING CAPABILITIES

Even if the policy mandate could be made more coherent, it is by no means clear that the police mission would suddenly become possible. There are real doubts about the capacity of the police to perform adequately the basic functions assigned to them.

Surprisingly, the greatest weaknesses are in the domain of their most commonly assigned mission: crime fighting.[14] The current dominant strategy of policing relies on three principal operational methods to control crime. The first is patrol (random or targeted), designed to deter crime and intercept criminal acts in progress. The second is rapid responses to calls for service. The third is retrospective investigation of criminal offenses. The first two functions are generally carried out by a uniformed patrol force that typically comprises 60 to 70 percent of a police department.[15] The patrol force is linked to citizens through an elaborate network of telephones, dispatchers, and radios. The third function is usually performed by a detective bureau that comprises 10 to 15 percent of the force. The detectives are aided in the solution of crimes by their own extensive experience with criminal offenders, by elaborate files of previous cases and recidivists, by forensic laboratories, and by a variety of standard investigative methods.

Although this apparatus is extremely impressive in its operations, and although great progress has been made in deterring and solving crimes, there are reasons to believe that this strategy is not nearly as effective in controlling crime as once believed. Experiments have revealed that motorized patrol neither prevents crime nor reassures citizens.[16] Varying the levels of patrol in communities by a factor of two results in no changes in levels of crime or in levels of fear.

Research has also cast doubt on the efficacy of rapid response to calls for service.[17] The problem is not that offenders flee before the police can arrive at the scene. In most cities, the police are about five minutes from any point in an emergency situation. However, victims and witnesses do not call the police while the crime is occurring, or even shortly after. Many offenses are not noticed by witnesses; many witnesses decide not to become involved. And after an attack, when the victim has the first opportunity to alert the police, his or her first call is usually to someone else—a relative, a friend, or an advisor. As a result, a fast response time is wasted. As the police often put it, they arrive in time to hold the hand of the victim—a task they resent since it keeps them from apprehending the victimizer.

Finally, studies of retrospective investigation of crimes reveal that most cases are solved, not by deduction, or physical evidence, or informants, but by very specific identifications of the offender by the victim or witnesses.[18] This reflects the fact that many times criminal and victim know each other; it also leads to the sad conclusion that little is known about how to solve crimes that happen between strangers.

In sum, the principal techniques relied on by the police to deal with their primary objective seem surprisingly ineffective. Moreover, it is by no means clear that more resources would help. Additional money (in the form of more police on the street) or additional power to search do not obviously improve police performance. The far more valuable resource seems to be an effective partnership with the community to ensure that what the community knows will be available to the police.[19] But the police cannot command that; they must earn it by working to create trust and confidence between themselves and the community. Their current techniques do not approach this goal. There may be some promising alternatives, but they are so far largely untested.

Police capabilities in other domains seem stronger. The police do seem able to still citizens' fears by being regularly available on a face-to-face basis. They do seem able to promote order by using their authority to regulate disorderly and disruptive conduct on the street. They do routinely provide emergency medical services because their training equips them for the task. In the area of crime prevention, the police are also beginning to make progress, but often at the expense of their traditional methods. One new approach is called "problem solving."[20] To illustrate, let us suppose the police discover that truant teenagers are behind a rash of daytime burglaries in a particular area. More effective enforcement of truancy laws ends the problem, but the department is accused of spending an inordinate amount of time on minor offenses like truancy.[21]

A far more difficult domain is emergency social services. The police have little patience for problems that cannot be solved by an arrest, and little training or knowledge that equips them to respond in some way other than through arrests. They do not want to become social workers. And even if their responsibilities are limited to emergencies and they are not required to sustain a relationship with the people or the situations that keep producing the emergencies, they still are not comfortable with this mission. The police are constantly drawn into these problems; they often contribute by resolving the dispute; and they could contribute more through referrals. Yet this awareness does not budge them from their basic distrust of such services. It is true, of course, that the police alone cannot actually solve these problems. At best, they can provide "trauma care" and "referrals" to those who can treat the underlying troubles.

So, there is a mismatch between police operational inclinations and capabilities on the one hand and the police mission on the other. In areas that they and the society regard as essential, their capabilities are strikingly limited. In areas that are potentially important but underemphasized, their capabilities are stronger.

LIMITED MANAGERIAL CONTROL

Beyond their liability for inconsistent objectives and their reliance on inadequate capabilities, police leadership is further handicapped by a startling lack of operational control over officers. The department functions under a carefully constructed illusion of control created to satisfy citizen demands for accountability. There is a bulky manual setting out policies and procedures that detail what officers should do in performing their varied tasks. There is a well-defined chain of command separated by narrow spans of authority that seem to provide dense supervision. And there is extensive investment in training. It appears, then, that the conduct of officers is under tight administrative control.

The reality is quite different, however. For the most part, the police operate on their own.[22] Although they must be responsive to dispatchers, they tell the dispatchers when they are available for service and where they are located. Their supervisors are often absorbed with other duties and cannot always find them. Supervisors respond to calls with the officers only on the most important occasions. These conditions establish an irreducible degree of discretion for police officers.[23] As a practical matter, although the written procedures and hierarchical structure create deterrents for misconduct, the officer controls most of the information about his or her whereabouts and activities, and that fact defeats the effectiveness of these control arrangements.

To complicate matters, police officers often have a substantial degree of power they can wield against their immediate and higher-level officers, some of it founded on mutual blackmail. Paradoxically, the dense framework of rules means that virtually all officers are guilty of some infraction some time in their careers. This is as true for supervisors as for officers. Knowledge of the infraction, sometimes even evidence, is often held by one's subordinate. In the worst cases, superior and subordinate have colluded to cover up some offense. In these situations, the supervisor's power to control the subordinate is checked by the implied threat to reveal the incriminating information. The practice is referred to as "dropping a dime," and its threat blunts a great deal of supervisory authority.

At a more positive level, most police managers recognize that they need the cooperation of their officers. Indeed, it is very unsettling to preside over an organization of several thousand officers who roam the streets carrying guns.

Every police manager is keenly aware of the fragility of his or her control—how easy it would be for the officers to cause a lot of trouble in a short period by either failing to do their jobs or doing them too zealously. To ensure the cooperation of the troops, they express deep concern about "maintaining morale." And when they make a decision that is unpopular with their troops, they are warned ominously that "morale will go down."

Although there are perfectly good reasons for worrying about esprit in an organization like a police department, the obsessive concern with morale often has a darker side. To some extent, the warning that morale will go down is a threat that if the police executive asks the officers to do something they do not want to do, they will begin behaving badly on the street. This possibility sometimes leads police executives to back off from demanding things from their officers that should be demanded on behalf of the public. In cases of police corruption and brutality, for example, the police routinely expect their leaders to "support" their troops against the charges. Sometimes these pressures are quite intense, and police executives yield to the expectations of their subordinates.

The effective independence of the police force from close managerial control is greatly reinforced by formal arrangements as well as working conditions and informal threats. The civil-service system establishes performance standards and protects people with those competences. The restrictions can be overcome only with the aid of enormous political and administrative effort. In addition, many departments now have police unions, with explicit contracts and official grievance procedures.[24] This factor adds to the complexity of making general or specific changes in organizational procedures of personnel policies. It also compounds the political difficulties, for police unions are often politically powerful. In many northeastern cities, police personnel and their many relatives vote reliably to ensure that their elected leaders are responsive to their desires. It is the public sector version of having employee stockholders. Police executives are thus quite cautious in challenging their own organizations—despite the illusion of power that comes from their gold braid, the chain of command, and their tough disciplinary procedures.

Ironically, this situation has worsened as a result of making the police independent of politics. Police departments were separated from mayoral control and accountability as a means of guarding against political corruption. But police leaders did not really become independent. They became dependent on, and responsive to, the aspirations of their own troops. They began to define their jobs in terms of supporting the profession of policing. Without a countervailing public pressure that would focus their attention on the performance of *public* duties, they were powerless to resist the demands and expectations of their own subordinates. As a result, the police have substantial informal powers over their own leaders, who find it particularly hard to stand against a police force that can mobilize its own political constituency against them.

An alternative approach to managing police organizations would be to shift from a "command and control" system to one built on "professional responsibility.''[25] In this concept, the irreducible discretion of officers would be officially recognized. They would be trained to exercise this discretion wisely not only through instruction on the techniques of their profession (e.g., the skilled, disciplined use of force) but also through inculcation in the values that should guide their activities.[26] Moreover, control would be exerted through after-the-fact examinations of their conduct and performance, rather than before-the-fact establishment of rules followed by direct supervision to ensure compliance. They would be liable to citizens whose rights and interests they had violated in the performance of their duties.

The first difficulty with shifting to this style of organizational control is that it is not certain it would succeed. Other barriers are no less considerable: The public is unwilling to grant police officers the status and pay associated with professionalism; neither the community nor the police executives who represent the community are clear on what purposes and values should guide officers; and the officers themselves prefer the protection of the organization, its rules, and its informal understandings to the vagaries of consumer satisfaction and liability judgments. Indeed, some police unions have opposed requirements that officers wear identifying name plates or badge numbers, to escape direct accountability to citizens.

In sum, it is not clear that police managers *can* direct their own troops even if they know what they should do and have suitable technologies for accomplishing their purposes. The mechanisms of command and control are unreliable in the face of discretion and countervailing power. The potential for professionalism in the field is limited by the reluctance of the public to rely on and pay for this alternative means of control, as well as by the desire of the police themselves to assume the prerogatives of professionalism but escape the responsibilities.

SUMMARY

Perhaps I have exaggerated the difficulty of leading a police organization. If one sets high enough standards and concentrates exclusively on the drawbacks of an enterprise, anything can be made to seem impossible. But there are two pieces of objective evidence I would offer to buttress the analytic case made above that leading a police organization successfully is very difficult, if not impossible.

First, there is the nagging sense throughout the country and within the police profession that something is not right in policing. Certainly many communities and departments seem to be well satisfied with one another; there the police are confident in their operation. However, there are numerous other places where the claims of success seem more like desperate bravado than quiet confidence, and quite a few departments—including some of the largest—where disappointment, sullenness, and defensiveness seem dominant. Indeed, it may be one measure of public confidence in police and public perception of their success that the private security sector is growing much faster than the police industry.[27]

A second piece of evidence is the vulnerability of police executives. It is not unusual for them to stay in their jobs for less than three years.[28] While brevity may indicate insufficient training or competence in the job, it may also reflect community uncertainty about what it wants from its police department and its leader. In the latter reasoning, police executives become scapegoats for unresolved conflicts within the community about the purposes, methods, and operations of the police department.

APPROACHES TO THE JOB

Despite the difficulty or impossibility of the job, some police executives have succeeded. They have earned reputations as successful managers. They have stayed on the job. And they have improved the performance of their organizations. To suggest how successful police executives cope, the strategies of three such leaders of three organizations are examined: Darryl Gates, chief of police in Los Angeles; Lee Brown, chief of police in Houston; and Kevin Tucker, police commissioner of the Philadelphia Police Department.[29]

DARRYL GATES: PROFESSIONAL POLICING

Darryl Gates became the chief of police for the City of Los Angeles in 1978.[30] His distinguished predecessors included William Parker, who served as police chief from 1950 to 1966, and Ed Davis, who was chief from 1969 to 1978. Such long terms are not the norm in American policing. They are common in Los Angeles because there the position is protected by civil-service restrictions. The job is filled through an independent police commission established for the express purpose of appointing a chief. The members base their decision on tests and interviews of candidates. The person who is selected cannot be removed except for cause. The position pays $80,000 per year, making the chief of police in Los Angeles one of the highest paid civil servants in the country.

Since he became chief, Darryl Gates has given no cause for dismissal. Indeed, he distinguished himself as the very model of a modern police executive: cool, tough, exacting, self-disciplined, and purposeful. He was sufficiently popular with the citizens of Los Angeles to be considered a plausible candidate for mayor—perhaps even governor. He had enough respect from his troops that his was one of the few big-city departments that has not yet unionized. And he had great standing within his professional community: In a confrontation with the redoubtable Federal Bureau of Investigation over who would assume primary responsibility for guaranteeing security for the 1984 Olympics held in Los Angeles, Gates prevailed.

His department had an enviable reputation for integrity, professionalism, and efficiency. He took office just after Proposition 13 passed in California. The effect was to shrink the police force from about seventy-five hundred officers in 1975 to about sixty-six hundred in 1980. Meanwhile, the population and calls for service increased dramatically. Moreover, the city's neighborhoods were becoming more heterogeneous and often poorer. Fueled by the easy access to supplies of heroin, cocaine, and marijuana from nearby Mexico, drug use continued to increase. Despite these circumstances, crime rates did not rise, clearance rates (i.e., the fraction of reported crimes that are solved with an arrest) remained steady, no major corruption or brutality scandals were uncovered, and the neighborhoods remained calm throughout the hot summers. The question thus arises: How was Gates able to do the impossible job?

The simple answer is that Gates was able to represent the performance of his organization to the citizens of Los Angeles, the broader police profession, and his own troops in terms that were consistent with the traditions and ideals of his department. The values that he articulated, and the performance he demanded from his organization, were right at the center of both previous traditions and current expectations. Values and performance conformed to public, professional, and subordinate hopes and expectations for the department. To comprehend Gates's success, we must understand how he fit into the historical context of policing in Los Angeles.

The foundation for Gates's success was laid by William B. Parker. Parker built the political constituency for a professional, crime-fighting police force by identifying three important values that could command public enthusiasm and support: first, an urgent public desire to curb crime and disorder; second, public hope that professionals and experts could solve problems; third, a determination to keep police departments free from the potential corruption of political influence. The image of nonpartisan, incorruptible, well-trained crime-fighters was the perfect expression of these enduring public aspirations. In this respect, the concept of independent, professionalized policing was one of the best political ideas ever invented by a police executive: It gave the police broad community support, high standing, and wide autonomy.

Parker also established the administrative structures to support this style of policing. To emphasize crime fighting, Parker (1) stressed crime statistics and clearance measures as the key indicators of organizational and individual performance; (2) shifted his patrol force from foot beats to patrol cars that could respond quickly to calls for service; (3) centralized and strengthened his detective division; and (4) eventually established the nation's first Special Weapons and Tactical Teams (SWAT) to deal with particularly dangerous and violent criminals. To guard against corruption, Parker (1) produced and distributed elaborate manuals detailing policies and procedures; (2) created a centralized internal affairs division; (3) replaced old division boundaries corresponding to political or sociological groupings by boundaries corresponding to census tracts; and (4) routinely dispatched and transferred officers from one division to another.

To ensure the professionalism and expertise of the department, selection standards were made more stringent, training was expanded and improved, a planning and research division was established, a statistical method for deploying patrol officers was designed and used, and performance statistics on crimes, arrests, citations written, and response times began to be tabulated. Over Parker's sixteen-year term, these efforts created a highly professionalized, autonomous police force committed to crime control through efficient and fair law enforcement—the epitome of what most people thought a police department should be.

The outstanding reputation of the Los Angeles Police Department (LAPD) survived until 1965. On August 11, the Watts riot exploded. The LAPD could not meet the challenge. As one veteran of that era recalls: "Everything we believed would be effective didn't work. We withdrew officers; that didn't work. We put more officers in; that didn't work. We used all our black and liaison officers; that didn't work."[31] After a week of rioting, thirty-one civilians were dead, and much of Watts had been burned to the ground. Order was restored only with the assistance of fourteen thousand National Guardsmen.

What the riot revealed to those inside and outside the department was that the police force had become increasingly isolated from the community. No one had any sense of the deep anger and resentment that had been building in Watts. No credible capacity existed for controlling the trouble once it began. Police liaison efforts had focused on clergy and business groups and thus had failed to provide information to the police about emerging problems. Nor could these weak links bestow legitimacy on police operations designed to quell the riot. The police lacked standing in important parts of the city.

To respond to this problem, the LAPD established a Community Relations Program. The program consisted of a group of lieutenants assigned exclusively to community liaison work in areas where the department's community ties seem to have eroded. Their job was to arrange meetings between the police captains responsible for given areas and representatives of local citizen groups; to organize youth groups; and to set up "phone trees" to be used for rumor control. Since the department was committed to effective crime control, these measures were understood within the department principally as intelligence-gathering efforts.

In 1969 Ed Davis became the chief. In personal style, he was more flamboyant and outspoken than Parker, but he stood for many of the same values. He affirmed his commitment to crime control by suggesting that skyjackers should be hanged at airports "after a fair trial." He insisted that the LAPD did not discriminate, because it shot more whites than blacks in the course of its operations. Such views aroused antagonism from civil libertarians and minority representatives in Los Angeles and nationally and suggested a degree of recklessness that was out of keeping with disciplined professionalism. However, Davis's opinions were not entirely unsuited to a conception of police as expert crime-fighters. And there were many in Los Angeles and elsewhere who wanted that kind of police force. Indeed, in the polarized mood of that period, the enmity of civil liberties and minority groups might have enhanced Davis's popularity. Independence and crime fighting remained good politics.

But Davis had another idea as well. The lesson of the Watts riot had not escaped him. He became convinced that policing could be strengthened if officers could be made to feel responsible for the territory they policed and if they could mobilize the local communities to assist them. Consequently, he changed the organization of the LAPD to emphasize geographic responsibility.

At that time, the management of the LAPD patrol force was accomplished by having a certain number of sectors, each covered by a patrol car. The department was organized in three shifts. It was the responsibility of the watch commanders in each sector to ensure that the patrol cars were staffed. The patrol cars were then sent out to the streets to keep watch and to respond to calls for service that came from a central dispatching unit. Because the police were divided into three shifts with minimal communication across the shifts and were centrally dispatched without much regard for their "home beats," they developed little sense of responsibility for a given territory and little connection with the people who lived there.

Davis proposed two changes that would give a territorial overlay to this basic pattern of deployment. One change was called "the basic car plan," in which areas were divided into sectors that could be covered by a single patrol car. That car (and the nine or so officers that were required to man it twenty-four hours a day, seven days a week) would be more or less permanently assigned to a given area. To the extent that additional cars were needed to respond to calls for service, they would be supplied and designated as X cars. The watch commander thus had the responsibility for staffing the "basic cars" and the "X cars." The number of basic cars remained stable; the number of X cars varied according to fluctuations in the demands for service. Basic cars always had first priority in responding to calls in their areas; X cars served in a back-up capacity. The expectation was that the officers who staffed the basic cars would become more familiar with their areas.

The second change involved the designation of one officer among those assigned to a basic car as the senior lead officer. His or her job was to ensure the effective, round-the-clock management of the basic car and to meet with neighborhood groups to learn what crime problems concerned them. In effect, the lead officer planned the activities of the car and its officers to make the maximum contribution to the crime problems the community singled out for police department attention. His or her plans could be overridden by centrally dispatched calls for service. But in the periods in which the car was not responding to calls for service, it was supposed to work on the issues identified by the senior lead officer.

The changes did not receive wide publicity, since, in keeping with the portrayal of professionalized competence, these arrangements were considered matters of internal organization and efficiency. But they brought into the LAPD a new way of relating to the community.

In 1971 Davis went one step further. He tasked his senior lead officers with the responsibility for creating neighborhood watch groups to assist the police in their crime control efforts. In the process, the police discovered an important fact: What actually concerned citizens was rarely what the police thought concerned them. They heard relatively few complaints about serious crime, and many more about vagrants, rowdy teenagers, abandoned cars, and vandalism.

This created a dilemma for the police. If they were going to show good faith in forming partnerships with the community, they would have to take these concerns seriously. On the other hand, responding to such minor problems did not match their image of a professionalized, crime-fighting police force. It seemed to detract from their capacity to deal with violent crime. In addition, the amount of time spent in meetings was trying the patience of watch commanders, who continued to be responsible for deploying the patrol force and keeping response times low.

Consequently, a crack appeared in the organization of the LAPD. On one side were the senior lead officers who were committed to close collaboration with the community and who sought to direct the attention of officers to the problems the community nominated. On the other side were the watch commanders, most of the patrol force, and even some senior lead officers who thought that the job of the police was to respond to calls for service and deal with serious crime and who sought to have as many officers ready for dispatching as possible so that when the crime calls came, the LAPD would be ready.

By 1973 Davis was ready for the next move toward establishing geographic responsibility. He introduced into the LAPD a concept known as "team policing." The city was divided into seventy units, each unit comprising three to five basic cars. In addition, the various functional groups that had previously been centralized (e.g., detectives, narcotics, juvenile offenders, and traffic) were distributed across these new units. A lieutenant was placed in charge of each unit and was expected to operate like a "mini-chief" for his or her area. Essentially, this change reversed the trend toward centralization that Parker had begun, making it possible for local neighborhoods to provide more effective guidance to the police department than ever before.

These changes were not unanimously supported. There remained an undercurrent in the LAPD throughout this period that wanted the department to continue as the powerful crime-fighting organization it had been in the late fifties and early sixties. Several factors kept this spirit alive in the department, perhaps the most important of which was simply the desires and expectations of the officers themselves. They had joined to patrol the streets, solve crimes, and lock up criminals. Their training continued to emphasize the skills associated with law enforcement and crime fighting. The detectives were still a high-prestige unit, and promotion to detective was based partly on the production of felony arrests. Hence the principal performance measures remained measures of enforcement activity such as arrests and citations.

Moreover, the mid-level managers in the department were somewhat ambivalent about "community relations" and "team policing." They too wanted to be crime-fighters more than politicians, and they were still being evaluated on reported levels of crime and response times. Neither the chief nor the public seemed terribly excited about the changes that had been made in the department. What the police continued to be admired for was their courage and competence as crime-fighters.

Many of the underlying tensions in the LAPD—between centralization versus decentralization, autonomy versus community partnerships, rapid responses to calls for service versus community meetings, serious crime fighting versus dealing with neighborhood complaints—came to a head about the time that Darryl Gates became the chief. One catalyst was the ambivalence within the police department itself. It was hard to claim the mantle of an independent, professional crime-fighter while responding increasingly to minor community complaints. As one senior officer remarked:

> I was in the locker room working out, and I heard two guys who were senior leads. One was talking to the other about how he needed cookies for his meeting, and he was really concerned about "dammit, I can't find the cookies." And the other one needed a movie projector, and I looked at these two kids, good looking and good cops, and I thought, oh my God, what have we done with our finest.[32]

In addition, however, resource constraints were beginning to bind. Davis had committed the organization to "team policing" on the assumption that the LAPD would receive up to one thousand additional officers. Those hopes were dampened in 1973 when Thomas Bradley—a political opponent of Davis—was elected mayor and chose not to increase the budget of the department. They were dashed in 1978 with the passage of Proposition 13. Consequently, just at the time Gates took office, the pressures on the police department had risen to the boiling point.

Gates's response was swift and decisive. He abolished team policing in 1979. Patrol officers and detectives were put back under separate commands, and specialists were recentralized under headquarters commands. The operational objective was to maintain the organization's capacity to respond to calls for service in the face of declining resources. The connections to the communities were supposed to be maintained by captains who once again assumed the public liaison responsibility and by the senior lead officers who remained in charged of the basic cars.

In reality, however, the functions that had been developed under Parker atrophied as the department retrenched. Many captains were uninterested in community relations. There was no one at headquarters who kept track of how well captains and senior lead officers were performing their community liaison duties. And there was a general air of resentment against the community that had failed to support the LAPD with the resources it thought it deserved. As a result, the senior lead officers "went into a drift."

In the 1980s Gates attempted to revive community relations functions as the department worked through the effects of Proposition 13. Starting in 1984, two areas designed and began to operate Community Mobilization Projects, which relied heavily on senior lead officers and which gave them and their projects priority in calls for service. In 1986 a high-level policy paper issued by the powerful Office of Operations recommended an organization-wide commitment to the senior lead officers and the community liaison/mobilization effort. Pressure once again began to be exerted from the top for the restoration of this function. The interesting result was that many senior lead officers who had enjoyed the rank but not the special duties began transferring out of these jobs, and those who liked both the rank and the function began transferring in.

These initiatives did not conclusively resolve the conflict between geo-graphically-based, community-oriented policing on the one hand and centralized crime-fighting policing on the other. Indeed, the tension remained sharp. And when administrative concerns about crime and response times periodically reas-serted themselves, the department would again shift away—at least temporarily—from the community relations functions.

In fact, just such a surge of administrative concern damaged a promising Community Mobilization Project in the Wilshire Division. There, a two-year project focused on street people, prostitution, and graffiti and based in a locally established police station had succeeded in cleaning up the area, thus earning the gratitude of local citizens. On the other hand, its response-time statistics had decreased to become the worst in the city. Under pressure from police headquar-ters to improve its response time, the local commander reassigned some key senior lead officers to regular patrol functions. Both the lead officers and the neighbor-hood were unhappy. But in the eyes of Darryl Gates, acting for the citizens of Los Angeles, the requirements of professionalized policing had to be met. In the end, that was what successful policing in Los Angeles demanded.

LEE BROWN: COMMUNITY POLICING

Lee Brown became the police commissioner for the Houston Police Department in 1982.[33] He was the seventh chief in eight years.

Those eight years had been stormy ones. The department seemed to oscillate between tight (some would say arbitrary) discipline and broad indulgence. Her-man Short, the police chief from the mid-sixties to 1973, had been an autocrat who stood for tough crime fighting but who also brooked no errors of judgment or discipline in his department. In 1973 a liberal coalition elected Fred Hoffheinz mayor, and Herman Short resigned. He was replaced by Carroll Lynn, an executive within the department. Lynn's regime was marked by little more than internal power struggles. He resigned within two years, after being indicted, and was replaced by Pappy Bond—a "policeman's policeman" in the eyes of his numerous supporters in the department. Bond's principal objective seemed to be to reassure the police officers of Houston that they were valued and supported. Discipline slackened.

During the mid-seventies, the Houston Police Department earned a national reputation as a "cowboy" department. In a period of rapid expansion, the department had advertised nationally for police officers who "wanted to be close to the action." Lenient dress codes and regulations, introduced by Pappy Bond, had resulted in police officers wearing cowboy hats and boots to work and equipping themselves with weapons of their own choice—such as pearl-handled automatics. To round out the image, during the mid-seventies, the Houston Police Department held the record for shooting more people in the course of its duties than any other department. In the first three months of 1977, thirteen people were killed in three months. Then, in 1977 the Joe Campo Torres case erupted.

Torres, a Mexican-American, had been taken from a bar by five Houston police officers, beaten badly, and then thrown in a swamp. As an officer involved later testified, Torres had been thrown in the swamp because one of the other officers had "always wanted to see a wetback swim." Torres drowned, and when his body surfaced two days later, an investigation disclosed the involvement of the Houston police officers.

The Torres case subjected the Houston Police Department to a great deal of outside pressure. The United States Attorney's office assumed responsibility for the Torres case and began to watch the Houston Police Department's activities much more closely. The Texas State Legislature passed a civil rights statute making it a felony for a police officer to injure or kill a prisoner in his or her custody. The Harris County District Attorney's office created its own Civil Rights Division. And an Internal Affairs Division was set up within the Houston Police Department and became active in investigating incidents of police misconduct.

In this milieu, Harry Caldwell became the chief. Caldwell, like his predecessors, was an insider. Indeed, he was described by many as the brains behind the previous succession of "good old boy" chiefs. Now at the helm himself, Caldwell finally had the opportunity to mold the Houston Police Department into his vision of a modern, effective department. He viewed his primary mission as "establishing accountability." He built up the Internal Affairs Division and used it to investigate all police shootings. He wrote new policies and procedures about the use of force—prohibiting officers from shooting at fleeing felons, moving cars, and burglary suspects. He required officers to register all firearms they carried to facilitate investigations in shooting incidents. And he eliminated cowboy hats and boots.

Caldwell's efforts began to reestablish the legitimacy and credibility of the Houston Police Department within the city and the criminal justice system, but they severely antagonized the officers who were accustomed to more supportive regimes in which they could wield more influence over their chiefs. Early in Caldwell's term, the Houston Police Officer's Association (HPOA) invited Caldwell to a meeting to discuss policies and procedures. Over three hundred officers attended. Caldwell clarified his position: "I'm a goddamn dictator, and if you don't like it, you can hit the fucking door."

A little later, in an apparent effort to reopen communications, Caldwell commissioned a study of officer morale by the union. When the report was presented, however, Caldwell tore it up, threw it in a wastebasket, and once again explained:

"This is not a popularity contest. We're going to run it the way I say, and if you don't like it, you can get the fuck out." In response, the HPOA voted never to meet with Caldwell again. They also decided that since they were "going to have to be a bear, they might as well be a grizzly."

In the end, Caldwell got tired. His vision of a professionalized Houston Police Department did not seem to connect powerfully enough with either outside or inside constituents. There was enthusiasm externally for his stance on deadly force, but it was outweighed by internal anger—the result of his allowing little opportunity for the officers to express their point of view or have their fears and worries addressed. Caldwell also sought to increase the force's sensitivity to the community by training officers in Spanish, but he regarded federal demands for affirmative action in hiring as undermining his drive for high professional standards.

Perhaps most important, Caldwell seemed to believe he had to do everything himself. He gave three hundred speeches a year. Even though he had opportunities to fill key positions within his own department, he was forced to reach way down into the ranks of the sergeants to find anyone who seemed to share his purposes. Caldwell could simply not roll the stone up the hill, and he resigned after about two years to take a rest.

Caldwell was replaced by B. K. Johnson—a choice that won the approval of Pappy Bond. As he explained to reporters, "What Houston needs is a chief like Johnson who will concentrate on protecting the city from criminals." The minority groups were concerned that Johnson would allow the police to run amok again. They were not reassured when Johnson was overheard reciting parts of *Little Black Sambo* to test a microphone at a luncheon speech; nor when he dispatched tactical squads of foot patrols to round up "vagrants" in poor areas; nor when, in response to requests from the Hispanic community for improved police action in dealing with homicides, large numbers of police cars began crisscrossing their neighborhoods. From the community's perspective, Johnson seemed insensitive and heavy-handed.

Surprisingly, the union was not particularly happy with Johnson either. Over the years, the Houston Police Department had changed. It included more women and minorities, it was better educated, and it had learned and repented from the disgrace of the Torres case. The union had begun representing the police officer's interests in more constructive forms than simply lobbying for more license to roust people on the street. Bob Thomas, the president of the growing Houston Police Patrolman's Union, proposed innovations gleaned from other departments to improve working conditions: discipline policies from Los Angeles, the four-day workweek from Kansas City, mandatory physical fitness, and participatory management. Johnson responded by telling Thomas, "I intend to stay here forever, and nothing is going to change."

As it turned out, Johnson was wrong. In November 1981 Kathy Whitmire was elected mayor of Houston. She consulted with Bob Thomas to get his views on what should be done with the department. Johnson resigned, accusing Whitmire of "being in the pocket of the union." Whitmire appointed Assistant Chief John Bales as acting chief and began a national search for a new chief. In April 1982 she chose Lee P. Brown, then commissioner of public safety in Atlanta, to be Houston's police chief.

Brown began with many strikes against him. He was the first outsider ever appointed to the job of chief. He was also the first black. And he held a Ph.D. The union vigorously opposed his nomination, claiming that he was unqualified. The only ones who seemed to support Brown were Whitmire and the minority community of Houston—not a group that had previously been important in setting police policy.

Four years later, Brown had raised the department from national disgrace to incipient acclaim. Moreover, in the mayoral election of 1985, both candidates pledged to keep Lee Brown as chief if elected. Whitmire won again, but as one city editor observed, this time her victory was on Lee Brown's coattails. The issue, of course, is how this feat was accomplished.

Brown's success seems to have been built on several pillars. First, from the outset, his approach to the job was nonconfrontational and forward-looking. He was not interested in the past or in the question of who had failed in leading the Houston Police Department. He deflected all such discussions and instead repeated his ambition to make the Houston Police Department the best in the country. No doubt the fact that two previous chiefs remained in high positions within the department made such a stance necessary as well as wise. But the point is that he was uniformly constructive. He focused attention on future performance rather than past blame.

Consistent with this approach, Brown labored hard to develop a specific plan for moving the Houston Police Department into the future. He commissioned the internal staff to analyze the current state of the organization and its performance. When that plan failed to meet his exacting standards, he sought help from an outside consultant named Robert Wasserman. Over six months, Wasserman and Brown undertook to diagnose the current strengths and weaknesses of the department and to develop a strategy that exploited its strengths and shored up its weaknesses. That plan was presented to the principal managers of the department in a private, day-long internal meeting. None of the department's "dirty laundry" was paraded for public view.

While working within the organization, Brown was simultaneously working externally in the same constructive vein. He published a set of "values" that would guide the organization under his stewardship (see Table 5.1). In addition, once his assessment and plan had been reviewed inside the department, they were published for outside discussion and comment. Through the general values, the assessment of the department, and the plan for the future, Brown made himself externally accountable to the community of Houston. If his behavior was not consistent with his published values, if there were not improvements in the directions indicated by his plan, he would be exposed to failure. Such accountability revealed to his subordinates the general course he planned to take. Moreover, since Brown himself was staked to these objectives, they knew that he would remain constant in pursuit of them. Finally, since these plans won widespread outside support, they created some urgency within the department. They became a reality to which the organization had to adapt rather than mere suggestions offered by a short-term chief.

In addition, Brown was able to use two significant new projects to both symbolize and give material substance to his plans. One project was the opening of a new police substation, which demonstrated his commitment to decentralizing police operations and moving them closer to the community. The second involved managing an "anti-fear experiment" funded by the National Institute of Justice. This project engaged the police in activities such as directed contacts with citizens, community newsletters, and visits to victims of crime, all designed to bring the police into close contact with the community and alleviate citizens' fears.

Finally, and most significantly, Brown began building an administrative framework that would accomplish the operational goals of bringing the police closer to the community and allowing them to work on the problems that the community nominated for their attention rather than the problems the police thought were important. He called his plan Directed Area Response Teams (DART). Brown organized the city into discrete areas and assigned groups of police officers to be responsible for peace and order within those areas. Their job was to establish and consult with local citizen groups representing these areas and

Table 5.1 Values of the Houston Police Department

The Houston Police Department will involve the community in all policing activities which directly impact the quality of community life.

The Houston Police Department believes that while crime prevention is its primary goal, it should vigorously pursue those who commit serious crimes.

The Houston Police Department believes that policing strategies used must preserve and advance democratic values.

The Houston Police Department believes that it must structure service delivery in a way that will reinforce the strength of the city's neighborhoods.

The Houston Police Department believes that the public should have input into the development of policies which directly impact the quality of neighborhood life.

The Houston Police Department is committed to managing its resources in a careful and effective manner.

The Houston Police Department will seek the input of employees into matters which impact employee job satisfaction and effectiveness.

The Houston Police Department will maintain the highest levels of integrity and professionalism in all its actions

The Houston Police Department will seek to provide stability, continuity and consistency in all of its operations.

---

to handle as best they could the problems confronting the communities. Many specialized police resources that had previously been centralized were decentralized so that they would be available to the local areas. The police were held accountable not so much for staffing patrol cars, keeping response times low, and producing arrests as for creating a sense of security, order, and responsiveness in the minds of the citizens whom they served.

These actions built a substantial base of support for Lee Brown and the Houston Police Department. Their articulated values connected with the values of the city. The attention given to allaying fear and consulting with the community reassured the community that the police would be responsive to their concerns and available to them when needed. The political strength generated by these successes meant that the police themselves would have to accommodate to this new regime, since it was clear that Brown would be around for a while and it was hard to attack the values he represented and the constituency he had built.

This reality may have reconciled many police officers to Brown's vision. But it is also true, and somewhat unexpected, that the police officers themselves found that they liked Brown's style of policing. One hard-boiled patrol officer who had been a hero in the old days of cowboy policing explained why the new regime of community policing was better:

In the old days when we were mostly locking up bad guys and responding to crime calls, I got the feeling that everyone was a jerk. Now that we're dealing with citizens who are interested in making their communities better, I see a whole lot of good people in the society.

With broad support from outside and within the department, and with an organization that is innovating in community relations, fear reduction, and crime prevention, Brown is succeeding in doing an impossible job.

KEVIN TUCKER: THE NEW DAWN

In 1986 Kevin Tucker was named commissioner of the Philadelphia Police Department.[34] His appointment came in the wake of two major scandals: the disastrous MOVE operation in which the Philadelphia Police Department accidentally caused a fire that destroyed several blocks of low-income housing when they unwisely tried to flush a militant black group out of a fortified house with a smoke bomb; and a far-ranging corruption investigation which had resulted in the indictment of high-level officials in the department.

Such events were not entirely out of line with the department's prior reputation. In the late 1960s their leader Frank Rizzo had earned a national reputation by carrying a revolver and a nightstick everywhere—even to formal occasions. He then became mayor because of the popularity of his uncompromising stand against rioters and hoodlums.

With a former police commissioner as mayor, it would be logical to assume that the police department would benefit, and to a degree, it did. Rizzo's legacy to the department seems to have been increased manpower (but with no corresponding increases in facilities or equipment), improved pensions, looser disability rules for retiring from the police force, and undiscriminating support for officers on the street. The net effect of this boon on the department was to create an organization that was self-indulgent and undisciplined. It was not surprising, then, that events such as MOVE and the corruption scandal occurred.

Tucker's appointment signaled a change in the orientation of the city and the police department. Tucker was the first outsider to become commissioner of the Philadelphia Police Department. He was the choice of the business community of Philadelphia, who admired his federal enforcement experience and the image of integrity and professionalism that he projected. He was also supported by a small group of progressive police professionals who had long been embarrassed by the Rizzo regime and frustrated by the parochialism of the nation's fifth-largest department.

To be successful, Tucker had to capitalize on these slender assets. His "coping devices" included the following. First, he had an exceedingly good personal touch and rapport with his officers. He went to retirement dinners, funerals, and baptisms. The officers liked him and believed that he would try to better conditions for the cop on the street. Consistent with this general stance, he was able to form a good working relationship with the head of the union.

Second, he commissioned a "study task force" to review the organization of the department and compose a "management blueprint" for improving its performance. This task force was funded by contributions from city foundations and businesses. Members of the task force included prominent Philadelphians and nationally recognized experts in law enforcement and policing.

Originally, the goal of the task force was to produce a detailed management plan under the assumption that a substantial mandate for change existed in Philadelphia—a mandate that would empower Tucker to implement the proposed changes. Gradually it became apparent, however, that the mandate for reform was weak and fickle. Consequently, the task force had to create and sustain a constituency that supported change as well as define the particular ways in which the department would be changed. This altered the conception of the task force report from a management blueprint to a more thematic political document addressed to the general Philadelphia community and the police department, which outlined both a broad vision of policing in Philadelphia and a detailed plan for effecting it.

The published report attracted widespread local and national attention. The task force found that the department was "unfocused, unmanaged, and unaccountable," and it committed the department to a new strategy of community-based, problem-solving policing. This document gave Tucker a foundation from which he could command and deploy additional funds from a tight-fisted city administration.

Third, Tucker decided to invest heavily in management training for his mid-level officers. With some increased resources in hand, Tucker contracted with the Police Executive Research Forum to teach a version of their three-week executive training program designed specifically for Philadelphia. An important theme in that program was the role of mid-level management in an organization that was undergoing a basic change in its overall strategy.

Fourth, Tucker continued but revamped the study task force. All of the non-Philadelphians who had served on the task force were thanked for their services and dismissed. A new group was established, composed entirely of Philadelphians, some of whom had served on the initial task force and some who had not. Renamed the Implementation Committee, this group provided continuing oversight of the police department, lobbying the mayor on key issues and maintaining the pressure for reform by issuing a nine-month "Progress Report." Eventually, the group modified its name and its function and became the Commissioner's Advisory Committee, while still serving as a constructive political force for change.

These coping mechanisms generated a great deal of ferment within the police department, which in turn opened significant opportunities for change. Reform was nowhere near completed, however, when a mayoral election intervened. The future of the police department became particularly uncertain when it turned out that the major challenger to incumbent Wilson Goode was none other than former mayor and commissioner Frank Rizzo. While the election hung in the balance, the reforms ceased within the department.

Interestingly, no direct attacks were made by Rizzo on the changes that Tucker had initiated. They were popular enough to withstand challenge during the campaign, but there was little doubt in anyone's mind that if Rizzo were to win the election, much of what Tucker had begun would be halted. Fortunately, and perhaps somewhat to the credit of Kevin Tucker, Goode won the election by a narrow margin and soon reappointed Tucker. He also raised Tucker's annual salary from $55,000 (which was less than his principal assistants were making as civil servants) to $80,000. When Tucker left in 1988, he was able to pass the baton to Deputy Commissioner Willie Williams, who pledged to continue the reforms within the Philadelphia Police Department.

DOING IMPOSSIBLE JOBS

What these stories have in common is the success of individual police commissioners in building a favorable reputation for themselves and their departments in a world where it is in principle impossible to succeed at that job. What they also have in common is the fact that the managers worked very hard to make themselves accountable to the public by defining their purposes in broad terms and then by trying to keep their own actions, and the actions of their organizations, consistent with those broad purposes. In short, they fit themselves and their organizations to public expectations of their performance.

There are two fundamental differences in these stories, however. One is the extent to which the managers strived to shape the public expectations and mandates within which they then operated. Gates, in Los Angeles, inherited a tradition and stayed within it. This was quite natural since his organization was perceived to be working well. Brown and Tucker, on the other hand, had the obligation and the chance to reshape their mandates, for their organizations were seen to be in crisis. They seized the opportunity by proposing a new contract between them and the communities they policed: Brown through his values and management plan; Tucker through his study task force and advisory committee.

A second key difference is in the substantive nature of the police strategies pursued. Darryl Gates continued the strategy of professionalized crime fighting, which consisted of emphasizing crime control, relying on rapid responses to calls for service, and centralizing command. Eventually, he adjusted his department's operations to make room for crime prevention, order maintenance, and community consultations, but professionalized crime fighting remained the dominant theme of the department. Whenever response times and professional independence came into conflict with order maintenance and community consultation, response times and professional independence won.

Lee Brown and Kevin Tucker pursued a different strategy of policing—one that allowed for crime prevention, fear reduction, order maintenance, and emergency services as well as rapid response to incidents of crime. Their strategy also called for close consultation with local communities rather than professional distance. To a degree, this program of policing represented a tactical innovation because it was a shift away from the orthodox ideas that had dominated the profession. As such, it carried substantial operational and political risks. It was by no means clear that this strategy would be better in controlling crime, reducing fear, and serving the people than traditional professionalized crime fighting. But both Brown and Tucker thought it was worth trying and had the liberty to do so precisely because their organizations' previous methods had been so discredited. So far, they have been successful in persuading others that this strategy is superior to the old one.

It is also worth noting that Brown and Tucker relied on different managerial tactics to alter the strategies of their departments. Tucker turned to a formally established outside commission to develop a new mandate for the police department. Brown relied principally on internal discussions and analyses to set the stage for his reforms (though these discussions occurred against the backdrop of a dismal past record, Brown's articulated values, and with the assistance of an outside consultant). Tucker used management training as the principal device for transforming the department. Brown took advantage of an experiment in fear reduction, a new station house, and the detailed specification of a new program (DART) to instruct his organization about what he wanted. Tucker spent a lot of time with his troops and stayed close to the union. Brown was more aloof and distant.

In sum, the key to success in the impossible job of managing large urban police departments seems to be fitting the strategy of the department to the historical context, to the current expectations of the community, and to the capabilities of the organization. There may be many styles of policing that can "succeed" in a given city. What is important, then, is for the manager to find not only a strategy that guarantees his or her individual success, but also one that creates values and secures substantial public benefits for the resources expended.

Some value-creating strategies are riskier to pursue than others because they are new. The public has not yet demanded them, nor have the organizations produced them. Brown and Tucker distinguished themselves not only because they discovered a successful strategy of policing but also because they chose a riskier, more innovative path. That risk was "financed" by their hard work with the citizens to "capitalize" their venture. Gates followed a more conservative course. Still, both innovative and traditional strategies produced successes for managers, and it remains unclear which type holds greater value for the citizens over the long run.

NOTES

1. I am following a line of analysis first developed in Philip Selznick, *Leadership in Administration* (New York: Harper and Row, 1957). For a more "nuts and bolts" discussion of how to succeed as a police executive, see Michael S. Scott, *Managing for Success: A Police Chief's Survival Guide* (Washington, D.C.: Police Executive Research Forum, 1986).

2. Basically, there are three approaches to measuring the value of public sector activities. The most ambitious is "benefit cost analysis." For a basic treatment, see Harley H. Henrich and Graeme Taylor, *Program Budgeting Cost Analysis: Cases, Texts and Reading* (Pacific Palisades, Calif.: Goodyear, 1969). A second approach is "program evaluation." For a comprehensive treatment of this subject, see Carol H. Weiss, *Evaluating Action Programs* (Boston, Mass.: Allyn and Bacon, 1972). A third approach is measuring the quantity and quality of activities produced. See, for example, Paul K. Brace, Robert Elkin, Daniel D. Robinson, and Harold I. Shinberg, *Reporting of Service Efforts and Accomplishments* (Stamford, Conn.: Financial Accounting Standards Board, 1980).

3. See, for example, Commission on Accreditation for Law Enforcement Agencies, *Standards for Law Enforcement Agencies* (Fairfax, Va.: Commission on Accreditation, 1988).

4. Philadelphia Police Study Task Force, *Philadelphia and its Police: Toward a New Partnership* (Philadelphia: Philadelphia Police Study Task Force, 1987).

5. For the techniques of controlling police corruption, see Allen N. Kornblum, *The Moral Hazards: Police Strategies for Honesty and Ethical Behavior* (Lexington, Mass.: D. C. Heath, 1976).

6. For a wider view of police functions, see Herman Goldstein, *Policing a Free Society* (Cambridge, Mass.: Ballinger Press, 1977).

7. Mark H. Moore and Robert J. Trojanowicz, *The Police and Crime,* Perspectives on Policing (Washington, D.C.: National Institute of Justice, 1988).

8. Patsy Klaus and Carol Kalish, *The Severity of Crime,* Bureau of Justice Statistics Bulletin, January 1984 (Washington, D.C.: U. S. Department of Justice, 1984).

9. For a theoretical discussion of this issue, see Egon Bittner, "The Police on Skid-row: A Study of Peace-keeping," *American Sociological Review* 32 (October 1967): 699–715. For a recent example of how this can become an important political issue, see David Kennedy, *Neighborhood Policing: The London Metropolitan Police Force,* Kennedy

School of Government Case #C15-87-770 (Cambridge, Mass.: Kennedy School of Government, 1986).

10. Mark H. Moore and Robert J. Trojanowicz, *Fear and the Police*, Perspectives on Policing (Washington, D. C.: National Institute of Justice, 1988).

11. Wesley Skogan, "Fear of Crime and Neighborhood Change," in *Communities and Crime*, ed. Albert J. Reiss and Michael Tonry, vol. 8 of *Crime and Justice: A Review of Research* (Chicago, Ill.: University of Chicago Press, 1986), p. 222.

12. Anthony M. Pate, Mary Ann Wycoff, Wesley G. Skogan, and Lawrence W. Sherman, *Reducing Fear of Crime in Houston and Newark* (Washington, D.C.: Police Foundation, 1986).

13. Mary Ann Wycoff, *The Role of Municipal Police: Research as a Prelude to Changing It: Executive Summary* (Washington, D.C.: Police Foundation, 1982).

14. Moore and Trojanowicz, *The Police and Crime*.

15. Michael T. Farmer, ed., *Survey of Police Operational and Administrative Practices* (Washington, D.C.: Police Executive Research Forum, 1978).

16. George L. Kelling, Tony Pate, Duane Dieckman, Charles E. Brown, *The Kansas City Preventive Patrol Experiment: A Summary Report* (Washington, D.C.: Police Foundation, 1974).

17. *Response Time Analysis* (Kansas City, Mo.: Kansas City Police Department, 1977).

18. Peter W. Greenwood, Jan M. Chaiken, and Joan Petersilia, *The Criminal Investigation Process* (Lexington, Mass.: D. C. Heath, 1977); John Eck, *Managing Case Assignments: Burglary Investigation Decision Model Replication* (Washington, D.C.: Police Executive Research Forum, 1979).

19. Wesley Skogan and George E. Antunes, "Information, Apprehension and Deterrence: Exploring the Limits of Police Productivity," *Journal of Criminal Justice* 7 (1979): 217–41.

20. For the theory of "problem-solving," see Herman Goldstein, "Improving Policing: A Problem Oriented Approach," *Crime and Delinquency* 25 (1979): 236–58. For practical applications, see John Eck and William Spelman, *Solving Problems: Problem Oriented Policing in Newport News* (Washington, D.C.: Police Executive Research Forum, 1987).

21. This example was discussed by Chief Darryl Gates of the Los Angeles Police Department during the discussions of the Harvard/NIJ Executive Session on Policing, 6 November 1987.

22. James Q. Wilson, *Varieties of Police Behavior* (Cambridge, Mass.: Harvard University Press, 1968), chapter 4. For a more anecdotal account, see Jonathan Rubinstein, *City Police* (New York: Farrar, Strauss and Giroux, 1973).

23. The concept is borrowed from Richard Elmore. See Richard Elmore, "Organizational Models of Program Implementation," *Public Policy* (Spring 1978): 187–228.

24. Steven A. Rynecki, Douglas A. Cairns, Donald J. Cairns, *Police Collective Bargaining Agreements* (Washington, D.C.: Police Executive Research Forum, 1978).

25. George L. Kelling, Robert Wasserman, and Hubert Williams, *Police Accountability and Community Policing*, Perspectives on Policing (Washington, D.C.: National Institute of Justice, 1988).

26. Robert Wasserman and Mark H. Moore, *Values in Policing*, Perspectives on Policing (Washington, D.C.: National Institute of Justice, 1988).

27. William C. Cunningham and Todd H. Taylor, *Private Security and Police in America* (Portland, Oreg.: Chancellor Press, 1985), pp. 105–16.

28. Donald C. Withan, *The American Law Enforcement Chief Executive: A Management Profile* (Washington, D.C.: Police Executive Research Forum, 1984).

29. The data on the "coping" strategies of these three police executives come from three different sources: case studies of the organizations; personal interviews and discussions with the executives; and personal participation in the activities.

30. The story of Darryl Gates and Los Angeles is based primarily on David Kennedy, *Neighborhood Policing in Los Angeles,* Kennedy School of Government Case #C16-87-717 (Cambridge, Mass.: Kennedy School of Government, 1987). It is supplemented by informal discussions with Chief Gates in meetings of Harvard's Executive Session on Community Policing.

31. Ibid., p. 2.

32. Ibid. p. 5.

33. This story is based principally on Zachary Tumin, *Lee Brown and the Houston Police Department* (Cambridge, Mass.: Harvard University Program in Criminal Justice, 1989). It is supplemented by many discussions with Chief Brown in meetings of Harvard's Executive Session on Community Policing and by visits to the Houston Police Department.

34. The Philadelphia story is based on my personal participation in the Police Study Task Force and on sustained professional assistance to Commissioner Tucker.

6

A State Mental Health Commissioner and the Politics of Mental Illness

Gary E. Miller and Ira Iscoe

Most people avoid thinking about mental illness until they are forced to do so by virtue of its unwelcome appearance in oneself or a family member. For people with means or a good insurance policy, mental illness entails office visits to a private psychiatrist or psychologist or perhaps a short stay in a private mental hospital or psychiatric unit of a general hospital. But for the large number of people with limited resources and more disabling mental illnesses, the only place to turn for help is the public mental health system. The institutions and community-based programs that comprise the public mental health system are nominally under the direction of an official whose title varies from state to state but whom we shall here refer to as the "state mental health commissioner."

Mental illness is one of the most serious public health problems in the United States. Approximately 19 percent of the population suffers from some form of mental disorder ranging from phobias, to personality problems and stress-related conditions, to major illnesses like schizophrenia and manic depressive disease.[1]

Although diagnostic classifications, causal theories, and treatment methods have changed over the centuries, mental illness seems to have been a constant feature of humankind's presence on earth. Society no longer considers psychotic people to be possessed by demons or able to endure torture without feeling pain; nor does it condone lifelong incarceration of people with mental illness in human warehouses. Nevertheless, it would be a mistake to conclude as the final decade of the twentieth century opens that society has discovered the most effective way of caring for its mentally ill citizens or that the stigma attached to mental illness has been eliminated. The confusion and controversy that surround mental illness treatment (whose accepted euphemism is "mental health services"), together with society's failure to agree on the role that government should play in caring for mentally ill people, are among the leading contributors to the impossibility of the task of the state mental health commissioner. The commissioner has to achieve the unachievable and meet demands that cannot be met. The impossibility of the job arises not only from the nature of mental illness and limits in treatment technology but also from the unique political context in which the commissioner operates.

It would be difficult enough for a mental health commissioner to deal with the usual politics surrounding the allocation of roles and resources among state agencies and disputes about policies. The politics of mental illness, however, are charged with emotion. Parents of a young adult with recurring and seemingly intractable antisocial behavior are understandably frustrated and exasperated because the mental health agency has been unable to find a permanent solution to their problem. Local elected officials, concerned about safety, call state legislators to complain about a plan to move state hospital patients into a halfway house in a residential neighborhood. With equal vehemence, advocacy lawyers criticize the commissioner for denying other state hospital patients their freedom by not releasing them into the community. Dedicated proponents of a particular treatment ideology are moved to publicly demand the commissioner's resignation for a perceived lack of enthusiasm for their preferred approach. A newspaper armed with few facts launches a crusade to reform an allegedly archaic mental health system, blaming the commissioner for conditions the commissioner neither created nor condoned.

The emotions that activate the politics of mental illness are to some extent a product of the fear that everyone has of losing their mind or of encountering disabled mental functioning in a family member or close friend. The political world of the state mental health commissioner reveals that many people—even those well educated, including mental health professional themselves—are profoundly ambivalent in their attitudes toward the mentally ill. We are frightened by them and we seek distance and protection from them, yet we also feel compassion toward them and we urge sympathetic care and protection of them.

HISTORICAL DEVELOPMENT OF MENTAL HEALTH CARE

A brief historical review of services to the mentally ill helps put the task of the state mental health commissioner in perspective. The history of care of the mentally ill is characterized by cycles of reform and neglect, each cycle bearing a similarity to its predecessors. Community-based care is shifted to state government-controlled care. "Out of sight, out of mind" attitudes result in mental patients being locked away in remote state hospitals. Exposés about conditions in these institutions raise the social guilt quotient; more tax money is then spent to upgrade care or to return the mentally ill to the community. The stage is set for the next cycle of neglect and reform.

Era of State Mental Hospitals

Mental health care in the United States in the late eighteenth and early nineteenth century was the product of a reform movement that began in western Europe and signaled the era of moral treatment.[2] Proponents of moral treatment advocated abandonment of the chains and shackles that had been used to control institutionalized mentally ill people. The essence of the moral treatment movement was the belief that if the mentally ill were treated in a humane fashion, their symptoms would subside to the point that many could be released from institutions and possibly resume productive lives. The most noteworthy event of the era was Phillippe Pinel's unchaining of severely disturbed mental patients in the Bicêtre asylum in Paris in 1793.[3]

Although the first public and private mental hospitals in the United States tried to preserve the philosophy of moral treatment, the young nation was soon swamped with more mentally ill patients than could be cared for properly in existing facilities. Many of these people were recent immigrants who suffered not only from mental illness but also from lack of marketable job skills and failure to assimilate into the predominant culture. The situation had further deteriorated by the 1840s, when reformer Dorothea Lynde Dix discovered county jails and poor houses across the country crowded with mentally ill, criminal, mentally retarded, blind, deaf, syphilitic, and tuberculous people, as well as others who were simply poor or elderly—all living together in filth and degradation.

It was under Dorothea Dix's leadership that state governments were persuaded to take over the care of the mentally ill from local governments, charities, and religious organizations.[4] The result was the opening of state government-operated institutions to provide treatment as well as sanctuary or asylum to the mentally ill. Samuel Gridley Howe, Dix's colleague and counterpart in the field of care of the blind, deaf, and mentally retarded, played a similar role in urging state governments to establish institutions for people with these disabilities.[5]

However, the growth in the number of patients admitted to the newly constructed state hospitals quickly outstripped their capacity to provide adequate housing and care. Conditions worsened during the first decades of the twentieth century. By the end of World War II, articles began to appear about inhumane living conditions in state mental hospitals, exposing the inadequate budgets, overcrowding, unsanitary and unsafe buildings, lack of medical care, and so forth. Perhaps the most important influence in drawing the nation's attention to the dismal situation in state hospitals was the publication in 1948 of Albert Deutsch's *The Shame of the States*.[6] The stage was set for a new era of reform.

Era of Deinstitutionalization and Community Care

The deinstitutionalization movement and its corollary—community care of the mentally ill—have together been the dominant influence on state mental health policies and practices since the early 1960s and will likely continue in that role for the remaining years of the twentieth century.[7] With the introduction in 1955 of chlorpromazine, the first of a new class of medications for the treatment of schizophrenia, the population of state mental hospitals began to decline for the first time in history.[8] This remarkable phenomenon paved the way for a national movement that has been responsible for major improvements in care of the mentally ill, but also, as we shall discuss later, for some problems that contribute to the impossibility of the mental health commissioner's task.

The new medications permitted treatment of many people with serious mental illnesses like schizophrenia in such community settings as general hospitals, outpatient clinics, and day hospitals. Although these pharmaceuticals do not cure psychiatric disorders, they frequently reduce disabling signs and symptoms so that patients can behave in a more socially acceptable fashion, communicate more effectively with others and learn new skills.

It was a combination of the newly emerging community care movement and the recognition of the inadequacies of many state mental hospitals described in *The Shame of the States* that led Congress to appoint a Joint Commission on Mental Illness and Health in 1955. The 1961 report of this commission, *Action for Mental Health*, recommended smaller, more specialized state psychiatric hospitals and a network of community treatment centers.[9] With the urging of President John F. Kennedy, Congress acted on the recommendations of the report by passing the Community Mental Health Centers Act in 1963.[10] Over a period of sixteen years, the federal government awarded grants to hundreds of local agencies, creating a nationwide network of over seven hundred community mental health centers (CMHCs). Although the community centers became a permanent part of the national scene, many of the goals and dreams of *Action for Mental Health* were not realized.

During the 1970s there was mounting criticism of the community centers for ignoring the plight of people with more serious and disabling forms of mental illness.[11] National studies identified breakdowns in continuity of care and lack of coordination among government agencies with responsibility for serving the long-term and severely mentally ill.[12] One particularly needy subset of those with chronic mental illness is that group lacking a domicile who are thus considered the "homeless mentally ill."[13]

The Mental Health Systems Act of 1980, an effort to redirect community mental health resources toward the seriously mentally ill and make CMHCs more accountable to state government, was essentially repealed shortly after its passage and replaced with a system of block grants to the states.[14] The effect of the new block-grant program was to eliminate the federal government's role in directing the activities of CMHCs, thus enabling each state mental health agency to formulate policies and priorities for the entire state mental health system, not just for state hospitals.

State mental health commissioners responded to this opportunity by placing their highest priority on the expansion of community services for people with severe and chronic mental illness.[15] Progress in this direction required increased state government influence over CMHCs, which have been traditionally more responsive to local government and the federal bureaucracy. Commissioners, therefore, have had to enter a political minefield and gingerly attempt to impose state priorities on relatively autonomous local entities. Commissioners have struggled to create a mental health system out of a collection of locally run CMHCs and state hospitals whose superintendents have generally preferred to think of themselves as independent of the state mental health agency. That struggle is one of the impossible tasks of the state mental health commissioner.

THE JOB OF COMMISSIONER

The state mental health commissioner is the chief executive officer of an organization that usually has direct responsibility for management of state institutions (such as state hospitals) and somewhat less direct responsibility for management of CMHCs. There is considerable variation from state to state as to the composition of the mental health agency, the scope of the commissioner's nominal responsibility and actual power to direct mental health programs, and the organizational locus of the mental health agency vis-à-vis other human-services agencies of the state government.

Some state mental health agencies are independent while others are combined with social services, public assistance, public health, and rehabilitation agencies to form a comprehensive organization, often referred to as an umbrella agency.[16] The mental health agency, whether independent or a division of an umbrella agency, may be concerned solely with services to the mentally ill. Alternatively, it may be charged also with responsibility for serving people with substance abuse disorders (alcohol and drugs); mental retardation; or mental retardation and other conditions (including autism, epilepsy, and cerebral palsy) collectively referred to as developmental disabilities. Of the fifty state mental health agencies, twenty-seven have additional responsibility for the state's mental retardation or developmental disabilities program and twenty for the state's substance abuse program.[17] State mental hospitals are typically under the direct supervision of the state mental health commissioner, while CMHCs are usually operated by private not-for-profit organizations or local governmental units that negotiate contracts with or receive grants from the state mental health agency.

Some mental health commissioners are appointed by and report to the state's governor; others answer to a board of lay persons. The commissioner of a state mental health agency that is a part of an umbrella agency usually reports to the commissioner or secretary of the umbrella agency. In umbrella agencies that separate program services from line management, the mental health commissioner may lack real authority over mental health programs, instead serving mainly as an advisor or consultant to other executives in the agency who actually supervise the programs.

Although as recently as the late 1960s, every state mental health commissioner held a medical degree (and usually specialized in psychiatry), today's commissioners have diverse educational backgrounds. Academic credentials range from medical degrees with psychiatric specialization, to doctorates in psychology and a variety of other fields, to master's degrees in social work, health care, business, or public administration, to bachelor's degrees.[18]

During the 1950s and 1960s the role of state mental health commissioner was relatively uncomplicated. Except for an occasional media exposé, a commissioner could run the agency almost as if it were a private company, with little interference from outside forces. Few members of the general public were aware of what actually transpired in state mental hospitals. Although knowledgeable legislators knew of the dilapidated condition of some of these institutions and the generally inadequate staffing and funding, commissioners were seldom blamed for these conditions, required to explain their actions, or asked to justify publicly their budgetary and programmatic decisions. Few advocacy or consumer organizations had sufficient visibility and clout to pressure the commissioner to demand additional funds from the legislature or to modify some policy or practice in the mental health system. The era of class-action litigation against state mental health agencies did not begin until 1972, when the *Wyatt v. Stickney* decision in Alabama resulted in massive changes in state institutions pursuant to a judicially determined "right to treatment."[19]

Budgets were usually organized by line items with specific dollar amounts appropriated for each state hospital and the agency central office. Almost all of the money came from state appropriations; federal funding was limited to relatively small formula grants under the Comprehensive Health Planning Act, hospital improvement project grants (of up to $100,000 per hospital), and, beginning in 1963, CMHC grants provided directly to the community centers. Although the federal Medicare (Title 13) and Medicaid (Title 19) programs were initiated in 1965, use of Medicaid for adults ages twenty-one through sixty-five in state mental hospitals was prohibited by federal law. The Medicaid intermediate care facility–mental retardation program (ICF-MR), which contributed significantly to the financing of state institutions for the mentally retarded, did not begin until 1974.

In this period, it was still neither required nor expected by the publc, governors, or legislatures that state mental health agencies have the sophisticated fiscal management capability now considered essential. Peer review, quality assurance, and patient-rights protection systems were not yet obligatory in state mental hospitals or state mental health agencies. Since mental health agencies were less complex and demanding, commissioners without management experience were frequently hired. Psychiatrists from the world of private practice or academia were expected to quickly transfer their skill in managing the therapy of individual patients to managing systems providing care to thousands. Presumably, the necessary expertise would be acquired via on-the-job training.

During the 1980s the role of state mental health commissioner changed dramatically.[20] The commissioner is now supposed to possess a range of skills and knowledge that is rarely, if ever, found in a single person: management abilities suited for running a multimillion- (sometimes multibillion-) dollar organization; knowledge of the clinical and technical aspects of mental health service delivery; an ability to conceptualize, develop, and administer multifaceted systems of care; familiarity with hospital administration; comprehensive financial knowledge that covers such complex federal programs as Medicare and Medicaid; skill as a public speaker including the ability to testify before legislative committees; skill in communicating with the news media; a working knowledge of mental health law, litigation, and legal strategy; skill as a negotiator in dealing with unions and employee and professional organizations and with citizen, parent, and advocacy groups; an ability to convey such elusive attributes as "leadership," "charisma," and "creativity"; and, finally, mastery of the political process and of the political intrigue that almost always surrounds the office of state mental health commissioner.[21]

Why the Job Is Impossible

The impossibility of the commissioner's task is only partly the result of the complexity of the job and the diverse range of abilities required. If success were merely a matter of hard work and skill in the several areas listed above, a knowledgeable, intelligent, and reasonably competent person willing to put in about sixty hours a week could be expected to master the job of commissioner over time and to receive at least passing grades from the many people who stand ready to evaluate the commissioner's performance. Unfortunately, this is not the case. The commissioner must deal with powerful people and constituencies who place demands on the mental health agency that are both unreachable and contradictory. Because any commissioner, even an exceptionally skilled one, cannot satisfy all such demands, the commissioner is invariably seen by at least some observers as failing to carry out the responsibilities of the position.

We should qualify our remarks by pointing out that the number and intensity of the demands on a mental health commissioner vary from state to state and are sporadic within a single state. The commissioner's ability to improve the mental health system or survive in the job for a reasonable period of time may depend on such variables as the political and economic climate in the state, the political debts incurred by the governor or the umbrella-agency head to whom the commissioner reports, the personalities of the leaders of citizen and employee organizations, the ownership and editorial stance of the newspapers, and the personal relationship of the commissioner with key elected officials in the state.

Even under the best of circumstances, the impossibility of the job eventually takes its toll. The average tenure for the state mental health commissioner is 2.61 years.[22] The following discussion demonstrates the unreasonable and contradictory demands that make the commissioner's job impossible.

INTRACTABLE CLIENTS

Curing the Incurable

The commissioner deals on a regular basis with people who cannot accept the fact that psychiatry has limitations. One especially important point is not widely recognized: The major mental illnesses of people in public mental health systems can sometimes be partly controlled, but they are chronic in nature and generally not susceptible to cure. Most people with symptoms of such chronic medical disorders as diabetes, cancer, and heart disese remain in the community with warm social support; yet the person who persists in exhibiting signs of mental illness causes almost unbearable distress to many citizens and thereby symbolizes the inadequacies of the mental health system. Many responsible community leaders believe that even the most seriously disabled mentally ill persons can be treated successfully in the state mental hospital and restored to the community to live independently and symptom-free indefinitely. Continued hospitalization, "crazy" behavior in the community, or return to the hospital after discharge are regarded as signs of the bad judgment of the officials of the system. The absence of any treatment methods that could achieve total and permanent restoration to mental health tends to be ignored by these critics. They apparently believe that if the agency were better managed, had more doctors and other treatment personnel (or perhaps better ones), or had more money, it could cure the incurable.

The Homeless Mentally Ill

The mental health commissioner is also expected to solve some of the most difficult issues in our society. The case of the homeless mentally ill presents the quintessential example of unrealistic expectations, since the mental health system actually gets much of the blame for the problem.

There is no escaping the media reports of the desperate plight of the nation's homeless—people who survive by panhandling and eating out of garbage cans, who huddle over subway grates in the winter and sleep in doorways and under bridges. Not surprisingly, a significant percentage of these people have symptoms of a mental illness. In fact, the same can be said about 19 percent of the general population.[23] This association between homelessness and mental illness has led to widespread publicity attributing the problem of homelessness to state mental health agencies and their policy of deinstitutionalization. The implication is either that these people did not stay in the hospital long enough to be cured or that they should be gathered up and put into mental hospitals—which are, after all, residences of a sort.

The logic of the connection between deinstitutionalization and homelessness is faulty.[24] Although about 25 to 40 percent of these people have a history of mental illness, it does not follow that the problem was created by the mental health system.[25] It is true that in the 1950s state hospitals served as warehouses for thousands of people who had no other place to live. Yet several contemporary factors beyond the control of the mental health commissioner, including both laws and professional standards, make it inconceivable that state hospitals could ever be used in that fashion again.

Medications now enable the vast majority of mentally ill people to live outside of hospitals. Mental illness does not imply an automatic need for hospitalization any more than does physical illness. As in chronic physical disorders, hospitalization is required only when symptoms are acute and when medical supervision and continual nursing care are necessary. It is not only clinically improper to house mentally ill people in hospitals when they do not need hospitalization; it would also break the budget of most states. With accreditation of state hospitals now requiring staffing levels that may cost several hundred dollars per patient day, it would make little sense for the state mental health agency to herd homeless people into hospitals.

Even if a commissioner were disposed to attempt such a solution to the problem of the homeless mentally ill, the law would impose a formidable barrier. Since the early 1960s, federal courts and state legislatures have modified commitment laws to mandate as a condition for involuntary admission to a state mental hospital both the presence of mental illness and a judicial determination that the patient is either "gravely disabled" or exhibits behavior that poses a serious physical danger to the patient or another person.[26] Even in the case of a homeless mentally ill person who requires hospitalization, a determination that the patient is "in need of care and treatment" (the previous standard for commitment) would not satisfy the current, more stringent legal criteria. In the continuing conflict between individual freedom and the protection of health by the state, freedom currently commands a very high priority.

State mental health agencies *do* attempt to provide psychiatric treatment (although not necessarily in a state hospital) to homeless mentally ill people, to the extent that they agree to accept such treatment and within budgetary constraints. But even when these people receive psychiatric treatment, they remain the "homeless mentally ill" because their illnesses, although perhaps improved, will endure and because psychiatric treatment cannot create a home for them. Neither can psychiatric treatment address some of the root causes of homelessness: poverty, social isolation, and lack of a human services "safety net."

Members of the homeless population often have serious medical and social as well as psychiatric problems. Substance abuse has always been a major contributor to their situation. The homeless also have poor nutrition, tend to be school dropouts, and lack job skills. How often, however, is homelessness identified as a medical problem, an educational problem, or a problem for the state public welfare agency, the vocational rehabilitation agency, or the housing authority? The mental health agency and its commissioner are often expected to absorb the criticism engendered by society's failure to meet the basic needs of its poor and disabled members.

The Dangerous Mental Patient

Accused of lack of diligence, the mental health system and its chief are also blamed for violent crime, or at least the violent acts of those who were previously institutionalized. Although it has been established that mentally ill people as a group are no more dangerous than other groups, the public has been conditioned by the media (including movies about mad killers) to believe differently.[27] A person who was once in a state hospital and who later commits a violent act is routinely characterized as a "former mental patient," suggesting that the hospital and mental health agency are somehow responsible. The agency's psychiatrists are expected to know when a patient might become violent and then either to cure the patient before discharge or keep him or her locked up indefinitely. It is, of course, impossible for the agency to comply with these expectations. In the first place, as noted before, even the best hospital treatment cannot cure people of serious mental illness. Second, neither a psychiatrist nor anyone else can accurately predict the future behavior of another person, whether or not the person is mentally ill.[28] Third, it is illegal to keep a mental patient locked up indefinitely in an institution solely because the staff believe the patient might someday exhibit dangerous behavior.[29]

If a patient in a state hospital or special forensic hospital (for the "criminally insane") no longer meets the legal standards for commitment, the mental health agency is not simply *allowed* to release the patient; it is *required* to release that patient—even if he or she has previously committed a violent act. The agency's psychiatrists face a "catch-22" situation. If they continue the confinement of a patient who does not seem to be dangerous now because they think he or she might someday hurt someone, they face the wrath of the civil libertarians and patient-rights advocates. If they release the patient, they are certain to be denounced if the patient commits some violent act in the future. In the final analysis, patients will be discharged from both civil and forensic mental hospitals because they must be. Occasionally one of these people will commit a violent act. When that happens, the state mental health commissioner is likely to surface as the official who bears at least some indirect responsibility for the violent act.

The discovery by the media that "dangerous" people are being discharged can lead to harsh criticism of the mental health agency. Legislators and newspapers with a law-and-order agenda do not always distinguish between convicted criminals and patients who have not been convicted. Such patients have been found incompetent to stand trial or acquitted on the ground of insanity. When the state mental health commission authorizes the release of dangerous patients from forensic hospitals, as the law often requires, the commissioner must take the risk of being accused of endangering the public.

Deficiencies in the mental health system are also alleged in the case of particularly horrendous crimes such as mass or serial murders perpetrated by people who have never received psychiatric treatment. A better mental health system would presumably have identified potential criminals in advance, sent them to the appropriate kind of therapy, and prevented the tragic occurrences. Needless to say, no conceivable state mental health system could accomplish such a feat.

CONSTITUENCIES IN CONFLICT

Institution versus Community

One of the most divisive issues faced by the commissioner is community care of the mentally ill versus care in the state hospital. It is clear from both history and current research that although the majority of mentally ill people can be well served in the community, some cannot.[30] Some people with severe and refractory disabilities need institutional settings like state hospitals that afford twenty-four-hour psychiatric and nursing care and that protect the patient and others from confused or aggressive behavior. If logic prevailed, state hospitals (referred to in some states as psychiatric centers or mental health institutes) would be assigned responsibility for mentally disabled people whose illnesses require the structured environment of an institution; others with less severe conditions would be assigned to community programs such as community mental health centers. The size and budgets of the facilities would be based on estimates of the number of mentally ill people requiring treatment in each type of setting. Unfortunately, a logical analysis of this kind would run headlong into the politics of mental illness.

Quite understandably, the directors and governing boards of CMHCs have formed statewide councils to lobby the mental health agency, legislators, and the governor for increased appropriations to the centers. These organizations and their paid lobbyists typically call for a reallocation of funds from state hospitals to community care programs. It is argued, for example, that while state hospitals may receive about 70 percent of the mental health agency budget, they serve only 30 percent of the patients. The implication is that the dollar allocation should be altered to reflect the patient load at each setting.

However, such statistics compare apples and oranges.[31] The number of patients served in an accredited mental hospital, professionally staffed around the clock, cannot be legitimately compared to an outpatient caseload that includes patients who may be seen in an office for a few minutes every three months. Furthermore, a shift of dollars from a state hospital to a community program does not automatically cause a state hospital's census (and thus its costs) to decline. The hospital's census is determined by a variety of factors. One is the effectiveness of the community program in preventing admissions. Another is the severity of the illnesses of patients being admitted. Still another is the number of mentally ill people in the hospital's service area at risk of relapse. In addition, changes in the private healthcare and insurance industries can cause people to lose their access to private psychiatric care.[32] Nevertheless, when a commissioner defends a state hospital appropriation request necessary to meet minimal standards of care, the commissioner may be accused by community care partisans of being institutionally oriented and not supportive of community programs.

As troublesome as the procommunity and anti-institutional forces are to the commissioner, the political hazard of being perceived as a less than staunch defender of institutions is even greater. Institutions are the principal employers in the rural communities where many of them are located. A plan to scale down a state hospital or (heaven forbid!) close one that has outlived its usefulness is likely to present a real economic threat to that community. It may incite a political shooting match with most of the guns aimed directly at the commissioner. The legislative delegation from the community in which the state hospital is located, as well as its mayor and other city and county officials, may express their concern to the commissioner. More often, however, in trying to garner the most influence, they will notify the governor or the board that appoints the commissioner about the detrimental economic consequences of the commissioner's action. These local and state officials will be joined in coalition by the unions and public employee associations that always have their vocal champions in the state legislature and perhaps even in the governor's office.

The commissioner's problem is compounded by the fact that the enlightened and scientifically valid approach to mental health care consists of expanding community services to severely mentally ill people and reducing their dependence on the state hospital. The expected by-products of pursuing the "right" approach are (a) smaller state hospitals with fewer employees and reduced budgets, (b) the closing of some hospitals that are no longer necessary, and (c) expansion of CMHC programs and budgets. Although the commissioner may shift attention and resources from hospital care to community care and back again, it is impossible to act in the interests of all who are appropriately and understandably concerned.

For mental health commissioners whose responsibility includes mental retardation services, the institution versus community controversy can become an emotional battlefield. The expectation that the commissioner can somehow both expand and diminish the role of institutions is as present in mental retardation as in mental health. There is, however, an additional dimension to the conflict in the mental retardation field: an altruistic, ideological commitment on the part of both pro-institution and anti-institution advocates that makes their struggle resemble that between right-to-life and prochoice supporters. Any action a commissioner is likely to take will be wrong in the eyes of one or the other group. A reasonable position, for example, would be to expand community alternatives for all but the most severely handicapped, mentally retarded people, reserving state schools (also called training centers or developmental centers) for those with the most severe disabilities, especially people with serious physical complications and behavior problems.

This position, however, would be abhorrent to both the anti-institution groups (typically state and local chapters of the Association for Retarded Citizens [ARC]) and pro-institution groups (typically organizations of parents of state school residents). To the anti-institution, procommunity groups, any action short of phasing out state schools is unacceptable. Development of the full potential of retarded citizens, these advocates would argue, is possible only in a "normal" community setting. In their view, not only do institutions hinder personal development, but they cause regression. State school residents can become less autonomous, increasingly dependent on the institution, and lose skills already acquired. Anti-institution advocates reject passionately the proposition that state schools should specialize in caring for the most severely disabled, because they construe such a policy as a form of discrimination based solely on degree of handicap and as a denial of the potential of *every* person to grow and develop. The position of this group is, in short, that all institutions are bad institutions and that therefore every person should live in the community.

Parents of residents of state schools express as much passion and conviction as their anti-institution counterparts when they argue for the institution as a proper place to care for some disabled people. They would view the proposed strategy as the beginning of the end, a first step toward closure of state schools. Their reasoning: State schools that serve only the most severely disabled would have fewer residents and higher per-resident costs, thus tempting state legislatures to close or consolidate these institutions. Both their fear of institutional closure and their anger at the mental health agency for its basically procommunity policies are understandable. The state stepped forward years earlier to assume a *parens patriae* responsibility for their disabled son or daughter. Furthermore, that responsibility, in the eyes of the parents, has been carried out reasonably well. Usually, the dormitories on the campuses of the institutions are clean, attractive, and well maintained; staff are caring and attentive; medical and dental care are provided; and recreational, social, and religious needs are met through chaplains' services, athletic games, dances, field trips into town, and so forth. The institution offers security to aging parents who are worried about the long-term future of their son or daughter. They see in the state school with its spacious grounds and impressive buildings a sense of permanence and of commitment by the state government to the welfare of their child.

It is not surprising, therefore, that when professional staff members suggest to parents of a state school resident that he or she should be placed in a community residential program (group home), the typical response is panic. Why would parents be willing to trade a safe and secure setting for their child for an uncertain future in a small home on an ordinary street? The staff may explain that a relatively unstructured and less closely supervised group-home setting would pose acceptable risks when compared with the benefits of community living. These arguments, although supported by research, usually fall on deaf ears.[33]

A recent example from Texas illustrates the dilemma. During a two-year period, the Texas Department of Mental Health and Mental Retardation placed over fifteen hundred mentally retarded people from its thirteen state schools (with surprisingly few objections from their parents) into small-community group homes. A statewide anti-institution advocacy organization (ARC/Texas) grudgingly acknowledged the placements but continued its harsh criticism of the agency for not actively seeking closure of state schools, not placing more people into the community, and allowing the state school staffing ratios to improve (although to levels that were still less than ideal).

At the same time, a pro-institution group (Parents Association for the Retarded of Texas—PART) chastised the agency and its commissioner for undermining the "state school system," forcing the deinstitutionalization of people who had previously been well cared for in the state schools, and threatening their lives and well-being by exposing them to a more hazardous community environment. The PART members were not persuaded by the improved staffing in the state schools or by the findings of an independent study that said parents and guardians of mentally retarded people placed in the community from Texas state schools were pleased with the new group homes and considered them preferable to the state schools.[34]

In sum, the issue of institution versus community demands huge amounts of the commissioner's time and energy. The result will always be active conflict, for a single "correct" solution to the problem does not exist.

Tyranny of the Laity

A virtual army of citizens stands ready to advise the commissioner on policies and actions and to criticize the commissioner if the advice is not taken. The citizens may speak for themselves or perhaps imply the existence of a large following with similar views. In most states, they are organized into a number of consumer or advocacy groups which may employ full-time staff members. The advent of such groups in the mental health and mental retardation fields is, on balance, a positive development, for it ensures that public mental health agencies receive feedback and guidance from those who are most directly affected by their services.

Although commissioners recognize the importance of communicating effectively with advocacy and consumer groups, the stridency with which some groups project their demands, the unreasonable nature of some of the requests, and the sheer number of groups make this task of the commissioner particularly challenging. Even if a commissioner manages to establish good relations with the advocacy groups, maintaining their support (or at least avoiding their overt hostility) is still not an easy job.

As we have seen from the example of ARC/Texas and PART in the previous section, the groups can pull the commissioner in opposite directions. The commissioner faces a similar conflict when the expectations of a state chapter of Alliance for the Mentally Ill (AMI), representing primarily the interests of parents of the mentally ill, differ sharply from those of the mentally ill themselves—the "primary consumers," whose self-advocacy is a major new force in the mental health field. A commissioner may also be blamed by advocacy groups for inadequate funding of mental health programs, for the commissioner makes an easier target than the state legislature, which actually has the responsibility for appropriating funds.

Advocacy organizations can improve their effectiveness by increasing the size of their membership and budget. To accomplish this, the groups frequently draw the attention of current and potential members to serious deficiencies in the mental health agency. They then proceed to work with state officials to overcome these failings and improve patient care. However, less honorable techniques are some-times used. An advocacy organization may exaggerate the deficiencies and main-tain that they can be corrected only through its intervention. This creates a sense of crisis, rallying the members to a common cause and bringing nonmembers into the dues-paying fold. If an executive director of an advocacy group, for example, can convince the membership that his or her militant posture is all that stands between the group and some disaster, both the vitality of the group and the tenure of the executive director are likely to be enhanced. From the perspective of the mental health commissioner, however, this tactic does not really help to correct the true deficiencies of the department, and it is devastating to the morale of its employees. However many and vexing the actual problems, there is little pleasure in seeing one's agency constantly depicted as riddled with terrible cracks that urgently need fixing.

A fortunate commissioner may be able to forge an alliance with some of the advocacy groups to press for new legislation or increased appropriations. But if the commissioner is not sufficiently sensitive to the view of the groups or is unskilled in negotiating, or if the groups have selected leaders who are unremit-tingly hostile to the mental health agency, the commissioner will have difficulty in obtaining the support of the groups and may even find them actively opposing the policies of the mental health agency. The difficulties will not be limited to the commissioner's relationship with the advocacy organizations, for their views on the mental health system—and the commissioner—will be conveyed to powerful people upon whom the commissioner must depend for support: the governor, the mental health agency's governing board, and state legislators.

The work of the mental health commissioner is also affected by citizens' groups protesting the opening of a new group home or halfway house for people with mental illness or mental retardation. Although such protests are not an everyday occurrence, most commissioners have encountered at least one instance of or-ganized opposition to a residential program from citizens who fear that a home occupied by mentally disabled persons will cause a decline in the quality of their neighborhood and possibly threaten their safety or that of their children. The neighborhood groups may employ both legal means (relying, for example, on local zoning ordinances) and political means to block the opening of a community residential program or to remove it after it has opened.

This perceived threat to neighborhood quality and safety is a volatile issue that must be handled with care by a commissioner. The commissioner's success in resolving the problem requires that he or she be sensitive not only to the rights and needs of the mentally disabled persons seeking to move into the community home but also to the opinions and fears of their prospective neighbors. A commissioner who dismisses the protests of neighborhood groups as manifestations of ignorance and prejudice does so at considerable risk. Local legislators and municipal officials backing the neighborhood groups will avoid any suggestion in their public statements that their opposition is a form of discrimination against the handicapped. Instead, they will emphasize the commissioner's ill-advised deinstitutionalization policy, the poor planning of the new community residence, the insufficient preparation of the neighborhood, the lack of staff to properly supervise the residents, the residents' need for more care than can be provided in a community home, and the danger that residents will be taken advantage of by other people. Privately, however, supporters of the "not in my neighborhood" movement may work hard to remove the problem by removing the commissioner.

LIMITS ON THE COMMISSIONER'S POWER

The Commissioner as Commander-in-Chief

State mental health commissioners usually have considerably less authority than their statutory responsibilities or their agency's table of organization may suggest. A commissioner's freedom of action is limited, for example, by his or her need to gain support from constituencies external to state government, among them citizens' and advocacy groups, labor unions, and professional organizations. But numerous other constraints exist within state government and even within those elements of the state mental health system ostensibly under the commissioner's control.

During the past twenty-five years, the legislatures of many states have restructured their state agencies in an effort to save money and achieve greater efficiency and uniformity in state government operations. The reorganization takes two general forms: establishment of centralized administrative service agencies, and consolidation of groups of related agencies into larger umbrella agencies. Both developments restrict the commissioner's ability to direct the employees and programs of the mental health agency.

Centralized administrative service agencies (for example, state personnel departments, budget agencies, and centralized computer operations) control resources essential to the day-to-day management of every other state agency. As a result, these centralized agencies become extremely powerful, protecting that power by husbanding the resources they control and dispensing them with great care and selectivity to client agencies. For example, the state personnel agency must approve the salary and position description of every classified state employee. If the commissioner wishes to establish a new position within the agency, he or she is required to submit to the personnel agency a request for approval of the position, which includes a position description and compensation level as well as evidence that funds are available to pay the salary. Depending on the state, the personnel agency may have the authority to modify the position description, reduce the compensation level, or deny the position entirely. The personnel agency also controls employee grievance procedures and may be authorized to make the final decision in cases where an employee challenges a personnel action of the mental health agency.

State comptrollers or budget agencies may have the power to restrain the commissioner from spending funds already appropriated by the legislature or to actually reduce appropriations. Commissioners rarely have the flexibility to move money between line items (for example, between institutional and community budgets) but must seek approval from the budget agency. Finally, a commissioner who wishes to automate an agency function must first convince the chief of the centralized computer service that the mental health agency's needs are at least as important as those of other agencies.

It should be obvious that under these circumstances a mental health commissioner is not free to manage the agency's human and financial resources in accordance with his or her policies and the needs of the mental health system. The commissioner must allocate time to lobby the chiefs of centralized administrative service agencies in competition with the commissioners of every other state agency. A mental health commissioner who is successful at this task will win some favorable decisions from the centralized agencies, but at a high cost in time taken from the commissioner's primary responsibilities. Even under the best of circumstances, the commissioner must endure lengthy delays while administrative service agencies process the commissioner's various requests.

The commissioner of a mental health agency that is a part of an umbrella human-services agency faces a unique set of problems. Secretaries of umbrella agencies are likely to be political appointees who usually cannot and need not understand mental health services or their inherently controversial nature. When the going gets tough, the mental health commissioner may discover that he or she is receiving less than the complete support of the secretary. Also, it is not uncommon to find intense competition between the mental health agency and its peers within the umbrella for resources, power, and the approval of the secretary. Finally, in addition to losing the resources under the control of centralized administrative service agencies, a mental health commissioner may forfeit to the umbrella agency secretary such vital functions as planning and employee training.

The weakest mental health commissioners are those in states like Florida, where a deputy secretary for operations supervises all of the umbrella agency's programs (including mental health) through substate regional or district offices. The mental health commissioner is essentially staff, reduced to writing proposals, giving advice, and commenting on programmatic issues. If there is a bright side to this arrangement, it is that the commissioner is spared many of the conflicting and unrealistic political pressures discussed in this chapter, since it is well known that he or she is little more than a figurehead.

Even if a commissioner is a ''commander-in-chief'' who has formal line authority and is able to develop a reasonable base of external support for a policy, carrying out a program requires the cooperation of the superintendents of state institutions and the directors of community centers. To obtain that cooperation, the commissioner must rely primarily on leadership and persuasion, for these people almost always have an independent power base with which they can oppose the commissioner's policies.

We have already mentioned the statewide political alliances of CMHCs that can effectively lobby state legislators and the governor. One of the most difficult tasks of a commissioner is to convert the various programs managed by the agency into a true mental health system, in which CMHCs play a major role by diverting to community care some patients who would otherwise be admitted to state hospitals and by providing after-care to patients leaving the hospitals. The prerequisite is that the community centers have to yield to the commissioner some of their traditional prerogatives—namely, deciding which programs to operate, which patients to serve, and how to serve them. Since in almost every state CMHCs retain a considerable degree of autonomy, a commissioner must be skilled in managing large-scale change if he or she is to achieve these vital agency goals. Successful commissioners usually engage the CMHCs and their statewide alliances in a participatory process in which CMHC leaders work together with state mental health agency staff in planning for change and designing the specifications of new programs.

Institutional superintendents may technically answer to the commissioner, but they can be almost as independent of the state mental health agency as CMHC directors. The superintendents may occasionally work through informal statewide alliances resembling the councils of CMHCs, but their power comes mainly from their local political connections. As major employers, superintendents of state hospitals and state schools have substantial influence with local government officials and legislators from the area. Although this influence can be used to help the state mental health agency pursue its goals, it can also be used to oppose state mental health policy (or the commissioner). The commissioner must therefore carefully cultivate the support and allegiance of institutional superintendents. Even when a commissioner accomplishes this, there will probably be one or two recalcitrant superintendents who believe their interests are best served by refusing to cooperate with the commissioner. They may even decline to abide by state mental health policies. Depending on the locale and the strength of the political ties of these people, the commissioner may face anything from a nuisance to a serious threat to his or her survival.

On Being Investigated

One of the least pleasant aspects of being commissioner is the almost constant scrutiny of the mental health agency by some type of oversight or investigating committee. The committees are usually created by governors or legislatures in response to a controversy that has reached the media. A committee's purpose ranges from learning more details about a problem in the agency, to eliciting information upon which to base changes in state law, to just satisfying the constituency of an elected official that something is being done about an issue. Even personnel matters can result in investigations. In Texas, for example, a legislative investigating committee was appointed in 1982 because legislators were unhappy about the dismissal of an institutional superintendent.

Commissioners know that it is impossible to run a large system of institutions and community programs without problems. There is always the possibility of physical or sexual abuse of patients by hospital personnel, improper psychiatric treatment of a patient, or misuse of state funds by an employee. Patients sometimes do commit suicide or injure other patients, even when all of the professionally accepted precautions have been taken. State mental health agencies employ a multiplicity of internal controls and other devices to reduce the likelihood of such occurrences. Among them are patient-rights and abuse committees, quality assurance and professional peer-review programs, internal audits of facilities, screening of new employees for criminal records, uniform training and orientation of all employees, written rules and regulations, toll-free hotlines for patient complaints, and so forth. Inevitably, however, in every state mental health system an incident occurs that leads to the appointment of an investigating committee. Although these committees and the public hearings through which they conduct their business are integral to a system of open government, they nevertheless have a vast potential for creating adverse publicity, damaging the credibility of the system, and possibly shortening the tenure of the commissioner in charge.

Even in the absence of controversy, mental health agencies are studied and reviewed by a variety of groups. Standing committees of the state house and senate typically oversee operations of the mental health agency. Sunset committees, a special challenge for the commissioner, are ostensibly concerned with determining whether a mental health agency should continue or be abolished, but they are usually more interested in restructuring the agency. At their invitation, professional organizations, consumer and advisory groups, and members of the general public testify about their views of how the state law that established the mental health agency should be changed. A commissioner who lives through the time-consuming and stressful ordeal of a sunset review may wind up with a very different agency and possibly a different kind of job.

Living under Lawsuits

Lawsuits are a fact of life for a state mental health commissioner. For example, there are about fifty to sixty lawsuits pending at all times against the Texas Department of Mental Health and Mental Retardation, many naming its commissioner as the lead defendant. Sometimes plaintiffs seek not only a form of equitable relief but also personal damages against the commissioner and other state officials. Some of the most serious difficulties faced by a commissioner arise when class-action lawsuits in the federal courts are settled by means of a legal document, usually called a consent decree, which requires monitoring or supervision of the state mental health agency by a "special master," "monitor," or "expert" appointed by a federal judge.

Class-action suits are typically initiated and perpetuated by advocacy lawyers who recruit patients to serve as representatives of a class of allegedly deprived or abused people. Patients play a relatively minor role in such litigation, however; the lawsuits are primarily vehicles for advocacy lawyers to pursue causes in which they strongly believe. The lawyers' ideological objectives have probably been endorsed by a federal court, thus creating a precedent upon which plaintiffs base their demands.

The ideological goals differ from suit to suit. In one action, advocacy lawyers may argue that people confined in mental hospitals have a right to treatment. This translates into an effort by advocacy lawyers to obtain court orders forcing the state agency to meet specified staffing ratios, establish new programs, and increase funding of the affected facilities. On the other hand, another lawsuit may seek the right of even the most disturbed psychotic patients to *refuse* treatment prescribed by state mental hospital psychiatrists. In a "least restrictive environment" lawsuit, the focus is less on institutional programs or staffing than on having every mentally disabled person treated in the "community," in the belief that all institutions—even adequately staffed ones—are bad places.

When these lawsuits are settled in lieu of a trial, the consent decree invariably includes a special master or monitor appointed by the judge to look over the shoulders of state officials to ensure that they meet the requirements of the decree. As a consequence, the commissioner is subjected not only to the administrative and political pressures described previously but also to demands from a person who, although lacking accountability to state government, is empowered by a federal district judge to exercise considerable authority over state government operations.[36]

Those unfamiliar with this type of negotiation over implementations of court decisions may view the federal district court as a dispenser of justice, a regulative agent that analyzes objectively both sides of an issue and makes a reasoned decision to accept or reject an implementation. Federal judges are obligated to base their decisions on their interpretation of the consent decree, the United States Constitution, federal law, or previous court decisions. They and their monitors, however, are free to play the same political game as other government officials, but without the attendant risks that provide moderation and balance—namely, the risk of not being reelected or reappointed to a position or of being fired.

A commissioner who advocates a vigorous legal defense of the state's interests in a class-action lawsuit may be accused of defending the indefensible or of undermining the state's best hope for additional mental health dollars. Why should the state contest the lawsuit when, after all, a victory by plaintiffs would result in more money being appropriated to state mental health programs—something everyone would deem desirable? On the other hand, state lawmakers would look askance at possible collusion between a state mental health commissioner and outside legal advocates aimed at the state's "taking a fall." If legislators became convinced that the commissioner was attempting to use a lawsuit to force the legislature to appropriate additional funds to the mental health agency, the commissioner would very likely experience considerable political difficulty.

If a state fails to put up a good legal defense and instead yields to all of the demands of monitors and advocacy lawyers, the effect on the agency is invasive. The federal judge and the monitors do not limit their role to making findings and ordering changes in the mental health system or its expenditures; they are in the business of managing the agency—determining how its programs will be run and how state tax dollars will be spent.[36] Mental health commissioners and their staff members are no longer free to design and operate programs in accordance with their training and professional judgment. The fate of the patients in their care will depend less on their view of proper treatment than on the opinion of outside monitors and consultants who are free to test their ideas on a captive state mental health system and yet bear no responsibility for the consequences.

This has been the experience of the Texas Department of Mental Health and Mental Retardation in contending with two class-action lawsuits: *RAJ v. Miller,* dealing with mental health services, and *Lelsz v. Kavanagh,* dealing with mental retardation services.[37] Although both lawsuits were filed in 1974, discovery was prolonged until 1981 (*RAJ*) and 1983 (*Lelsz*) when negotiated agreements that we shall refer to as consent decrees were approved by the courts. These decrees, ordinarily considered devices for settling lawsuits, have instead allowed the litigation to grow to the point that it dominates virtually all policy- and decision-making in the state mental health agency. These are but two examples of many such cases.

In *RAJ* a three-person panel of monitors reported to the judge that there was too much violence in the Texas state hospitals, that aggressive acts by severely mentally ill patients could be predicted and prevented by behavior management, that there were too few aides on the hospital wards, and that the hospitals were relying too much on medication and too little on social therapies. The panel recommended that the judge find the mental health agency in noncompliance with the consent decree, even though the panel's claims bore little relationship to the language in the decree that described what the mental health agency's responsibilities should be. The allegation of excessive violence, for example, was linked to a phrase in the decree requiring the hospitals to provide a "clean and safe environment," which was specifically intended by the parties to refer to the physical surroundings.

The injury reports prepared for a number of years by the state mental health agency were the only possible source for a claim of increased violence in the hospitals. These reports demonstrated a progressive decline in the rate of serious injuries. To overcome this problem, the panel emphasized in its report a tragic incident that had occurred several months earlier: A patient in one of the state hospitals who had always been docile gouged out the eyes of another patient, an aggressive person who was being held in restraints. The panel's report did not consider the cause of this incident or who, if anyone, might be at fault; rather, it used the incident as emotional leverage for its position, implying that it was typical of all of the agency's state hospitals.

The overwhelming majority of injuries reflected in the agency's statistics were not the result of aggressive acts, yet the panel chose the word "violence." The inflammatory tone of that term played well in the press when the panel distributed its report to the media and freely gave interviews in which its position was elaborated. There was little that the mental health commissioner could say in response that would not be construed as supporting violence or inadequate staffing.

At the federal court hearing set by the judge to consider these matters, it turned out that there was little evidence to support the panel's allegations; they represented, for the most part, the opinions of panel members. State officials and expert witnesses argued that the agency's injury reports did not demonstrate excessive violence, that the overwhelming majority of the injuries were extremely minor (scratches and bruises), that the agency had instituted an innovative training program throughout its state hospitals designed to reduce injuries, that it had in fact significantly lowered the rate of serious injuries over a three-year period, and that it was not fair to accuse the agency of an excessive injury rate in the absence of any baseline of national, state, or individual hospital injury rates. The state agency's experts pointed out that the panel's views on behavior management, social therapies, and medication were professionally naive. Moreover, the fact that all eight state mental hospitals were fully accredited by the Joint Commission on the Accreditation of Hospitals should have served as evidence that the hospitals' treatment programs were of acceptable quality. Finally, while acknowledging that the state hospitals could benefit from additional personnel, the state argued against a rigid system of court-ordered staffing ratios that would eliminate the flexibility to staff wards according to changing patient populations and clinical needs.

The state mental health agency lost on every count. The agency was found "guilty" of excessive violence, inadequate treatment programs, and an insufficient number of aides working on the hospital wards. Among the several remedies ordered by the court was imposition of a rigid staffing formula (psychiatric aides to patient ratios of 1:5, 1:5, and 1:10 on the three shifts), although no evidence has been presented at the court hearing to support this or any other ratio. As a result of the court order, nursing personnel and supervisors lost their ability to modify employee levels based on changing needs in the department's eight state hospitals. Because the court-ordered ratios for these psychiatric aides are among the richest in the country, the agency's limited funds have been consumed in meeting the mandate, leaving insufficient dollars to hire adequate numbers of professional personnel such as psychiatrists, registered nurses, and psychologists.

The second example of what a consent decree can trigger involves the *Lelsz* lawsuit, in which the Texas mental health agency faced three opponents with strong anti-institution positions: the plaintiff's lawyer, ARC of Texas (an intervening party), and Advocacy Incorporated (also an intervenor). These parties filed a motion asking the judge to order the mental health agency to place a minimum number of mentally retarded people from state schools into community programs within a specified period of time. The court's monitor supported the motion for mandatory deinstitutionalization but recommended that the department place fewer people than originally suggested in the motion.

At the court hearing, the department noted that it had assigned many people to community programs, each placement based on a determination by agency professionals that the person would benefit from the experience. Department officials and expert witnesses argued that imposition of a quota would force professionals to place indiscriminately rather than in accordance with the needs of individual mentally retarded persons.

As in the *RAJ* decision, the federal judge rejected all of the state agency's arguments, accused it of dragging its feet in community placements, and ordered that 279 people from just three state schools be placed into the community within a one-year period. The Texas mental health agency appealed this ruling to the Fifth Circuit Court of Appeals, which agreed with the agency that the district judge had exceeded his authority. The appeals court struck down the offending court order, but by the time the department had won its victory, the 279 people had been placed and the agency had already been subjected to the unreasonable pressures and distortion of its service system that resulted from the court-ordered quota.

The normally difficult job of dealing with parent organizations over the institution versus community issue was greatly complicted by this court order. Even though the commissioner's options were limited by a federal court order, this did not reduce the commissioner's responsibility for actions taken by the agency or the ease with which the commissioner could be accused of acting contrary to the interests of the various groups.

Perhaps the most powerful effect of class-action lawsuits is psychological. The employees of the mental health agency are depicted in the legal pleadings of their opponents as the "bad guys," intent on providing poor care and depriving defenseless mental patients of their rights. The advocacy lawyers and monitors perceive themselves, on the other hand, as champions of the mentally ill and mentally retarded, standing up to an insensitive bureaucracy. This propaganda is not limited to briefs filed in the federal courts; monitors and plaintiffs' lawyers openly cater to the press. The intemperate statements of these critics are news in themselves and frequently capture the front page or the first page of the state section of metropolitan newspapers. Any retort that a commissioner might make under these circumstances would appear defensive or self-serving. This is a case where there is simply no correct response.

As one would expect, employee morale is undermined by litigation-inspired publicity about allegedly horrible conditions in state institutions. Most of the staff working in these facilities are unsung heroes who care for very disturbed and disabled people under difficult conditions, earn little money, and yet are subjected to media "exposés" that bear little relationship to their daily experience. Although they understand that exaggeration and distortion by the state's adversaries are a part of the litigation game, they find it hard to accept that the general public is told that they provide poor treatment, are uncaring, or abuse and neglect their patients.

The lawsuits support a litigation industry consisting of plaintiffs' attorneys, expert witnesses, court monitors, and the staff and consultants hired by the monitors. These people have little incentive to find the mental health agency in compliance with consent decrees when their salaries and fees are dependent on continually discovering more problems and deficiencies that require further monitoring or new legal motions. For example, the 1983 consent decree in *Lelsz* specified that the court monitor would receive $40,000 per year and work only on an "as needed, part-time basis." Over the course of the three-and-a-half years since the monitor was hired by the court, her budget has increased to $465,000 per year. Instead of one part-time monitor, the Texas mental health agency must now deal with a substantial bureaucracy dedicated to identifying "problems" that can be used to justify further expansion of the power of the monitor as well as the size of her staff. Unfortunately, it is the taxpayers of the state of Texas who must foot the bill for this growth industry.

The Media

Most mental health commissioners work hard to establish cordial relationships with representatives of the media. They attempt to be open with the press and accessible to reporters who have questions or wish to conduct interviews. Some mental health commissioners have people on their staff whose main job is to communicate with the media on behalf of the agency. These efforts usually lead to some good press—for example, coverage of innovative program or in-depth articles about such issues as the homeless mentally ill—but they cannot protect the mental health agency from adverse publicity. The issues and controversies that make the commissioner's job impossible inevitably lead to bad publicity that can have a deleterious effect on a commissioner's reputation and tenure.

In October 1984 the Texas Department of Mental Health and Mental Retardation published some press clippings about mental health agencies across the country that were collected over a period of approximately one year.[38] Out of numerous inflammatory headlines, here are a few representative selections:

"Is CPI [Cleveland Psychiatric Institute] a Dangerous Place to Be?"

"Mental Patients Tied to 12 Killings: Warnings Ignored"

"Chronic Mental Cases Locked Out"

"Housing for Ex-Mental Patients Remains Big Problem"

"Suit Accuses State of Violating Rights of Retarded People"

"2 Quit Drugs Controlling Violence: Patients Can't Always Be Forced to Take Medication"

"Audit Criticizes Management of State Program: Care of Emotionally Disturbed Children Costly"

"Funding Cut Could Force Closing of Mental Health Center"

This small sample of typical headlines gives an idea of the kind of publicity commissioners confront. Even if the reporting is conscientious and not sensational, it can rebound adversely on agency personnel and on the perception of the agency held by the governor and legislators.

Evaluating the Commissioner's Performance

How do we know if the commissioner has done a good job? In the private sector and even in some public agencies, it is relatively easy to measure the performance of the chief executive officer. For example, increases in revenues or profits or the introduction of successful new products are objective indicators that permit stockholders or the board of directors of a corporation to assess the achievements of its leader. On the other hand, in state mental health agencies there are few objective measures to evaluate the performance of the commissioner. In fact, there is not even agreement as to what constitutes success. A major new program is seen as a significant advance by some of the commissioner's constituents and as a dangerous or regressive step by others. Achievement of accreditation by all state hospitals, one of the few objective standards available, is useless in a state like Texas where this goal has already been reached.

Because of the lack of objective criteria to gauge a commissioner's performance, the commissioner tends to be judged not on accomplishments but on how he or she is viewed by other people. In the private sector an executive may not be especially well liked by company directors, peers, or employees, but if the executive is making a lot of money for the corporation, it is inclined to forgive the executive's unpopularity. In the case of the mental health agency, the commissioner's survival is almost entirely dependent on how the commissioner is regarded by key politicians and leaders of various constituency organizations.

There are numerous examples of commissioners who have significantly improved services to the mentally disabled (in our opinion) and yet were forced to leave for purely political reasons unrelated to job performance. Virtually any move in any direction by a commissioner elicits some degree of dissatisfaction from at least one constituency—for example, advocacy groups, parent organizations, labor unions, federal courts, legislators, the governor, and so forth. Therefore, a commissioner must be exceptionally skilled in negotiating, compromising, placating, and horse-trading just to stay in the job long enough to make a difference.

COPING STRATEGIES

Every commissioner who lasts more than a few months in the position develops strategies to cope with the pressures and impossibilities described in this chapter. Some of the strategies are of necessity tailored to the unique circumstances of a particular state at a particular time; others are more general, applicable to the situations faced by most state mental health commissioners. Here are a few of the latter.

A Sense of Humor

A good sense of humor is one of the most important and yet least appreciated attributes of a successful commissioner. If a commissioner cannot put into perspective the alternately ridiculous, ironic, and bizarre world of the state mental health agency—if he or she takes the job too seriously—that commissioner may not only lose the job but wind up among the clientele of the agency.

Constituency Building

The reader can infer from much of this chapter that a considerable amount of the commissioner's time must be spent dealing with internal and external constituencies. Skill in constituency building enhances both the commissioner's tenure and ability to carry out agency policies. A commissioner cannot avoid occasionally making some group or powerful person irate and upset because the commissioner has either taken or not taken a certain action. The commissioner's political and public relations skills are therefore taxed to the utmost in trying to ensure that as few people as possible (or the least credible people) are angry at the commissioner at any one time.

Participative Management

Dealing successfully with impossibility requires that the commissioner enlist the support of the forces that make the task impossible. A commissioner must be proficient in participative management; that is, involving agency employees, state facilities, CMHCs, and consumer and advocacy groups to achieve change and progress. In the fall of 1984, for example, the Texas mental health commissioner used a large-scale inclusive management process to gain support for a major new mental retardation policy. Since the policy entailed an increase in the number of mentally retarded people placed from state schools into the community, restrictions on admissions to the state schools, and fiscal transfers from the schools to community programs, it was expected to generate considerable controversy among advocacy organizations and agency employees. Numerous meetings distinguished by much give-and-take were held with representatives of each affected group. Their suggestions were solicited, leading to over a dozen redrafts of the policy. The final version, in spite of many compromises, retained the essential features of the original. The policy was approved in December 1984 with a minimum of conflict.

Progress out of Adversity

An effective commissioner must be a creative opportunist. Some of the most innovative mental health programs have arisen as a response to a crisis. In Texas, for example, a cut in the budget of the mental health agency became a net increase in agency dollars when the commissioner was able to trade the moderate reduction in appropriations for greater budgetary flexibility. In another action, an adverse court order made it possible to put into place a revolutionary fiscal incentive system in which Texas's community mental health–mental retardation centers are allotted extra money for reducing use of state hospitals.[39]

Leadership

There is no substitute for leadership skills.[40] One of the most vital coping strategies for a commissioner is letting people in the agency and other interested parties know what the organization stands for and where it is going. Although, as previously noted, there is a price to pay for going in *any* direction, a commissioner who cannot motivate people and give them a vision, a sense of direction, and a feeling of belonging to a greater enterprise may survive for a while but will probably accomplish very little.

WHY STAY ON?

Why persevere in a position in which it is impossible to satisfy the expectations of all the various constituencies and the general public? Why subject oneself to attacks by the press, advocates, politicians, and governing boards? Why tolerate contradictory demands to provide high-quality services with inadequate budgets? Obviously, there are types of people who can withstand these unreasonable pressures, absorb the criticism, and somehow acquire the necessary strength to continue. Some clinicians might consider a mental health commissioner a masochist who delights in being attacked. It is more likely, however, that commissioners learn to tolerate criticism as a necessary price to pay for the rewards of the job. Accepting such opposition becomes a modus operandi for a commissioner, a condition of life in which the censure, while not necessarily rolling off his or her back, is at least blunted and eventually adjusted to.

What rewards can possibly compensate for the gut-wrenching criticism and impossibility of the commissioner's job? Clearly the status and power of the position (as in the case of a chief executive officer of any organization) are a part of the answer. But there is also a sense of mission, a drive to improve a system of care and thus benefit the lives of thousands of people. Perhaps, as the sociobiologists would contend, there is no such thing as pure altruism. Yet mental health commissioners frequently behave as though they are motivated by an altruistic desire to help disabled people and to do so at high personal risk.

Although a cynical world may view with suspicion such words as dedication, commitment, and sacrifice, many mental health commissioners give generously of themselves to achieve goals that they believe in. Instead of being narrow-minded bureaucrats, they are often creative, far-sighted people with a vision of an improved mental health service system and the fortitude to pursue it, sometimes with both evangelical zeal and practical imagination. The willingness of the mental health commissioner to continue in an impossible job may be partly a function of what psychologists call "intermittent reinforcement" which means simply that the commissioner occasionally "wins" one. Such reinforcement schedules make behavior quite persistent and difficult to "extinguish." A small victory encourages the commissioner and staff to carry on and hope for another. Ultimately, political forces conspire to make the commissioner's position untenable and to force his or her departure, a process attested to by the short terms of these jobs.

LIFE AFTER COMMISSIONER

There is life after serving as a commissioner. Former commissioners frequently go on to more financially rewarding and less stressful positions, usually in the private healthcare or academic sectors, where their experience as human-service professionals and administrators is put to good use. Interestingly, many erstwhile commissioners mourn for their previous post and, despite the grueling battles, low pay, and high stress, are willing to reenter the public mental health arena.[41] The reason is that many feel they were not able to accomplish their goal of improving services to the mentally disabled. Some miss the challenge; others miss being in the public eye. Since few commissioners actually return to their old position, their expertise and accumulated experience are usually lost to the public mental health systems of this nation at a time when experienced leadership is increasingly demanded and certainly needed.

NOTES

1. J. K. Myers et al., "Six-month Prevalence of Psychiatric Disorders in Three Communities," *Archives of General Psychiatry* 41, 10 (1984): 959–70.

2. G. Zilboorg and G. W. Henry, *A History of Medical Psychology* (New York: W. W. Norton and Company, 1941).

3. W. Reise, *The Legacy of Philippe Pinel* (New York: Springer Publishing Co., 1969.

4. Zilboorg and Henry, *History of Medical Psychology*.

5. R. C. Scheerenberger, *A History of Mental Retardation* (Baltimore: Paul H. Brookes Publishing Co., 1983), pp. 101–4.

6. A. Deutsch, *The Shame of the States* (New York: Harcourt Brace Jovanovich, 1948).

7. P. Ahr and W. R. Holcomb, "State Mental Health Directors' Priorities for Mental Health Care," *Hospital and Community Psychiatry* 35 (1985): 39–45; G. E. Miller, "Future of the Chronically Mentally Ill,"in *The Chronically Mentally Ill: Research and Services,* ed. M. Mirabi (Jamaica, N.Y.: SP Medical and Scientific Books, 1984), pp. 307–27.

8. *Mental Health Statistical Note No. 165* (Rockville, Md.: National Institute of Mental Health, August 1983).

9. *Action for Mental Health: Report of the Joint Commission on Mental Illness and Health* (New York: Basic Books, 1961).

10. *Community Mental Health Centers Construction Act* (Public Law 88-164, 31 October 1963), United States Statutes at Large 94, pp. 290-99.

11. H. R. Lamb and V. Goertzel, "Discharged Mental Patients—Are They Really in the Community?" *Archives of General Psychiatry* 24 (1971): 24-34; *The Chronic Mental Patient: Problems, Solutions and Recommendations for Public Policy* (Washington, D.C.: American Psychiatric Association, 1978); *The Chronic Mental Health Patient in the Community* (New York: Group for the Advancement of Psychiatry, 1978): H. R. Lamb, "Roots of Neglect of the Long-term Mentally Ill," *Psychiatry* 42 (1979): 201-7; D. G. Langsley, "The Community Mental Health Center: Does It Treat the Patients?" *Hospital and Community Psychiatry* 31, 12 (1980): 815-19; G. E. Miller, "Barriers to Serving the Chronically Mentally Ill," *Psychiatric Quarterly* 53 (1981): 118-31.

12. *Returning the Mentally Disabled to the Community: Government Needs to Do More,* Report to the Congress by the Comptroller General of the United States, January 7, 1987 (Washington, D.C.: Government Printing Office, 1987); *Task Panel Reports Submitted to the President's Commission on Mental Health,* vol. 2, app. (Washington, D.C.: Government Printing Office, 1978), pp. 356-72.

13. L. Bachrach, "The Homeless Mentally Ill and Mental Health Services: An Analytical Review of the Literature," *Task Force Report of the American Psychiatric Association,* ed. H. R. Lamb (Washington, D.C.: American Psychiatric Association, 1984).

14. *Mental Health Systems Act* (Public Law 96-398, 7 October 1980), United States Statutes at Large 94, pp. 1564-1614, replaced by the *Omnibus Reconciliation Act of 1980* (Public Law 96-499, 25 December 1980), United States Statutes at Large 94, pp. 2599-2695.

15. Ahr and Holcomb, "State Mental Health Directors' Priorities for Mental Health Care," pp. 39-45; Miller, "Future of the Chronically Mentally Ill," pp. 307-27.

16. National Association of State Mental Health Program Directors (NASMHPD): Fourteen mental health programs are in "independent" agencies. NASMHPD State Report, March 4, 1982.

17. The numbers of agencies with additional responsibilities are derived from personal communication with H. Schnibbe, executive director of NASMHPD, March 1988; and *Location of Substance Abuse Administration/Treatment in Other States,* published by the Office of Strategic Planning, Texas Department of Mental Health and Mental Retardation, Austin, Tex., January 1987.

18. *Survey of State MH Authority/Academic Degree,* published by the Office of Strategic Planning, Texas Department of Mental Health and Mental Retardation, Austin, Tex., February 23, 1987.

19. *Wyatt v. Stickney,* 344 F.Supp. 373 (N.D. Alabama 1972).

20. M. J. Mills, "The Mental Health Commissionership: Major Changes over the Decade," *Hospital and Community Psychiatry* 36 (1985): 363-67.

21. G. E. Miller, "Mental Health and Politics," *State Government News* (August 1986): 14-15.

22. From NASMHPD studies done in July 1987 in Washington, D.C.

23. Myers et al., "Six-month Prevalence of Psychiatric Disorders in Three Communities," pp. 959-70.

24. H. R. Lamb, "Deinstitutionalization and the Homeless Mentally Ill," *Task Force Report of the American Psychiatric Association,* ed. H. R. Lamb (Washington, D.C.: American Psychiatric Press, 1984).

25. P. H. Rossi et al., "The Urban Homeless: Estimating Composition and Size," *Science* 235 (1987): 1336-41.

26. G. E. Dix, "Major Current Issues concerning Civil Commitment Criteria," *Law and Contemporary Problems* 45, 3 (1982): 137–59.

27. M. Krakowski, J. Volavka, and D. Brizer, "Psychopathology and Violence: A Review of the Literature," *Comprehensive Psychiatry* 27, 2 (1986): 131–48.

28. Ibid.

29. Dix, "Major Current Issues concerning Civil Commitment Criteria," pp. 137–59.

30. R. A. Dowart, "Deinstitutionalization: Who Is Left Behind?" *Hospital and Community Psychiatry* 31 (1980): 336–38; H. R. Lamb, "What Did We Really Expect from Deinstitutionalization?" *Hospital and Community Psychiatry* 32 (1981): 105–9; D. M. Engelhardt, B. Rosen, and J. Feldman, "A 15-Year Followup of 646 Schizophrenic Outpatients," *Schizophrenia Bulletin* 8 (1982): 293–503; J. E. Gudeman and M. R. Shore, "Beyond Deinstitutionalization," *New England Journal of Medicine* 131 (1984): 832–36.

31. G. E. Miller, "Institutionalization vs. Deinstitutionalization," *Impact,* Publication of the Texas Department of Mental Health and Mental Retardation, Austin, Tex., July/August 1986, pp. 8–11.

32. G. E. Miller, "The Public Sector: The State Mental Health Agency," *The New Economics and Psychiatric Care,* ed. S. S. Sharfstein and A. Beigel (Washington, D.C.: American Psychiatric Press, 1985).

33. S. Landesman-Dwyer, "Living in the Community," *American Journal of Mental Deficiency* 86 (1981): 223–34.

34. L. Willerman and C. M. Ford, *Consumer Satisfaction with Community Placement of Mentally Retarded Clients in the State of Texas: A Preliminary Report* (Austin: University of Texas at Austin, 1987).

35. G. E. Miller, *Living under Lawsuits,* Monograph published by the Texas Department of Mental Health and Mental Retardation, Austin, Tex., 1987.

36. Ibid.

37. *RAJ v. Miller,* Civil Action 3-74-0394-H, U.S. District Court for Northern Texas, Dallas Division; *Lelsz v. Kavanagh,* Civil Action 3-85-2462-H, U.S. District Court for Northern Texas, Dallas Division.

38. State mental health press clippings from across the nation. MHMR Media Update, Public Information Office, Texas Department of Mental Health and Mental Retardation, Austin, Tex., October 1984.

39. G. E. Miller and W. V. Rago, "Fiscal Incentives to the Development of Services in the Community" (from panel on "Economic Grand Rounds"), *Hospital and Community Psychiatry* 39 (1988): 595–97.

40. J. M. Burns, *Leadership* (New York: Harper and Row, 1978).

41. M. Greenblatt, K. D. Gaver, and E. Sherwood, "After Commissioner, What?" *American Journal of Psychiatry* 142 (1985): 752–54.

7

Managing the Social Safety Net: The Job of Social Welfare Executive

Laurence E. Lynn, Jr.

On October 13, 1988, President Ronald Reagan signed into law the Family Security Act (Public Law 100-485).[1] In the debate leading to enactment, supporters claimed that the act would initiate "a major change in our whole approach to the problem of welfare dependency."[2] The "old approach," the relief of poverty through public assistance payments, was to be abandoned as ineffective and too expensive. The new emphasis would be on "income from work rather than welfare" incorporated in a "new social contract" between society and those in need of public assistance.

The expectation of advocates for this new approach was that those in poverty would be given every assistance in preparing themselves for and obtaining jobs. Once this aid was accepted, however, recipients would be expected to work or face penalties. No public payment, moreover, was to be authorized "for failure or make-work activities"; legislators expected "tangible savings to the Federal Government" accomplished through program administration that is "hard-nosed about results."

Will these ambitious expectations be met? Programs authorized by the act are to be administered by the states in accordance with federal guidelines. Primary responsibility for implementing this new social contract—for demonstrating hard-nosed commitment to results—will be borne, therefore, by those executives in each state who are appointed by their governors to manage social welfare bureaucracies.[3] In addition to directing public welfare programs, these "social welfare executives" (as I shall refer to them in this chapter) are usually charged with carrying out social policy in other areas such as child welfare, developmental disabilities, services for older Americans, vocational rehabilitation, mental health and retardation, licensing and regulation of nonmedical care facilities, and maternal and child health.[4] Thus on these particular executives devolves a general responsibility for improving the well-being and functioning of vulnerable, needy, and dependent individuals and households, including welfare recipients and their families.

I shall argue that these jobs are extraordinarily difficult and that the primary reason is the inherent intractability of the political and administrative problems associated with carrying out mandates to improve human well-being and functioning. The sources of intractability are twofold: ambiguity in the nature of the results both sought and achieved, and indeterminacy in the institutions and processes by which the goals of public social welfare policy are formulated and implemented. The result of ambiguity and indeterminacy is that social welfare executives must contend with one managerial impasse after another, i.e., with problems that may have no solution widely regarded by watchful constituencies as satisfactory.

The few executives who are viewed as having accomplished significant results, I shall argue, are likely to be persons who exhibit an "entrepreneurial" rather than an "administrative" style of leadership, who are "innovators" or "developers" rather than "maintainers."[5] That is, they are apt to be naturally active and imaginative in seeking ways to create broad understanding of and political equity in their agency's mandates, thus establishing strong external and internal cultures of trust and support for program objectives and methods.[6] They are less apt to be nonpolitical administrators preoccupied with the more narrow managerial and tactical aspects of service delivery in their various programs.

This chapter is organized into four sections. The first provides a descriptive overview of the job of the social welfare executive. The second analyzes the difficulty of these jobs by viewing them as problems of collective choice in terms of securing both external support for agency efforts and cooperation from agency employees, contractors, and clients. The third describes strategies used by five actual social welfare executives to make headway against their problems. The final section appraises possible executive strategies in the light of both the general issues of collective choice and the lessons from actual cases, which take the temperament and skill of individual executives into account.

MANAGING SOCIAL WELFARE

State social welfare executives are responsible for implementing the provisions of federal and state laws that govern the social programs they administer. These programs include Aid to Families with Dependent Children; Medicaid; food stamps; general assistance, such as state supplements to the Supplemental Security Income program, emergency assistance, and low-income energy assistance; the Work Incentives (WIN) program; child welfare services, foster care, adoption assistance, Head Start, and child-support enforcement; grants for social services for such activities as day-care, delinquency prevention, and hospice care; vocational rehabilitation; mental retardation; maternal and child health; alcohol, drug abuse, and mental health programs; programs for refugees; and licensing and regulatory activities for a variety of facilities. In most states, social welfare departments are among the largest (and often *the* largest) in terms of size of budget and number of employees.

Social welfare executives are expected to see to it, for example, that the core tasks of social program administration are performed competently and in accordance with law for each of their programs. These tasks include determining eligiblity for benefits or services; establishing the appropriate level or form of the benefit; designing and delivering services; regulating the quality of service; evaluating results against goals or expectations; and, finally and perhaps most important, maintaining a balance between demands from clients and their advocates for service and the government's capacity to satisfy them.

However, in order for the core tasks to be competently executed—that is, in order for an adequate benefit check to be issued or an appropriate client served in a proper way at a specific location—a number of questions must be answered. What are the social goals or objectives (i.e., what are the specific changes in behavior or circumstances) toward which government efforts are to be directed and against which public managers are to be held accountable? Who is to receive the benefits or services—whose behavior is to be changed or condition improved? What kinds of benefits or services are to be offered in order to achieve the desired changes? How, where, and by whom are services or benefits to be delivered? How and by whom are benefits or services to be paid for?[7] Though federal statutes and guidelines may provide some of the necessary answers, many issues are typically left for the states to resolve.[8] Social welfare executives are expected to actively participate in their resolution, especially for programs, such as those affected by the Family Security Act, which are new or for which statutory or judicial mandates have changed.

It is in fulfilling this essentially policymaking role that the impossibilities confronting these executives begin to emerge in clearer focus. The requirements of federal laws and guidelines apart, social welfare executives are not free to do whatever they deem appropriate on behalf of their mandates. They are, in the first instance, agents of the elected executive who appointed them and must take this executive's views into account. But they must also be responsive to the legislators who authorize and commit funds for their programs; to federal officials who monitor their compliance with federal laws and regulations; to subordinate managers, supervisors, and field workers whose efforts produce the actual services; to representatives of particular interest groups, whose expertise, support or opposition may be important to their achieving their goals; and to newspaper and television reporters, who are conduits to a wider public and help shape their message.

Yet social welfare executives are not powerless. Though elected officials may be more powerful than appointed officials in higher-level decisions that establish broad purposes or funding levels, the influence of social welfare executives may be considerable in middle- and lower-level agendas involving the choice of programmatic approaches and the details of program design and execution.[9] Despite statutory, political, and organizational constraints and pressures, these executives are in a position to know more about and to have greater influence over their agencies than virtually any outside actor. Moreover, because none of their constituencies has the time or inclination or monitor everything they do, these executives have considerable potential latitude to choose what they will attend to and how they will carry out specific tasks.[10]

Almost any of the issues they face could absorb most of the social welfare executive's time and attention. But in a world of limited human capacity, managerial involvement has an opportunity cost. The problem for the social welfare executive is deciding how to allocate scarce time and attention among the competing demands associated with creating support for and producing social welfare services. A concentration on foster care and adoptions or on the efficient allocation of Medicaid resources, for example, may be at the expense of assuring appropriate conditions in nursing homes or designing work incentives for welfare recipients. Similarly, time spent generating support for promising new ideas may be at the expense of making certain that performance of agency routines is competent and efficient.

Because it is at the middle and lower levels of power that social policies acquire meaning for the public and attract the loyalty and support of agency constituencies, the executives who are influential at these levels are at the same time vulnerable to the kinds of focused conflicts and divergent concerns that continually arise in resolving programmatic issues.[11] Executives become lightning rods for discontent emerging from every direction. Thus what strategy they choose to guide their actions in inherently controversial matters is probably vital to their effectiveness.

MAKING PEOPLE BEHAVE

The kinds of mandates for which social welfare executives assume responsibility reflect the collective exercise of choice by citizens who pay for or benefit from social welfare policies, by their elected representatives, and by other actors in the policymaking process, such as interest group leaders, judges, and staff members in the executive branch and the legislature. Inherent in the institutions and processes of collective choice are a number of difficulties.[12]

• The taxpayers who provide the budgetary resources for agency services and the recipients of these services are not usually the same people. Thus, social programs generally involve redistribution, almost always a politically controversial activity.

• The recipients of social welfare services are often people—drug abusers, child molesters, unemployed welfare recipients, teenage mothers, destitute residents of urban ghettos, minority-group members—who are either unpopular with or of little concern to many voters and taxpayers, whose sympathy, patience, and loyalty to the social service enterprise cannot, therefore, be taken for granted.

• Equally often, program administrators, advocates for clients, direct service providers, and others whose efforts are necessary to the delivery of services disagree among themselves over the most appropriate help, treatment, or cure for those judged to be needy. Because they are accountable to different constituencies—supervisors, boards of directors, professional peers—these actors are often under no obligation to cooperate with one another or to subordinate their self-interest in favor of a more inclusive view.

- "Service" is typically the product of the interaction between service provider and client. Thus, the actual result when the "service" is "delivered"—e.g., the "treatment" received by a poorly motivated welfare recipient from an effective caseworker—is often difficult to observe. Moreover, since the goals and incentives of the two parties, as well as those of taxpayers, administrators, and advocates, often differ—clients seeking the assistance they "want," providers offering the services clients "need," others desiring to reduce the welfare rolls—the parties involved, as well as such outside observers as program evaluators, may interpret whatever transpires in quite different and conflicting ways.

Hence the "production function" for services involves many self-interested, independent-minded, and autonomous actors, from quality-control administrators in federal agencies, to service workers operating on contract out of neighborhood storefronts, to actual and potential beneficiaries. Because their efforts can be loosely coordinated at best, the ability of the social welfare executive to be "hard-nosed about results"—that is, to obtain cooperative effort toward agreed-upon results from these self-interested actors, with their diverse values, goals, and incentives and in the face of irreducible ambiguity—is tenuous. If bureaucratic measures are to achieve comprehensible results in an efficient manner, it is necessary to have coordination among service workers and clients, among bureaucrats at different levels of responsibility, among officials at different levels of government, and among taxpayers and their legislative representatives. Yet our "system" of collective choice frustrates achievement of that kind of cooperation.

It will be useful to elaborate on the troublesome dynamics underlying these problems.

The Ambiguity of Collective Demand

Governmental programs come into existence as a result of collective demand; i.e., a group of citizens and their representatives determine to provide a particular product or service—welfare benefits, resources for protecting children, treatment for drug users—to its members or to others whose interests are of common concern to them. Most publicly provided social welfare goods and services have the character of "collective goods." This means that their benefits—equality of access to social opportunities, full utilization of a society's human resources, safe and healthful neighborhoods, the guaranteed availability of help to those experiencing financial or personal crises—are enjoyed by all citizens whether or not they have actually contributed to paying for them.

Thus social welfare executives face the problem that the public at large (the potential electorate) may express general support for the collective goals of equity and assisting the needy but be reluctant either to tax themselves to pay for specific social programs or to place a value on the benefits they would derive from them.[13]

Compounding this ambivalence is the further problem that by their nature, collective goods contain important elements of ambiguity. Is the output that is valued the availability of a particular service, is it the altered behavior implied by its usage, or is it the consequences of the usage? The access working mothers have to quality day-care under the auspices of government, for example, may increase both the number of children enrolled in approved day-care arrangements and the number of mothers who are working. Potential supporters of the program may want to "purchase" the high quality, the increased usage by additional children, or the improvement in the employment or educational status of women (perhaps under the guise of making welfare mothers earn their keep). In another situation, enforcement of a regulation proscribing certain behavior may lead to punishment of violators (say, drug dealers), deterrence of destructive behavior (drug consumption), and the alleviation of problems (crime) associated with the proscribed behavior. Again, actual and potential supporters may value these outputs so differently that they will oppose one another over programmatic features.

Faced with such contradictions, social welfare executives must induce voluntary political approval for social programs by working out arrangements that attract or compel active political support for and belief in the value of certain kinds of output (for example, by child development specialists, welfare reform advocates, and potential employers of mothers of children). They must continually recognize and sort through the various ambiguities involved in any program and try to communicate an intelligible sense of purpose that somehow transcends or neutralizes destructive conflicts among a program's various constituencies.

In securing support, social welfare executives can assume an entrepreneurial role.[14] They can attempt, for instance, to recruit a subset of group members by offering them selective inducements; an example is designing programs in accord with the concepts of output of organized service providers such as physicians, vocational rehabilitation counselors, mental retardation or child development specialists, psychologists, or police. They can propose new program initiatives which combine the interests of several constituencies. More generally, according to Mancur Olson, "a leader or entrepreneur, who is generally trusted (or feared), or who can guess who is bluffing in the bargaining, or who can simply save bargaining time, can sometimes work out an arrangement that is better for all concerned than any outcome that could emerge without entrepreneurial leadership or organization."[15]

Alternatively, social welfare executives can seek to mobilize larger, more dispersed constituencies, such as interest groups representing clients or civic groups representing taxpayers. They might, for example, issue regulations that are broadly popular with influential parties: prohibiting physicians from charging Medicaid clients other than standard fees, or keeping single mothers from using unapproved day-care arrangements. Or they can offer the promise of rewards, such as the governor's support for coveted legislation or budgetary allocations.

However, by their nature, redistributive and regulatory policies such as these are relatively coercive.[16] What frustrates effective entrepreneurship is the awareness or suspicion by affected groups that entrepreneurial executives either cater to special interests to gain their support or coerce the citizenry: the public, whose earnings are being "confiscated" for the benefit of the poor; beneficiaries, whose behavior is being manipulated as the condition of survival; and service providers, who are being told how to practice or what prices to charge.

Moreover, the would-be entrepreneur might well be regarded as superfluous to goal achievement by self-interested actors. As Russell Hardin observes, "Groups can often control their own effects on policy more specifically when they actively lobby, campaign, or go to court than when they more nearly passively influence the choices of entrepreneurs."[17] The prevalence of negative attitudes toward their departments and their efforts, and the difficulties of overcoming them, explain much of the pressure and vulnerability associated with the social welfare executive's job.

The Indeterminacy of Bureaucratic Supply

The actual provision of social welfare services is also hampered by a number of obstacles. Even the identity of those to be served is often at issue: Does an official seek change in clients or in service providers, in parents or in their children, in job seekers or in employers? The greater the change being sought, the greater the pressure on program administrators is to demonstrate actual effectiveness (and the greater is their vulnerability to evidence of ineffectiveness).[18] Human-service organizations thus tend either to prefer clients for whom success is more likely, avoiding the most troublesome cases, or to emphasize their processing responsibilities, which are less problematic, at the expense of seeking change in the functioning of the difficult or recalcitrant.[19]

Further, in making a benefit or service available, social welfare executives necessarily alter the incentives facing those who are eligible and those administrative units that deal with eligible people. The result may be behavior quite different from what is desired. Certifying employable people as disadvantaged and thus eligible for a wage subsidy, for example, actually reduces their employment prospects, since employers shy away from applicants who bear the disadvantaged label despite the incentive of subsidy.[20] Making available publicly assisted day-care services may induce some people to abandon perfectly adequate private day-care arrangements in order to take advantage of subsidized care. Offering reimbursements for the cost of service to people who fall into certain categories of need encourages service providers to place people in these categories in order to increase the level of reimbursements even if such labeling is of questionable validity. These "moral hazards" produce unintended and onerous consequences, usually in the form of higher-than-expected costs and caseloads.[21]

The more fundamental problem, however, is that social welfare executives must achieve their service delivery goals by securing the willing cooperation of a dispersed network of self-interested agents—employees and contractors who, though they act on behalf and at the behest of the executive, may or may not share fully the executive's preferences and who are in positions deliberately or otherwise to frustrate the achievement of executive purposes. Management has the least influence over the bureaucracy's production of services when direct service jobs involve considerable discretion, when choices must be made among multiple objectives or work tasks, and when policy involves changes in practice in an established bureaucracy—three circumstances that are prevalent in social programs.[22] Disagreements between the principal and his or her agents may be sharp and, more troublesome, may remain covert or unexpressed.

The penalties or inducements at the executive's disposal may be insufficient to elicit the desired behavior from these agents. Financial incentives may be too weak to overcome existing reward systems. The agency's ability to enforce sanctions may be poor. Interest groups may know that continued resistance will be supported in the legislature. Injunctions and restraining orders may be sought by the aggrieved.

Having to rely on self-interested agents thus introduces substantial uncertainty into the prospect of achieving service production goals. Social welfare executives must attend to such tasks as structuring the relationships with clients or agents (for example, determining the form of contracts with proprietary or not-for-profit service providers), monitoring agent performance, and enforcing compliance, all of which are costly in terms of executive time and attention and have a low likelihood of being entirely successful.[23] Indeed, the participants in social program provision may have little motivation to cooperate in ensuring effective and efficient program performance, and there may be little the social welfare executive can do about it.

ENTREPRENEURS AND ADMINISTRATORS

When one compares the structural predicament facing social welfare executives with the capacities of actual people in these positions, it becomes more apparent why the odds are low that the typical executive will leave a measurable and unambiguous legacy of success. In the final analysis, after all of the systemic problems discussed in the previous section are taken into account, social welfare executives are individuals in their own right: men and women with aspirations, strengths, and limitations. Their recognition and successful use of their potential influence will bear the unmistakable imprint of their values, their personalities, and their styles of learning, making decisions, and conducting political relationships.

Success cannot be predicted or measured apart from the temperament and skill of the executive being evaluated. Many executives' capacity may be insufficient to permit more than survival; for others, significant accomplishments are conceivable. The range of possibilities is made clear by considering some specific cases.

"I spend most of my time on the unpredictable events that could bring everything crashing down around our heads. Issues are important, but we share responsibility for most of them with lots of people—with the Feds, with the legislature. The incidents are more important, often involve less tangible or real things, and are viewed solely as the responsibility of the department and the governor. *The management of incidents makes or breaks you.*"[24] With these words Steven Minter described his approach to managing the Massachusetts Department of Public Welfare, an approach that may be labeled "nonentrepreneurial" or "administrative" and that emphasizes the supply side of social welfare provision.

Minter's choice of approach was in part a product of two circumstances: His superior was a risk-averse governor, Francis Sargeant, who ignored the department except when trouble loomed, and there was constant potential for crisis surrounding departmental activities.[25] As a result, Minter construed his job as "doing the things that had to be done."[26] "I don't consider it my job to dream up dramatic new policy initiatives," he said. "Instead, I'm a process and procedures man."[27] In other words, Minter's strategy also appeared to reflect, as one observer put it, "Minter's own preferences and administrative style,"[28] a style that is "left-brain" and systems-oriented.

Minter was not, by nature, a change agent. At the top of his personal list of concerns were the matters that might cause the department to lose funds. Next came breakdowns in the system with political ramifications. At the bottom of his priority list were items, such as program initiatives, with little immediate payoff or threat. The result was not just *a* strategy; it was *his* strategy, one that appeared to suit not only the circumstances of a cautious superior but his own personality and inner aspirations. Because of his loyalty and obvious commitment to protecting the governor, Minter was "allowed broad discretion in ordering and managing the many pressing priorities with which the department had to deal."[29] Consequently, the strategy seemed appropriate; by successfully managing "incidents," the administration could claim competence in its stewardship of public welfare and avoid costly controversy. One analyst concluded nonetheless that "although Minter had both the skills and expertise the job of commissioner of public welfare required, the complicated nature of the department's task and the impossibility of defining what had to be done made the department impossible to 'run.'"[30]

Another social welfare executive whose "achievements were largely systems achievements concerning management information and planning" was Barbara Blum, commissioner of social services in New York State from 1977 to 1982 and an appointee of Governor Hugh Carey.[31] Blum's college degree was in mathematics, and like Minter, she was an experienced social welfare professional. Also like Minter, she emphasized process and procedures over new program initiatives.

"My mathematical training enables me to enjoy data. I think that you learn an enormous amount by watching trend data in particular. . . . The budget . . . was fun for me. . . . I have always operated with a fair amount of structure. . . . I feel very strongly that once your objectives are clear, people have to begin to fall into line. . . . You have to use your sanctions and try to force whatever can be had [from the local level]." She found legislative politics frustrating. "I don't like the state legislative process. I like the legislators, but I think the process is a disaster. . . . If there were trade-offs occurring, I didn't know what they were. It's just strange. People would worry about little sentences. . . . I never could understand some of those lengthy discussions about very minor issues."

Blum became known as one of a group of "strong commissioners" on whom the governor depended. "I had almost total autonomy," she said, but she also conceded that "if I had gotten into more trouble there might have been more supervision exercised." Echoing Minter, she pointed out that "the public and often the legislators themselves perceive the commissioner to be in control of whatever is happening down at the local level." The achievement in which she expressed greatest pride was a 15 percent increase in the basic welfare grant, an initiative of her department. Second on her list was implementation of the Child Welfare Reform Act, introduced by the legislature. When asked if the remote and seemingly indifferent governor had sponsored a program in the welfare area, she said, "I think the initiative logically came out of the department, but it was supported by the executive office. . . . [Hugh Carey] was amost overly generous in the human services area." Thus, like Minter, Blum's achievements can be measured largely in terms of the discretion allowed her by the governor, the state's reputation for general competence in program administration, and the avoidance of fatal mistakes.

Only partially successful with a similar strategy and style was David Pingree, secretary of Florida's Department of Health and Rehabilitative Services under two governors. Responsible for implementing a complex legislative reorganization of the department, Pingree resembled Minter and Blum in being oriented more toward preventing explosions that could damage a disinterested governor than toward being an agent of change. He often claimed that an important indicator of his success as a manager was the sharp reduction in the volume of complaints about departmental operations registered by state legislators. Unlike Minter, who was well liked, Pingree kept an emotional distance from his employees. He had a reputation as a tough, even volatile administrator anxious to maintain political control through his direct, forceful style.

Though he was skillful for several years at controlling departmental operations, at pursuing the complex goals of the reorganization, and at crisis management, Pingree resigned shortly before the issuance of a report by a panel of the National Academy of Public Administration (NAPA), which was sharply critical of his leadership.[32] "Of late," said the panel, "the avoidance of crisis which would harm the Governor and the deflection of crises away from him appears to be an overriding goal of departmental leadership. 'Anybody who has been around this department,' said one official, 'knows that to get attention you politicize the issue, leak stuff outside so advocates can create a crisis.' "[33] The NAPA panel concluded that "the Department leadership appears preoccupied with avoiding mistakes and quieting controversy: it offers little emotional support to departmental employees who are estranged and confused and little intellectual support for its programs."[34]

An approach quite different from those of Minter, Blum, and Pingree is Gregory Coler's strategy in directing the Illinois Department of Public Aid (IDPA)—a strategy that may be labeled "entrepreneurial" and that emphasizes the demand side of social welfare provision. Illinois Governor James Thompson appeared no more eager to embrace the welfare department and its "no-win" issues than the governors of Florida, New York, and Massachusetts. However, while they had appointed process-oriented executives to do "what had to be done," the moderately conservative Thompson selected a man to head IDPA who was recognized for his aggressive style. At the same time, Thompson announced a new policy toward welfare dependency in Illinois: "Not just a check, but a chance" encapsulated a determination to reduce welfare rolls and state welfare expenditures by actively assisting the needy toward economic self-sufficiency. Thompson evidently believed he had chosen an executive who could make his new policy succeed.

A former community organizer, New York state official, and head of the Illinois Department of Children and Family Services, Coler was well known for his apparently limitless energy and enthusiasm, his shrewd grasp of legislative response to "selective incentives," and his instinct for persuasive communication, both direct and symbolic.[35] The department he took over was suffering from low morale, rising workloads, and a poor reputation in the legislature. He immediately established a simple, effective premise for departmental administration: IDPA would serve its two masters—clients and taxpayers—by offering the needy opportunity as well as funds. But he also had specific programmatic objectives: Reduce the welfare rolls, reduce welfare fraud, improve child-support collection performance. In pursuit of his goals, Coler became a highly visible, forceful, and engaging presence inside and outside the department. "You must run for office in your own organization," he said.

By managing issues, such as workfare and child-support enforcement, rather than incidents or crises, Coler left an apparent legacy of improved employee morale and sense of purpose in Illinois. In addition to winning legislative support for his initiatives, he appeared to instill in many employees a more positive view of their jobs and greater awareness of their contributions to the well-being of both client and taxpayer in Illinois. His growing national reputation as a social welfare administrator earned him appointment to the National Academy of Science's Committee on National Urban Policy. Also, in a move widely regarded as a promotion, Coler became secretary of Florida's Department of Health and Rehabilitative Services, the position formerly held by Pingree, where within a year his entrepreneurial style raised his department to the top of the governor's budgetary priorities.

Yet it is possible to question the success of his policies. Coler's flamboyance—his taste for the good life, his habit of traveling with an entourage, his gift for hyperbole—was believed by many to obscure a lack of substance and a lack of commitment by both Coler and the governor to providing adequate financial support for social programs. In a report released after his departure, the Manpower Demonstration Research Corporation concluded that the workfare program was ineffective and that its goals were not achieved because it was inadequately funded.[36] He was, some have said, "more show than go."

Similar to Coler in style and approach was the late Gordon Chase, who headed New York City's Health Services Administration during the tenure of Mayor John Lindsay. Intense, competitive, even compulsive, Chase brought a passion for helping people in need and a commanding presence to bear on a relatively small number of new program initiatives in which he believed he could be successful and achieve favorable political impact.[37] He was the consummate program entrepreneur:

> He created a large program to test children for lead poisoning and correct lead paint hazards in dwellings[;] . . . established a vastly expanded city effort to discover and treat sufferers from hypertension, alcoholism, gonorrhea, and sickle cell anemia; provide methadone to tens of thousands of addicts as a safe and cheap alternative to heroin; provide health care in the city's prison system; control rats and thereby reduce the incidence of rat bites; and introduce such managerial reforms as performance contracts for the provision of mental health services.[38]

He lavished attention and publicity on pet programs—like Coler, he assiduously courted the media—and largely ignored others. For example, lacking the expertise of a physician, he was reluctant to tangle with the Health and Hospitals Corporation. His instruction to his subordinates was, "I don't care how you do it; just bring me results."

Gordon Chase inspired intense loyalty, not only among his circle of trusted subordinates but among a generation of researchers and practitioners who, since his untimely death, have viewed him as something of a paragon for his achievements and style. As a former Chase subordinate who was to become commissioner of public welfare in Massachusetts said of him, "There was no greater expert in applying the theories of how to make things work to government."[39]

Yet, as with Coler, Chase had his critics. Some believed his *ad hoc* attention to program issues was at the expense of the continuity and effectiveness of the agency as a whole. Keenly aware of his finite time in office, he emphasized short-term results, which caused him to neglect the more painstaking activity of building a constituency for his changes. Craving positive exposure, relying on a tight circle of intimates, and avoiding debilitating bureaucratic conflict, Chase, it has been argued, did not have lasting influence on his agency because he did not penetrate deeply enough into agency culture—changing routines, instilling new values, altering the ways in which agency professionals and their constituencies viewed their roles. Lindsay's successor as mayor was able to undertake what Christopher Leman calls a "wholesale reversal" of Chase's policies.

Each of these five public executives employed particular tactics and strategies in pursuit of their purposes. Their means included designing and enforcing specific performance goals; promoting internal competition to stimulate higher performance; choosing political battles carefully, but choosing some; using early and specific successes to build a reputation for competence; leveraging agency expenditures to obtain political support; managing projects outside of normal management routines for high-priority objectives; obtaining feedback on programs from focus groups of service recipients; being willing to investigate their own departments and announce the results; organizing internal routines so that staff offices serve, not control, program offices; not staking one's reputation on goals with a low probability of success; and using the media aggressively to publicize one's ideas. To be effective, whether as an administrator or as an entrepreneur, an executive must demonstrate recognizable skill as a manager, and each of these managers was proficient in his or her own way.

These cases also suggest fundamental contrasts between administrative and entrepreneurial strategies. The former strategies are internally focused and concerned primarily with improving the quality and efficiency of service delivery largely on a program-by-program basis. The latter strategies are externally focused and concerned primarily with generating and sustaining demand for, and therefore political equity in, new and existing social programs. Both strategies must contend with the kinds of structural problems—with the tendencies toward noncooperative behavior and inefficient outcomes—described in the preceding section. Either tactic might be appropriate in given political and organizational circumstances.

Yet the preferred strategy for managing social welfare must be understood as reflecting the administrative styles and choices of the elected governor or mayor on the one hand and the appointed social welfare executive on the other. The appropriateness and probable effectiveness of a strategy thus has two dimensions relating to individual capabilities: the "fit" between the elected and appointed executives and the fit between the appointed executive and the wider political environment. By attracting political support and resources, an entrepreneurial executive would appear to have an advantage in producing widely noticed programmatic achievements over an administrator who concentrates on solving internal problems (a point to which I will return in the concluding section). But to a governor who has little interest in the social welfare department, an executive who adopts an entrepreneurial strategy might seem to put too much of the governor's own political reputation at risk and come to be regarded as a liability.

Finally, these cases suggest that the question of executive strategy is dependent on the skill and temperament of the person holding the job. Gregory Coler could not have "chosen" Steven Minter's approach, which would have been contrary to his nature, nor could David Pingree have "chosen" Coler's or Blum's strategy. Of Gordon Chase it was said, "You couldn't imagine him doing anything differently." Thus, identifying and classifying their strategies is in many respects equivalent to classifying their individual capabilities and styles of leading and managing.[40]

Determining an appropriate strategy means matching an appointee and his or her style to a particular political context, even if the criterion is no more complex than choosing between administrative and entrepreneurial approaches. Illinois Governor Thompson wanted an entrepreneur; Massachusetts Governor Sargeant wanted an administrator. Had Thompson been paired with a Minter, or Sargeant with a Coler, each would probably have been dissatisfied. A successful strategy, therefore, reflects a favorable mix of personal styles and ambitions, political context, and circumstances.

Although strategic achievements are, to a significant extent, fortuitous, they are not by any means wholly so. The possibilities for success can be enhanced by purposeful efforts on the part of both elected and appointed executives.

ENHANCING SOCIAL WELFARE MANAGEMENT

Improving executive management of social welfare departments can be approached from either (or both) of two directions. Improvement can be viewed as a matter of upgrading the level, quality, and deployment of executive resources committed to social welfare management: choosing the right person to meet the demands of the job and the expectations of the governor or mayor. Alternatively, it can be viewed as a matter of changing the design of social welfare institutions and programs through reorganizing and restructuring in order to make them more manageable (i.e., in order to enhance the productivity of managerial resources). Neither approach has been evaluated in any systematic way against outcomes. However, on the basis of both theory and experience, a number of general observations on each approach are worth making.

Executive Competence

Except in a few places—Florida, Massachusetts, Wisconsin, and New York City, for instance—there appears to be little or no attention paid to the appropriateness (as opposed to the expediency) of appointments to social welfare executive positions in state and municipal government. It is doubtful whether the routine application of ordinary patronage criteria will produce any more than accidentally qualified executives. Unusually good performance in these complex and demanding jobs—measured by program performance and the creation of political equity, not simply by longevity in office or the suppression of political conflict—is likely to be a product of some combination of entrepreneurial qualities: a forceful intellect, a high level of energy, exceptional political acumen, imagination and creativity, and strength of character. All public executive positions would benefit from unusual talent, of course, but contributing in a positive and lasting way to the controversial, value-laden, and complex issues associated with social welfare administration virtually requires it.

Consideration of the characteristic demands and problems facing social welfare executives suggests that, differences in context nothwithstanding, the more effective ones will tend to be intuitive, "right-brain" types: flexible, optimistic, thematic, and persuasive more than systematic, thorough, and realistic; more clever than smart; warm rather than cool; more convincing than convinced. Executives who are more inner-directed, process-oriented, ideological, or narrowly specialized (and this group includes many who become candidates for human-service appointments owing to their professional credentials) will probably have greater difficulty coping with the ambiguity, indeterminacy, and conflict associated with social program administration than executives who are outgoing, imaginative, and pragmatic.

Organizational Design

But what of the service delivery issues? What of the quality and competence of administration? Surely these matters should not be neglected. Without doubt the structure of an organization and of the incentives facing its officials affects its performance, and the structure of interorganizational relations (for example, the relations between federal, state, and local human-service agencies) influences the performance of the entire social service system. But the question is, is it time well spent for an executive to emphasize organization design and improvement of program performance through structural measures?

Analysis of the problems of social program administration strongly discourages a search for organizational designs and incentives that will produce efficient results without close and time-consuming monitoring of subordinate behavior—that is, for a "hidden managerial hand," or a set of rules and incentives that harmonizes conflicting interests and moves the organization toward the efficient supply of collective goods. Such a search may not be worth the cost in terms of attention diverted from more entrepreneurial, equity-building activities.[41] The tensions between the self-interests of legislators, program administrators, direct service workers of varying professional orientations, and clients, on the one hand, and organizational interests, on the other, cannot be overcome solely or even primarily by structural measures. Attempts to eliminate one set of bureaucratic problems may well create new ones that escape detection.[42] Attempts to disentangle the overlapping incentives inherent in the federal system of social program administration and closely monitor the consequences can be exhausting and ultimately fruitless.

On these grounds and all other factors being equal, executive resources would appear to be better deployed on the demand side: in creating political equity in social programs. By virtue of their positions in the political system, social welfare executives have natural advantages in exerting influence at the middle levels of power to secure support for programs and to shape the programmatic directions of policy. They are in a position to have a comprehensive view of their departments, to gather information, and to identify strategic opportunities, since they know more about external politics than lower-level officials and more about their department's internal dynamics than legislators or the governor. They have sufficient control over information and budgetary and human resources to allocate them to advantage.

The crux of the most reasonable approach to the structural problems facing social welfare executives—whether they arise on the demand or supply sides of social service provision—is to resist viewing effective executive performance as dependent on making technically rational decisions on each program design issue. Rather, executive decisionmaking should be regarded as a process with broadly strategic consequences: a series of opportunities to build a reputation for trustworthiness that will lead to cooperation and more efficient results.

> Managers should look at their organizations as being composed of individuals with diverse interests who will inevitably find themselves in conflict on occasion. Their best response to this problem is to inspire among their own employees a willingness to cooperate and trust each other by setting an example of being concerned and trustworthy themselves. . . . Managers who can induce norms of cooperation and trust among employees can realize more of the gains from team production than can managers who rely on formal incentive systems only.[43]

In practical terms, a successful strategy for managing social services will include an emphasis on positive rewards, recognition, and publicity; measures to instill pride and motivate efforts; premises for action that can be easily grasped and that reflect widely understood values; an absence of defensiveness and a willingness to investigate and publicize mistakes; loyalty to employees, political allies, and anyone who assists in promoting executive goals; occasional support for other political actors whose goodwill and power may be helpful; believable arguments and reliable data; and the appearance of intelligently conceived movement and change.

Whether the end in view is inducing able-bodied welfare recipients to work, protecting children from neglect and abuse, enhancing the dignity and independence of the impaired elderly, improving the life prospects of infants in high-risk environments, or sheltering the homeless, leadership that is hopeful, outward-looking, flexible, and understandable has the best chance of making a positive difference.

NOTES

1. I want to acknowledge the valuable comments of Eugene Bardach, Evelyn Brodkin, Edward Lawlor, Stephen Smith, Michael Wiseman, and the volume's editors on earlier drafts.

2. This and subsequent quotes are from Robert Pear, "Senate Vote Encourages Welfare Change," *New York Times*, 3 April 1987. See also Robert D. Reischauer, "The Welfare Reform Legislation: Directions for the Future," in *Welfare Policy for the 1990s*, ed. Phoebe H. Cottingham and David T. Ellwood (Cambridge, Mass.: Harvard University Press, 1989), pp. 10–40.

3. The positions that are the concern of this chapter are basically the executives of the principal agencies identified in *Public Welfare Directory* 46, ed. Amy Weinstein (Public Welfare Association, 1985). They are variously called secretaries/commissioners/directors of public welfare/human services (resources)/social (and rehabilitation) services/employment security.

4. "Generally, the term 'human services' refers to the following eight areas of service: (1) public assistance/social services; (2) health; (3) mental health; (4) mental retardation; (5) corrections; (6) youth services; (7) vocational rehabilitation; and (8) employment services." Taken from Neil Gilbert and Harry Specht, *Dimensions of Social Welfare Policy*, 2d ed. (Englewood Cliffs, N.J.: Prentice-Hall, 1986), p. 187. The social welfare executives discussed here have responsibilities in virtually all areas except (5).

5. Sandra P. Schoenberg, "A Typology of Leadership Styles in Public Organizations," in *Organization and Managerial Innovation*, ed. L. A. Rowe and W. B. Boise (Santa Monica, Calif.: Goodyear Publishing Co., 1973), pp. 177–86.

6. Political equity means a source of political benefits to governors and their appointees. Cf. Norman Frolich, Joe A. Oppenheimer, and Oran R. Young, *Political Leadership and Collective Goods* (Princeton, N.J.: Princeton University Press, 1971), and Jean-Luc Migue and Gerard Belanger, "Toward a General Theory of Managerial Discretion," *Public Choice* 17 (Spring 1974): 527–47.

7. Gilbert and Specht, *Social Welfare Policy*, pp. 37–40.

8. States are required by Public Law 100-485, for example, to determine on a case-by-case basis when the provision of child care is necessary to enable a welfare recipient to participate in a job training program.

9. Laurence E. Lynn, Jr., "Government Executives as Gamesmen: A Metaphor for Analyzing Managerial Behavior," *Journal of Policy Analysis and Management* 1, 4 (Summer 1982): 482–95.

10. For an analysis of executive latitude and autonomy, see Laurence E. Lynn, Jr., *Managing Public Policy* (Boston, Mass.: Little, Brown, 1987), especially chapter 3.

11. Evelyn Brodkin, "Implementation as Policy Politics" (Processed September 4, 1987), p. 2.

12. I am indebted to Michael Wiseman for clarifying my thinking on these matters.

13. According to the logic of collective action, members of a group will voluntarily incur the cost of providing a produce or service (i.e., will express a demand for it) if and only if, for each member, the resulting benefit exceeds that cost. If it is infeasible to exclude any of a group's members from enjoying the benefits of a product or service once it is available—if, in other words, the products or services are collective goods—then individual members of the group usually have no incentive to bear the costs of providing it since, if others foot the bill, they will still benefit. See Russell Hardin, *Collective Action* (Baltimore, Md.: Johns Hopkins University Press, 1982), pp. 16–22, and Mancur Olson, Jr., *The Logic of Collective Action: Public Goods and the Theory of Groups* (Cambridge, Mass.: Harvard University Press, 1971), chapter 1. Group size is significant in that it is feasible for members

of a small group to bargain with one another until an agreement on obtaining an optimal supply of a collective good is reached; for large groups the transaction costs are usually too high for such bargaining to be feasible. But see Olson, *The Logic of Collective Action*, p. 176.

14. According to Russell Hardin, "Political entrepreneurs are people who, for their own career reasons, find it in their private interest to work to provide collective benefits to relevant groups." *Collective Action*, p. 35. For a discussion of the term *entrepreneur* in connection with the provision of collective goods, see Olson, *The Logic of Collective Action*, pp. 174–78; Hardin, *Collective Action*, pp. 34–37; Frolich, Oppenheimer, and Young, *Political Leadership and Collective Goods;* and Terry M. Moe, *The Organization of Interests: Incentives and the Internal Dynamics of Political Interest Groups* (Chicago, Ill.: University of Chicago Press, 1980), pp. 36–39.

In a more general vein, Eugene Lewis argues that public entrepreneurs are "people who reject normal system maintenance norms and attempt to expand the goals, mandates, functions, and power of their organizations in ways unprecedented or unforseen by their putative masters." See Eugene Lewis, *Public Entrepreneurship: Toward a Theory of Bureaucratic Political Power* (Bloomington: Indiana University Press, 1980), pp. 8–9.

15. Olson, *The Logic of Collective Action*, p. 176.

16. Theodore J. Lowi, "Four Systems of Policy, Politics and Choice," *Public Administration Review* (July/August 1972): 298–310.

17. Hardin, *Collective Action*, p. 37.

18. Yeheskel Hasenfeld, *Human Service Organizations* (Englewood Cliffs, N.J.: Prentice-Hall, 1983), p. 143.

19. Ibid., p. 143. Cf. Manuel Carballo, "Governance," in *The State and the Poor in the 1980s*, ed. Manuel Carballo and Mary Jo Bane (Boston, Mass.: Auburn House, 1984), p. 315.

20. Gary Burtless, "Are Targeted Wage Subsidies Harmful? Evidence from a Wage Voucher Experiment," *Industrial and Labor Relations Review* 39, 1 (October 1985): 105–14.

21. Edith Stokey and Richard Zeckhauser, *A Primer for Policy Analysis* (New York: W. W. Norton, 1978), pp. 300–301.

22. Michael Lipsky, cited in Evelyn Z. Brodkin, *The False Promise of Administrative Reform: Implementing Quality Control in Welfare* (Philadelphia, Pa.: Temple University Press, 1986), p. 135, n 3.

23. In more technical terms, externalities in the production of social services (e.g., problems of team production) are likely to be hampered by prisoner's dilemmas which inhibit optimal levels of performance by clients and service workers. See Gary J. Miller, *Administrative Dilemmas: The Role of Political Leadership*, Political Economy Working Paper (St. Louis, Mo.: Washington University, June 1987). "There will always be incentives for individuals to shirk, cheat, or follow their own preferences in ways that cumulate to organizational inefficiencies" (p. 32). See also Edward M. Gramlich, "Cooperation and Competition in Public Welfare Policies," *Journal of Policy Analysis and Management* 6, 3 (Spring 1987): 417–31, for applications of game theory to social policy design.

24. Martha Wagner Weinberg, *Managing the State* (Cambridge, Mass.: MIT Press, 1977), p. 127 (my italics).

25. Ibid., pp. 127–28, 141. Minter and the governor could be described as facing a prisoner's dilemma in which noncooperative strategies—avoiding mistakes on Minter's part, punishing mistakes on the governor's part—dominated cooperative strategies directed at program performance.

26. Ibid., p. 130.

27. Ibid., p. 128.

28. Ibid.

29. Ibid., p. 140.

30. Ibid., p. 216. In other words, a cooperative, efficient outcome in the sense of note 28 was impossible.

31. Gerald Benjamin and T. Norman Hurd, *Making Experience Count: Managing Modern New York in the Carey Era* (Albany, N.Y.: Nelson A. Rockefeller Institute of Government, 1985), p. 116. Material for this section is drawn from the extensive interview with Barbara Blum in this volume.

32. *After a Decade: A Progress Report on the Organization and Management of the Florida State Department of Health and Rehabilitative Services,* Report by a Panel of the National Academy of Public Administration, submitted to the Florida state legislature in April 1986. I was a participant on this panel.

33. Ibid., p. 17.

34. Ibid., p. 11.

35. Information on Coler is drawn primarily from two research papers prepared by graduate students of the University of Chicago: Bob Tate, "Gregory Coler at Illinois' Department of Public Aid: A Manager with a Mission" (Processed June 11, 1986), and Janet Gill Marsh, "Reorienting the Mission of the Illinois Department of Public Aid: A Study of the Management of Director Gregory Coler" (Processed June 9, 1986).

36. *Washington Post,* 12 December 1987, p. A23.

37. Much of this section is drawn from Christopher K. Leman, "Gordon Chase at the Health Services Administration: Lessons from a Successful Public Manager" (Processed October 1987), and from recollections of my personal conversations with Chase. See also Gordon Chase and Elizabeth C. Reveal, *How to Manage in the Public Sector* (Reading, Mass.: Addison Wesley, 1983), and Gordon Chase, "Implementing a Human Services Program: How Hard Will It Be?" *Public Policy* 27, 4 (Fall 1979): 385–435.

38. Leman, "Gordon Chase," p. 1.

39. Charles M. Atkins, unpublished remarks, January 19, 1980. Atkins is widely regarded as a Chase protégé. Of Atkins's approach to establishing and implementing a policy encouraging more work by welfare recipients in Massachusetts, Robert Behn has written: "They simply started off. . . . The department's leadership simply guessed at what a good program would look like and implemented that state-wide. Then when they learned from what the field did with that initial [program], they modified it. They fixed it. From the first year of the program, Atkins and company have managed [the program] by groping along." Robert D. Behn, "Managing Innovation in Welfare, Training and Work: Some Lessons from ET Choices in Massachusetts" (Processed September 4, 1987), pp. 16–17.

40. Cf. Weinberg, *Managing the State,* p. 217.

41. Cf. Herbert Kaufman, *Administrative Feedback* (Washington, D.C.: Brookings Institution, 1973), p. 54.

42. Miller, *Administrative Dilemmas,* pp. 25–30.

43. Ibid., pp. 44, 50. This proposition is derived from an analysis of optimal strategies in repeated games. A managerial strategy of promoting mutual cooperation—specifically, beginning a series of interactions with a cooperative move and thereafter adopting the opposing player's strategy on the previous move, the so-called tit for tat strategy—can be shown to lead to better results in repeated games than self-interested, short-term maximizing strategies. See Robert Axelrod, *The Evaluation of Cooperation* (New York: Basic Books, 1984). Axelrod argues that a property of high scoring strategies in repeated games is that "of being *nice,* which is to say never being the first to defect" from being cooperative (p. 33).

8

When a Possible Job Becomes Impossible: Politics, Public Health, and the Management of the AIDS Epidemic

Edward F. Lawlor

> *There is no quality in human nature which causes more fatal errors in our conduct, than that which leads us to prefer whatever is present to the distant and remote, and makes us desire objects more according to their situation than their intrinsic value*
> —David Hume[1]

An emerging interpretation of the Acquired Immune Deficiency Syndrome (AIDS) epidemic holds that public health officials failed in their jobs and that the spread of the disease could have been limited during the early 1980s if these officials had acted more vigorously and with greater competence. Despite the enormous stakes involved and the apparent clarity of the task, the public health establishment has taken several years to gear up for the epidemic; many observers of the early history of response to AIDS argue that public health officials missed the only opportunity to control the spread of the virus.[2]

To say that the public health officials have failed implies that success and failure are definable and measurable with respect to this disease and that public health officials are accountable for what has resulted to date. Although a verdict of failure may ultimately be warranted, it is important to place the actions of public health officials in a political and institutional context. Further, before holding individual public health executives responsible for the spread of AIDS, it is necessary to articulate their professional role regarding this disease.

Noone seems to be happy with the performance of state and municipal public health officials on the front lines during the early period of this epidemic. This chapter explores the idea that controlling the spread of AIDS during this phase was an impossible task for state and municipal public health officials. The argument is multidimensional: (1) Relative to the larger cycles of reform in public health, the "time" was not right for public health officials to act with the requisite authority, resources, and dispatch; (2) the spread of the epidemic had collective-action characteristics that precluded group mobilization for either prevention or political advocacy in the brief period of time available; and (3) both the epidemic

152

and the job of the public official were so muddied and complicated that an immediate, unilateral, and effective public health response may have been an unrealistic expectation. This chapter examines the experiences of three officials who confronted the archetypical issues of AIDS policymaking: closing bathhouses, dispensing free needles, and requiring antibody testing. Finally, some ideas for positive coping in the face of an impossible task are explored.

PUBLIC HEALTH AS A POSSIBLE JOB

The charge of the state and municipal public health executive is to protect the health and safety of the public. This job usually carries responsibility for collecting and analyzing epidemiological data and vital statistics, regulating much of the healthcare delivery system, encouraging the adoption of preventive health measures, participating in health planning decisions, and "doing what is necessary" within the constraints of public health law to control the spread of infectious diseases. The American Public Health Association has designated six activities as the purview of local health departments: vital statistics, communicable disease control, sanitation, laboratory services (such as those necessary for testing for sexually transmitted diseases), maternal and child hygiene, and general health education. At the state level, the responsibilities of a typical health department include health surveillance and health policy planning, supervision and promotion of local health coverage, setting and enforcing public health standards, and directly providing health services where they may be lacking.

In practice, health departments at the state and local level are extremely varied. Some state departments are primarily data-oriented and play little role in policy development or the administration of direct services. Others, especially some departments in the large industrial states, have multiple duties in both the conventional public health domains and medical assistance policy. As a result, some of these jobs make extraordinary intellectual and managerial demands: the commissioner of health in California, for example, is responsible for areas as diverse as toxicology and management of the Medi-Cal program (California's version of Medicaid), while also managing a $6.5 billion budget and a department with over four thousand employees. The commissioner of health in New York State, in addition to the traditional operations of public health, is responsible for regulation of healthcare facilities and the development and maintenance of healthcare reimbursement for a large and heterogeneous healthcare industry. Thus, in the course of his work as New York's commissioner, Dr. David Axelrod has had to defend controversial regulations against smoking in public places as well as oversee the design of a technically complex and politically charged hospital reimbursement system. At times, the responsibilities of public health officials can assume a stochastic quality, as random events that have the potential to jeopardize the public health take center stage. It is state and local public health officials, among others, who have to respond to product-tampering episodes, such as the infamous Tylenol cases. In California it was the health commissioner's task to reassure the public that fallout from the Chernobyl accident was not a threat to the population of the state.

Before the early 1980s the job of the public health executive had relatively low visibility and stature in state and municipal government. At a national level, the perception that public health problems such as legionnaires disease, the swine flu affair, and toxic shock syndrome had been successfully managed created a view that contagion was controllable. Even within the public health profession, there was an underlying belief that the control of infectious disease had been largely accomplished; one head of a state infectious disease unit began looking for other work because the task of controlling such contagion had become "routine."[3] In addition, many preventive measures, the so-called life-style changes of reduced smoking and improvements in cardiovascular fitness, had at least been recognized, if not adopted, by the public. In the early 1980s the center of gravity in the health policy debate was clearly on issues of cost containment and access to acute healthcare, not public health. Although the tasks of epidemiological monitoring, administering a large and technically complex bureaucracy, and, in some states, managing health financing and delivery programs are all difficult, few observers of state public health administration in the late 1970s would have labeled the executive's job "impossible" or "intractable."

By the criteria that define impossibility in this volume, public health executives did not serve, or at least were not perceived to be serving, a particularly unattractive or unpopular clientele before the mid-1980s. If anything, public health executives were in the business of protecting the "public good," and their actions typically did not provoke either intense support or intense opposition. Activities such as the conduct of epidemiological surveillance, the regulation of food establishments, or even the enforcement of quality assurance in health facilities do not directly engage clients or constituencies that are highly stigmatized, nor are they activities that raise the questions of deservedness or moral hazard that are prevalent in the administration of social services or corrections agencies. Where public health administration becomes most closely aligned with problematic clients, as in the area of maternal and child health, the emphasis is usually placed on the health of the children, thus diffusing somewhat the controversies over entitlement and incentives that are paramount in the large welfare debate.

Public health officials, generally medical doctors with additional public health credentials, also have benefited from the sovereignty and authority of these professions. Most issues of public health are technically and scientifically complex, and administrators with specialized expertise (or access to that expertise) in fields such as epidemiology or toxicology have enjoyed considerable hegemony over their enterprise and received substantial deference from legislators, budget officers, and the executive branch.

By these measures, the job of a public health official looks more possible than impossible. In John Glidewell and Erwin Hargrove's framework, the clients are "legitimate," the number of constituencies is limited, the intensity of conflict is low, and the public confidence in authority is high. Although the tractability of many clients may be low—many people will not cease smoking, will not wear seatbelts, and will not utilize appropriate prenatal care—the accountability of health officials for such behaviors is also low. Furthermore, the time horizon over which progress in these health indicators is measured is much longer than the expected tenure of any health official. The one exception to this picture of the manageability of a health official's job is in the event of a health emergency. If people become sick or die because of food poisoning or a viral outbreak and there are political consequences, then public health officials will be early candidates for scapegoat. Even so, although many of the responsibilities of public health officials are challenging, the overall job is manageable and possible. The prospect of essentially random outbreaks of infection or illness introduces a political hazard into the job that distinguishes it from many other public sector positions, but these events are relatively rare and usually self-contained.

AIDS AND PUBLIC HEALTH ADMINISTRATION

By the mid-1980s the job of the public health executive had moved into the eye of the storm. The massive media attention devoted to AIDS in 1983 forced public health officials to become preoccupied with controlling the spread of the disease. First identified in 1981 (though it is now clear that the virus was present and transmitted during the late 1970s), the Human Immunodeficiency Virus (HIV) was soon recognized as 100 percent fatal in those cases that displayed particular symptoms and was spreading at an exponential rate in selected areas of the country. Public health executives in New York and California, and their counterparts in New York City and San Francisco, faced the first wave of transmission, illness, and death from the virus. Soon thereafter significant numbers of cases began to appear in other parts of the country, bringing increasing pressure on public health departments to act.

From a historical perspective, epidemics have presented public health officials with the opportunity to shape and expand the public health enterprise. However, mere existence of an epidemic is insufficient. Its appearance must interact with a variety of ancillary factors: the climate of opinion about medical credibility and competence, the nature of the disease and its affected populations, the status of knowledge and belief about the epidemic, the standards and language of societal communication, and so on.[4] The best example of this institutional opportunism can be seen in the New York City Board of Health's intervention in the tuberculosis crisis from roughly 1890 to 1920, during which time it established an epidemiological capability, extended its police powers, expanded its regulatory scope and resources, and solidified its public visibility and credibility.[5]

The timing of the AIDS epidemic, however, probably could not have been worse for public health officials interested in a rapid and expansive response:

The individuals and institutions that comprise the health polity . . . were poorly prepared to take aggressive, confident action against a disease that was infectious, linked—in the majority of cases—to individual behavior, expensive to study and treat, and required a coordinated array of public and personal health services. . . . Everyone who worked in the health sector knew a crisis was occurring; so did attentive consumers of print and television news. Uncertainty about priorities, resources, and, most important, leadership pervaded the health polity. The AIDS epidemic was an additional element in an ongoing crisis.[6]

With the onset of the AIDS epidemic, controlling the spread of HIV infection became the dominant responsibility of many state public health officials and health commissioners in large urban areas. Before 1985 the technology of testing for antibody of HIV infection was not available, making it difficult to monitor the prevalence of infection in the population, much less to intervene to halt its spread. With the emergence of a somewhat reliable and relatively inexpensive test for HIV antibody (the ELISA test), enormous pressure began to mount on public health officials to act to stem the spread of the disease. Unfortunately, the availability of a testing mechanism for the presence of HIV antibody was a double-edged sword. It allowed (somewhat imprecise) identification of carriers of the virus, yet it suggested no compelling answers to the larger question of how to implement the test and what to do with the resulting information.

Thus, public health officials have been operating in a highly charged atmosphere of responsibility and consequence—in what Ronald Bayer calls a "matter of extraordinary social moment."[7] Because it takes some time for HIV infection to convert into symptomatic AIDS, gains that are made today in controlling the spread of the infection will not be exhibited in reduced sickness and death until many years out into the future. Strong efforts to limit the spread of HIV infection are largely invisible today, but they have enormous consequences for reducing deaths and they help buy time to develop better medical interventions. Public health officials who act aggressively during the early stages of the epidemic will have the greatest impact on the ultimate course of the disease; however, many of these officials will no longer be in office if and when any improvement begins to be noted. For the foreseeable future, public health officials will have no good news to share. Because the infection is already widely distributed in the population and there is no effective therapy within view, the loss of life and social devastation will continue to mount.

Nonetheless, combating the epidemic requires public health officials to act on several fronts: (1) to affect individual behavior, especially among gay men and intravenous (IV) drug users; (2) to mold the climate of public opinion and the set of legislative choices that determine the range of public health interventions; and (3) to develop administrative capacity and capture sufficient resources for managing AIDS policy over the long term. The job of the public health executive in controlling AIDS is unusual in its public management demands; it is primarily a task of external influence, not the management of internal agency functions and mission. The most important frontiers for the public health official are the framing of a legislative context that will allow the department to maintain accurate surveillance; the influencing of potential carriers; and the shaping of the larger milieu of public concern without triggering undue fear and backlash. These responsibilities place a premium on the political savvy and the public communications skills of the executive.

WHY CONTROLLING AIDS IS IMPOSSIBLE: A THEORETICAL PERSPECTIVE

The mandate of public health executives to control the spread of AIDS is a prototypical impossible task because it requires collective behavior before clear and significant payoffs are evident to individuals. Left unattended, this situation persists until the number of infected people becomes so great that the individual incentives to avoid contraction essentially reach a threshold at which individual preventive actions are very widespread and effective. Waiting for this to occur, however, is the worst possible coping strategy for a public health official.

There are actually two types of impossibility embedded in the public health executive's charge to control the spread of HIV infection. The first stems from the collective-action nature of the problem and is seemingly abstract, but in practice it stands as the most intractable obstacle to the successful control of AIDS. The second type of impossibility is more commonly observed in public management: It is the problem of meeting mandated objectives in an environment of competing goals, ambiguity, and legal and fiscal constraints—all under enormous demands on personal time, energy, and intellect.

A Strong Impossibility Theorem

AIDS cannot be controlled by the efforts of a public health official because at root there is a fundamental mismatch between the risks and rewards of individual behavior and the collective interests of the groups at highest risk.

To understand the impossibility of the public health executive's job in controlling the spread of HIV infection, it is necessary to sketch a model of the collective response to AIDS. This model, consistent with Mancur Olson's theory of individual and group behavior in the face of a collective interest, provides a partial but significant explanation for the apparently slow response of the high-risk groups to the threat of HIV infection.

The collective interest in controlling the spread of HIV infection may seem obvious, but it needs to be articulated for the purposes of the analysis. Because the virus is invisible and its consequences so socially and economically devastating, it would seem to everyone's advantage to promote measures that limit the spread of the infection. The diffusion of HIV infection out into the population can be viewed as a "collective bad": collective because it is effectively impossible to prevent large numbers of people from engaging in those behaviors that will bring them into contact with the virus and because many of the benefits of prevention will spill over to society at large.[8] The imagery of a collective bad is even more powerful since many people do not know they are infected (and can pass the infection on to someone else) and may remain asymptomatic for a long time.

The epidemiological evidence suggested early on that the spread of HIV infection was concentrated among a few groups: gay men, IV drug users, and their sexual partners. Some minority communities, by virtue of the numbers of people who fell into these categories, became areas of high prevalence in their own right. The early mobilization of any of these groups to control the spread of HIV infection is a function of several variables: the degree of perceived risk (and by extension the perceived value of risk reduction), the costs of risk reduction, the efficacy of risk reduction, and the size of the group.[9] Where the risk is perceived to be low, the group large, the efficacy of protection uncertain, and the "costs" of prevention high (in sexual freedom and in drug-taking ritual), little mobilization can be expected. This was essentially the situation during the early period of the epidemic. Alternatively, if risks were considered high, the group small, the efficacy of prevention certain, and the costs low, it would be reasonable to expect a mobilization to control the epidemic.[10]

Many members of the gay community and even some public health officials believed that control of the spread of the epidemic would be arrived at internally. In the face of the threat of AIDS, the affected groups, especially the gay community, would organize and develop workable prevention strategies on their own. The logic of collective action, however, suggests otherwise: As long as the perceived risk of infection remained low and the membership of the group was large, no mobilization of the group to control the spread of infection would be forthcoming.[11] In Olson's terms, the groups potentially affected by AIDS could be expected to remain *latent* until the calculus of transmission changed dramatically. Most people would not deem it in their interest to make the changes necessary to control the spread of the infection (i.e., engaging in "safe sex") when the potential reduction in personal and group risk appeared so small.

There are several additional explanations why the "payoffs" of these risky encounters might overwhelm the perceived harms. First, the carrier or partner may be ignorant of the presence of infection, or the person at risk may be ignorant of his or her partner's other activities. Second, even if people are aware of the possibility of infection, the probability of transmission may be quite small for a single encounter. Further, in situations of passion or craving, a one-in-one-thousand chance of transmission may not seem as consequential as it might be when viewed from a coldly rational perspective. Finally, the "rewards" of sex and drug taking are obviously powerful inducements to behave in ways that are clearly not in a person's long-term best interests. One has only to look at the recent history of efforts to control venereal disease, teenage pregnancy, or overall drug abuse to appreciate the stubbornness of these behaviors despite public interventions.[12] The problem of controlling the transmission of HIV among intravenous drug users is especially difficult because there are significant ethical and legal objections to preventing transmission without addressing drug abuse and because the behaviors associated with needle sharing are elusive and ritualistic.

Examining the collective-action aspects of the AIDS epidemic provides three important insights about the role and performance of public health officials. First, the underlying dynamics of the transmission of HIV infection suggest that no aggressive and rapid group response—especially among the IV drug-using population—would emerge early in the epidemic. Second, analysis of the collective-action properties of the epidemic suggests what kinds of public health strategies are indicated and what others are less defensible. Third, and more important for the public health official, an understanding of the collective-action dimension of this problem provides insight into the special political dynamics that will exist during the initial stage of the epidemic. In particular, public health officials should not expect the immediate formation of a constituency for a public-health-based "reasonable AIDS policy"; they should instead anticipate disproportionate influence from small existing groups with peripheral agendas. In many states a rapid and politically powerful response to AIDS was generated by groups with a conservative moral agenda not specific to AIDS. This phenomenon can be explained in part as "by-product" behavior; because such groups are fairly small, narrowly directed, and extant, it is relatively easy for them to shift their effort to an issue that overlaps many of their members' interests.

This theoretical discussion suggests that the choice whether to intervene or not is a choice between two equally ineffective alternatives. First, in order to intervene effectively, the commissioner must affect the risk/reward perceptions of people so as to alter their sexual and drug-taking behavior in very specific ways that violate strongly held social norms and values in the high-risk group. Such behavior change is unlikely, and the disease control, ineffective. Second, to refrain from intervention and let nature limit the disease will probably mean that the prevalence of AIDS will reach very high levels before it flattens out. There is some evidence that, without intervention, prevalence can reach levels above 50 percent in some communities, a disastrous outcome. When both these ineffective outcomes are considered soberly, the prospects for rapid and effective control of AIDS look extremely disheartening to a public health commissioner.

The theory that responds to problems of collective action suggests three possible resolutions to the AIDS quandary. Coercion, the exercise of the police powers of state, is a direct and obvious response. Public health officials are empowered both by statute and by tradition to employ coercive measures in the face of such a compelling threat to health as AIDS. For reasons that will be discussed below, however, the use of aggressive public-health police powers for this epidemic met with overwhelming political and logistical obstacles. A second response, based on the so-called by-product theory of organization, relies on the existence of an already-mobilized group to promote or take action for interests that are secondary to their membership. The already-organized gay community in San Francisco, for example, might have been expected to transfer their considerable organizational and political skills (as by-product behavior) to the fight against AIDS, but their response was delayed because fighting AIDS directly conflicted with many of the deeply held values of the gay population: sexual freedom, civil rights, and assimilation into the larger political community. The logic of collective action suggests something about the pattern of interest-group response during the early period of the epidemic: Groups that exist for some other purpose will be first and most effective in mobilizing a response. A public health official who perceives his or her role as a dispassionate broker of interests in AIDS policy should understand that there is no reason to expect those interests to be the same as his or her own or as those of other groups. The third theoretical resolution to this problem requires the emergence of political entrepreneurship. Although this attribute was evident in the leadership provided within groups, such as the Shanti Project in San Francisco and the Gay Men's Health Crisis in New York, and in the scientific research community, there are few striking examples of political entrepreneurship in state and municipal public health departments during the early experience with AIDS.

The meaning of all this for the job of the public health executive is primarily that mobilization to control the spread of AIDS should not have been expected to develop indigenously among the affected high-risk groups during the initial phase of the epidemic. People who engage in ''consensual'' risky behavior apparently had little to gain and much to lose by acting in the collective interest. The public health executive is, in effect, the steward of that collective interest. This role carries perhaps the most difficult public policy responsibility: altering individual behavior. Ronald Bayer poses this responsibility in stark terms:

> The only effective public health strategy for limiting or slowing the further spread of HTLV-III infection is one that will produce dramatic, perhaps unprecedented changes in the behavior of millions of men and women in this country. Such changes will demand alterations in behavior that are linked to deep biological and physiological drives and desires. They will demand acts of restraint and even deprivation for extended periods, if not for the lifetimes of those infected and those most at risk of being infected.[13]

The mobilization of groups is significant not only for the purposes of ''self-restraint'' but also for the purposes of exerting political influence on public health officials, state legislatures, and governors. The logic of collective action indicates that small groups, even those whose *raison d'être* may be peripheral to the development of AIDS policy, will dominate large, diffuse latent groups who are centrally concerned with or even defined by the AIDS epidemic. In addition to these factors, there are a number of other characteristics of the AIDS issue which further erode the public health officials' ability to respond. These features are weaker sources of impossibility.

A Weak Impossibility Theorem

In addition to being strictly impossible, controlling AIDS is effectively impossible because of the particular characteristics of the problem and the constraints on the office.

Technical features of the virus. The virus itself has characteristics that complicate the question of intervention. The overarching problem for public health officials is the absence of any solid data about the prevalence of HIV infection (as opposed to diagnosed AIDS) in the population, both nationally and in smaller geographical subdivisions. Until it manifests symptoms of opportunistic infections, the HIV virus is invisible to both possible carrier and potential receiver. Only through testing and retesting for antibody to the virus can people know if they have been exposed and are potential carriers. Even upon retesting there is no guarantee that person is not infected; there is some evidence that for certain people a considerable delay may occur between the time of infection and the generation of detectable antibodies. Uncertainty about the vehicles of transmission for the virus also has enormous implications for the conduct of state and local AIDS policy.[14] There is also uncertainty and disagreement among professionals about the efficacy of various forms of prevention, even the so-called safe sex measures that have been widely promoted as a response to AIDS.

Although it has been clearly established that the virus is not spread through casual contact, public health officials have had difficulty conveying the degrees of riskiness of transmission in terms that are meaningful to the public. In the Kokomo, Indiana, case in which Ryan White was denied admission to the local public schools because he was antibody positive, Dr. Woodward Meyers, the state health commissioner, was placed in the position of having to deny that there was "no risk" of transmission, even though the risk was extremely small relative to other hazards the students routinely face in the conduct of their daily lives. The fact that the public health commissioner could not guarantee the absolute safety of the other students did little to dispel the hysteria surrounding this case.

The difficulty of dispassionately articulating the risks of AIDS to the public— currently one of the key functions of public health officials—is further complicated by the rapidly changing nature and interpretation of the data. The early history of policymaking for AIDS has been marked by significantly conflicting evidence from "experts" about the extent of infection in the population, the modes of transmission (e.g., whether AIDS can be passed along through tears or by mosquitoes), and especially the risks of heterosexual contagion. Even the surgeon general has contributed to the confusion surrounding transmission, first warning that AIDS was about to "break out in the heterosexual" community and later reversing his position. As an example of how uncertainty has been fueled in the day-to-day media presentation, the CBS morning news in late 1985 presented an expert from the University of California who stated that heterosexual transmission from women to men was rare, followed by an expert from Harvard University who declared this statement to be incorrect.

Civil Liberties and the Limits of Public Health Law. Public health executives operate in an environment of law which provides only certain avenues of vested authority. Much of the law that authorizes and facilitates public health intervention predates the civil rights era, the Warren Court, and the associated vast body of constitutional interpretation that broadened the scope of individual rights and protection of privacy while weakening state police powers.[15] Larry Gostin, who has extensively examined the relationship of existing public health law and the policy demands of AIDS, concludes that

> procedural and substantive elements are conspicuously absent from most public health statutes, which have little regard for the price, in terms of restriction of individual rights, exacted by the exercise of compulsory powers. The powers provided in public health statutes are overly restrictive, largely reliant upon outdated concepts of full isolation or quarantine. . . . There are also no clearly stated criteria to guide public officials in the exercise of their powers. Thus society, through its legislature, has not enunciated the circumstances under which public health decisions are to be made. This leaves the delicate balance between public protection and individual rights to the unfettered, largely unreviewable discretion of public health officials.[16]

The absence of a contemporary legal framework for public health interventions for AIDS merely begs the larger question of how concerns for individual liberty, autonomy, privacy, and stigmatization should be balanced against the rights of society to restrain individuals in the name of controlling communicable disease. In the case of AIDS these are largely uncharted waters, and different states have struck markedly different bargains between the concerns of liberty and control. In Georgia the state pursued the legitimacy of employing antisodomy statutes all the way to the U.S. Supreme Court, ultimately prevailing over a divided bench. In the daily work of public health, however, there are no easy and direct answers to this dilemma of liberty and control, yet public health action requires implicit positions on these issues.

In the absence of new legislative initiative in public health, executives need to find ways of exploiting existing statutes. When Dr. David Axelrod, the commissioner of health in New York State, decided to take action against the bathhouses in New York City, he had to resort to some antiquated provisions of the state sanitary code to legally regulate high-risk behavior in bathhouses. As discussed below, Dr. Mervyn Silverman in San Francisco had questions about his legal authority to close bathhouses, and ultimately his actions were overturned by the court.

The Limits of Public Health "Technology." The traditional weapons of public health policy—testing, registry, quarantine, surveillance, and contact tracing (approaches that have had mixed success in the control of sexually transmitted and other infectious diseases)—have been at the center of the debate about public health policy. Each of these methods provides very limited and problematic weapons for a public health official attempting to control transmission.[17]

At a technical level there is great controversy over the meaning and accuracy of the testing procedure itself. The test indicates only that a person has antibodies to HIV infection, not that he or she has or even necessarily will develop symptomatic AIDS. However, people who are seropositive have the potential to pass on the AIDS virus and should be the focus of the control effort. Because the test is not perfectly reliable, a significant number of initial false positives will occur in a low-risk population. Positive findings have devastating effects on those tested, and the possibility that a majority of people identified as HIV positive would be incorrectly labeled is a strong counterargument to those who advocate testing in the general population as the first line of a public health strategy. To carry out such antibody testing and counseling in the population at large would be expensive, and many critics argue that public health resources could be much more efficiently employed in other prevention activities.

If the meaning and accuracy of the tests are troublesome, then the accumulation of test results in a registry compounds these problems. The list itself could be inaccurate, and opportunities would arise for breaches of confidentiality. Many fear that mandatory reporting combined with the existence of registries may discourage high-risk people from seeking out the test—in effect, driving high-risk behavior further underground. Colorado, for example, has required that all positive antibody tests be reported to state and local health departments on the grounds that these agencies need to know who is infectious. Carriers can then be counseled about their own status and the possibilities of transmission for epidemiological purposes as well as notified if and when an antiviral agent was developed.[18] Colorado has apparently managed to protect the confidentiality of these reports, but elsewhere there have been isolated incidents of disclosure that have fueled fears that invasion of privacy and discrimination may accompany registration of cases.

Contact tracing, a technique for identifying and counseling the partners of a known case, has been used to prevent the spread of sexually transmitted diseases since the early part of the century. A person identified as infectious is asked to provide names and addresses of sexual or drug-using partners, who are subsequently contacted and advised of the potential of infection. These techniques require a substantial invasion of privacy and cooperative effort. When a person becomes known to authorities as someone who continues to put others at risk, many have suggested the use of quarantine to isolate the infected man or woman and prevent further spread of the virus. Public health authorities in Florida and Texas have resorted to quarantine for brief periods, though the compulsory isolation of people pushes the boundaries of public health law and seriously infringes on individual liberties.[19]

In sum, the traditional arsenal of public health approaches leaves public health officials with a very weak and troublesome set of alternatives for combating AIDS. Identifying who is infectious, the foundation of any preventive effort, is problematic because of weaknesses in the test itself. Methods such as registration and contact tracing that build upon the identification of HIV-positive people perpetuate the weakness of the test and introduce new problems of confidentially, civil liberties, and ultimately effectiveness. One of the major challenges facing the public health executive is an intellectual one: how to develop, out of whole cloth, a new arsenal of public health strategies for dealing with this problem.

Constraints Imposed by the External Environment: Public Opinion. The climate of public opinion and fear is one of the most subtle instrumentalities of the public health executive's job. At a certain level of intensity and in certain forms, public attention is the greatest resource available to the public health executive. The only way to generate widespread behavioral change is by exposing the risks of transmission, yet it is exactly this exposure that can generate hostility, discrimination, stigmatization, and backlash toward affected groups. Interacting with public opinion surrounding AIDS is a subtle problem of rhetoric, where the choice of language has significant implications for the willingness of people to come forward and be tested and ultimately for the societal treatment of those with AIDS.[20]

At the state and city level, the major catalyst of public attention has been the emergent political debate about testing, reporting requirements, and quarantine. The vast publicity that has attended these debates, however, is a mixed blessing in the effort to control AIDS. Although the public health official wants to do everything possible to raise the consciousness of the populace about AIDS, there is a fine line where consciousness turns to hysteria. The regrettable treatment of children with AIDS who have attempted to register for school in Kokomo, Indiana; Arcadia, Florida; and New York City has demonstrated that a very subtle game of public education and public relations needs to be played in this area. The management of public opinion stands out as the most important and most difficult task of public health executives. Without raising sufficient concern, people will not change their behavior. When concern tips over into hysteria, however, both the political options and educational mission of the executive become extremely closely limited.

Resources. Although resource constraints are almost automatically on any list of what makes a public sector job difficult or impossible, the problem of resource constraints in policymaking for AIDS is somewhat unique. Many health agencies have experienced large infusions of funds to respond to AIDS but have had difficulty developing their organizational capability quickly enough to spend these resources intelligently and in a cost-effective manner. Between fiscal years 1984 and 1988, state-only funding for AIDS programs increased fifteenfold, from $9.3

million to $156 million. These funding levels do not include state and local use of federal funds, Medicaid, or municipal expenditures. The city of San Francisco, for example, reported spending $17.5 million of its own funds in fiscal year 1988.[21]

Further, although resources are increasing rapidly, the even more rapid increase in the numbers of infected and symptomatic people constantly outstrips the public effort. The New York City experience is instructive: In 1988, the city and state plan to spend about $15 million for prevention and education efforts. This effort is large relative to previous outlays but pales when one considers that there may be half a million people who are carriers of the virus. An expenditure of $15 million for prevention and education represents 6 percent of public spending on AIDS (including healthcare) and about .1 percent of all spending.[22]

Despite the significant increases in resources that have been captured by many public health departments, the successes and failures of public health officials in this epidemic have been largely defined by their performance in several test issues. In the public eye, the most significant questions during the early period of the epidemic have been the regulation of bathhouses, the dispensing of free needles to IV drug users, and the implementation of mandatory premarital screening for HIV antibody. These issues reveal the predicament faced by public health officials in three venues and illustrate the sharply divisive political responses that compound the already-difficult task of reacting quickly and forthrightly to the emerging epidemic.

CLOSING BATHHOUSES: DR. MERVYN SILVERMAN

No public health official was more visibly engaged in the early fight against the AIDS epidemic than Dr. Mervyn Silverman, the director of the San Francisco Department of Public Health. Silverman was in many respects all alone on the leading edge of the epidemic, trying to develop from scratch an educational, prevention, and treatment program during a period when knowledge about the epidemic was very sparse and there was enormous uncertainty about its future course.[23] Perhaps the paradigmatic example of managing both the political and public health dimensions of the early AIDS epidemic is the saga of regulating the bathhouses that serve the gay community in San Francisco. The regulation of bathhouses is an interesting study because it places in sharp relief the "old" traditions of public health against the modern view of public health management as an essentially political undertaking. Indeed, even in the sixteenth century public steam baths were a major target of the effort to control the spread of communicable disease.[24]

In the early 1980s the bathhouses in the San Francisco gay community were nationally if not internationally known enterprises for anonymous sex with multiple partners. Beginning in 1982 many in the public health community recognized that these sites could be contributing to the spread of infection, and there were numerous demands for the health commissioner to use the police power to close the facilities. Even Mayor Dianne Feinstein approached Silverman in 1982 about closing the bathhouses, fearing the contagion that might be occurring and possibly looking ahead to the image problems she might face later. For his part, Silverman saw the problem of managing the spread of the epidemic as more complicated than closing facilities; he wanted to maintain a relationship with the gay community that would be cooperative and supportive, not paternalistic.[25] He feared that a heavy-handed effort to close the bathhouses could simply drive high-risk behavior underground and make the long-term public health effort more confrontational. He argued: "If I'm going to change behavior, I have to do it as a protective measure, not as a policeman. You don't get people to change behavior too much as a cop."[26] He also had doubts about the health department's legal authority to regulate or close the bathhouses since the police department was responsible for licensing these enterprises.

The debate over what to do about the bathhouses in San Francisco was acrimonious and divisive. Opponents of the bathhouses were accused of being homophobic; supporters were accused of being homicidal. Silverman first undertook to encourage "voluntary" cooperation by the owners in the effort to control transmission. His second move was directed at eliminating sexual activity in these facilities. Not until October 1984 did Silverman order that several of the San Francisco bathhouses be closed. This step was taken after the mayor had dispatched her own undercover squad of policemen to gather evidence in the baths and then called on Silverman to "have the guts" to close the baths and "to not count hands to see what is popular." In November a judge in fact determined that the baths could reopen, though only under a set of rules designed to limit the practice of unsafe sex. Silverman announced his resignation in December after control of the health department was placed directly in the hands of the mayor.

Silverman's tenure in San Francisco demonstrates the extreme challenge that AIDS can present to a public health official. By all accounts, Silverman was a respected, competent, and effective public health official with exceptional political savvy. In the case of the baths, Silverman chose to rely on the autonomous action of the gay community as the vehicle of control. As late as 1984 he stated that "any action on [the baths] is going to have to come from the gay community, not my office." His approach presumed that the group would in fact mobilize and not remain latent during the critical period when the epidemic was spreading. Silverman saw himself as a broker of political consensus, not a policeman. However, the gay community remained bitterly divided over policy toward the baths, leaving Silverman with little tangible support for his "political" solution to a public health problem. In the end, few were happy with Silverman's performance: He has been criticized for being too timid and vacillating, as well as for being too aggressive and heavy-handed with the gay community.

DISPENSING NEEDLES: DR. STEPHEN JOSEPH

In New York City, a major route of transmission of HIV infection has been through the sharing of needles among the IV drug-using population. Making inroads into this source has stymied public health officials everywhere, but in New York City the problem is especially severe because of the extreme mismatch between the number of addicts and the number of treatment slots available. By 1988 there were an estimated two hundred thousand IV drug users in New York City, with 50 to 60 percent of them estimated to be already infected with the virus. There were, at most, about twenty-five thousand treatment slots. Advocacy for more treatment of IV drug users by public health officials raises a conflict between substance abuse programs and public health. Construing their public health mandate strictly, public health officials have been wrestling with the distribution of clean needles as a second-best approach to the transmission of HIV infection through IV drug use.

Dr. Stephen Joseph, the New York City health commissioner, followed his predecessor Dr. David Spencer in advocating the distribution of free needles, believing that the pace and consequences of the epidemic were more important than the obvious negative symbolism of a government seeming to promote drug abuse. Joseph had been publicizing the idea of a free needles program but had failed to convince Mayor Koch or State Health Commissioner David Axelrod. Numerous interest groups were also opposed to the message that was implicit in needle distribution. Dr. Beny J. Primm of the Addiction Research and Treatment Corporation argued that "if we had enough treatment programs and we made them attractive enough, we wouldn't need a needle program." Sterling Johnson, the city's special prosecutor for narcotics cases, suggested that "the next logical step would be the creation of city-supervised shooting galleries to insure that sanitary needles were being used. . . . Aren't you implicitly saying that New York is the place to come if you want to do drugs?" Even Archbishop John Cardinal O'Connor openly objected to the appearance of assisting drug abuse that is part and parcel of a needle dispensing program.

Nonetheless, Joseph continued to promote the concept of a needle distribution program both publicly and privately among city and state officials. His major political weapon became the numbers themselves, which showed substantial growth in the prevalence of HIV infection among addicts and considerable crossover of the virus to partners of IV drug users and their children. The public health intelligentsia had also given cautious support to the idea of dispensing needles, based on some evidence of its effectiveness in Europe.[27] The compromise struck in early 1988 was a test program in which two hundred participants in treatment would be given free needles. The rates of infection in this group would be compared to rates in a second group of two hundred that would not have access to free needles. For Joseph, the demonstration was a foot in the door, something that he hopes to expand into a larger program over time. Many critics believe the test program is a poor solution. Not only is the wrong symbolic message delivered, but the numbers enrolled will be too small to make an impact or demonstrate potential effectiveness.

The dynamic here is again instructive: Joseph, acting on his best instincts as a public health official, confronts opponents as diverse as federal drug officials and the Roman Catholic church. Any step he takes must have the approval of not only the mayor but also the state health commissioner and, by extension, the governor. On one side are the primary beneficiaries of this policy (IV drug users), who are not a "constituency" in the conventional sense and who have little legitimacy in the state political arena. On the other side are the pressure groups, mobilized against the needle distribution program as a by-product of their other agendas— law enforcement, resources for treatment, or the promotion of a certain morality. Any countervailing constituency of drug users who are potentially at risk of HIV infection is at best latent. The resolution to this quandary is a weak public health policy that satisfies noone.

MANDATORY PREMARITAL TESTING: DR. BERNARD TURNOCK

One of the best illustrations of the public health executive's predicament in confronting AIDS is captured by the experience of Dr. Bernard Turnock, the director of public health in the state of Illinois. The attempt to construct an AIDS policy in Illinois placed many of the social, political, and administrative issues visibly in a political context and set the stage for the development of AIDS policy elsewhere. As former Secretary of Education William Bennett indicated in 1987: "Illinois is a test case for the nation. What is decided by Governor Thompson will set the agenda for the nation." Turnock came into the AIDS debate with an excellent reputation as a public health official. He had taken over a department that was in disarray (his predecessor was dismissed after refusing to return from a vacation in Cancun during a salmonella outbreak in the state) and had built a competent organization. Many observers saw the appointment of Turnock as a movement toward depoliticization and professionalization of the department.

The effort to gear up for controlling AIDS in Illinois was conditioned in part by the experience of the states that sustained the first wave of exposure to AIDS— California and New York. In terms of numbers of cases, Illinois and Chicago were three to four years behind New York and California and their principal cities. In terms of public visibility, however, the climate for policymaking and control in Illinois was strongly influenced by the growing national media attention, especially the attention garnered by the highly publicized school cases in New York and Indiana. The Department of Public Health in Illinois responded in a forthright and mostly conventional manner. An interdisciplinary task force was created to advise the department about the content and resource requirements of a state AIDS policy. The department also developed a surveillance capacity, mounted an AIDS education campaign, established an informational hotline, conducted surveys of AIDS knowledge and of behavior increasing the risk of infection, and channeled state and federal funds to a variety of testing and control projects.

At each step, the development of an AIDS campaign was the managerial equivalent of walking on eggshells. For example, in the midst of implementing a wide-ranging educational program, Turnock and his department were stung by the revelation that among the publicly funded projects was the commissioning of a rap music jingle called "The Condom Rag," which had explicit and, to some, objectionable lyrics. In a press conference, the governor angrily demanded the shelving of the song, calling it "garbage, plain garbage." Although the jingle was a tiny piece of the overall plan, the highly publicized reaction served to undermine Turnock's management of the AIDS campaign. The episode illustrated once again the fragility of public and political sensibilities when it comes to sex and drugs, even in the face of a serious lethal epidemic.

In 1987 the AIDS policy, and eventually Turnock himself, became a cause célèbre in the state. Reflecting the fears and concerns of constituents, state lawmakers introduced sixty-nine pieces of AIDS legislation, with most of the bills directed at the prevention and control activities of the public health department. The major impetus for this onslaught came from a small but articulate group of conservative legislators interested in promoting a social agenda and protecting the population at *low risk*. State Senator Aldo DeAngelis, the author of a bill to require the department to trace the sexual partners of people who tested positive for AIDS and to quarantine some under court order, argued that strong medicine, even in the presence of low risk, was necessary. "My greatest concern is that the greatest increase in AIDS cases will be in the heterosexual population, and those people don't really think they are at risk. What happened is that the high risk groups took over the issue as exclusively theirs, and it isn't. AIDS education has worked very well for high-risk groups, but education alone won't work as well among heterosexuals, because most don't believe they will be affected."

Director Turnock initially opposed the conservative package of legislation that required compulsory premarital testing, contract tracing, and quarantine, contending that the department already had through existing law the power to conduct many of the measures proposed in the legislation and that legislative efforts would be more appropriately expended on education and prevention among high-risk groups. No sooner had Turnock expressed his opposition than his reconfirmation as director of the department was delayed, held hostage by proponents of the AIDS legislation. Despite the interests and efforts of the Chicago gay community, no countervailing constituency or alternative consensus emerged to defeat the legislature's public health strategy. Turnock subsequently dropped his public resistance to the legislation, noting that "after a discussion with the Governor, I saw that there was no overt harm in looking at it again. If we can show good faith in working with the General Assembly to codify our existing practices to reach a solution which does not cross the boundary of doing damage, we're ready to do it."

With his opposition relaxed, Turnock was quickly reconfirmed by the senate.

Of the sixty-nine bills introduced, seventeen were eventually passed and forwarded to the governor. After prolonged consideration, the governor took the middle ground, signing the least controversial bills, rewriting many provisions, and vetoing a law that would have required the Department of Public Health to trace contacts of HIV-positive cases back seven years. Under the legislative package that was enacted, the Department of Public Health was authorized to conduct voluntary contact tracing in situations where there is "reasonable belief" of HIV infection and, where there was a court order, to quarantine those who represented a significant threat to the public health. The most controversial element of this package was the requirement of mandatory antibody testing in order to obtain a marriage license. The requirement was nationally criticized (from an editorial in the *New York Times* to a statement by the surgeon general that "he could not imagine a worse way to spend your money") and drew widespread opposition within the state.

In the final analysis, however, Turnock and his department dodged a bullet. The legislative package made no overt and significant demands on the director to change existing approaches to the control of AIDS. The director retained his job. Moreover, the intensity of the public debate probably served to further enlighten a portion of the population about the risks and import of AIDS transmission. One interpretation of the AIDS drama that was played out in Illinois is that the outcome was secondary; the debate itself was a strategy of information, education, and prevention.[28] On the other hand, for all the explosive political discussion, little in the way of a new AIDS control strategy emerged from the legislation. The director paid a heavy personal price for his compromise and loyalty to the governor. This chronicle illustrates above all how limited and derivative is the authority of the public health director. At critical points in the development of an AIDS policy and in the evolution of the legislative package, the director's authority and ability to conduct a public campaign for the interests of his department was undermined by the governor.

COPING WITH AN IMPOSSIBLE TASK

If the logic of collective action is at work beneath the AIDS epidemic, then policymaking and public management that benignly rely on individual responsibility merely defer a collective response to AIDS until the level of infection in the population reaches chilling proportions. A passive stance by public health officials that expects people to incorporate the mounting evidence about risks of transmission can be likened to "waiting for Godot." In the end, it is a negative and irresponsible strategic response to this problem. On the other hand, public health executives have few political resources with which to wage the AIDS battle. In the early period of transmission, any constituency arising solely for the purposes of developing an AIDS policy can be expected to remain latent. Instead, what will surface are numerous small groups, particularly those with a moral agenda, who can mobilize quickly to promote their version of an AIDS response as a by-product of their primary group purpose. The political executive is unlikely to provide much support in this environment: In the cases of Drs. Silverman, Joseph, and Turnock, their respective mayors and governors were all opposing or undercutting their public health positions at significant points in the debate.

Arrayed against the seeming intractability of the problem of controlling AIDS are the enormous stakes involved as the virus spreads and its consequences begin to be felt. Coping with this situation at a personal level requires a strategic map, a benchmark against which executive choices and expenditures of time, political capital, energy, and intellect can be judged. The argument developed in this chapter suggests the following propositions for the conduct of the public health executive's job.

1) The job of controlling the spread of HIV infection is primarily a task of achieving external influence, ultimately attempting to affect the actions of people engaging in risky behavior.

The historical record in public health and in other areas of public policy suggests that behavior modification will at best be modest and partial and may ultimately have little to do with the actions of the policy leadership. Positive coping requires persistence in spite of these odds, as well as recognition that marginal differences in the trajectory of an epidemic that is fatal and exponential *are* consequential, even if no credit is given for marginal (and invisible) impacts.

2) The utilization of symbols is one of the few tools that the public health official qua individual has at his or her disposal.

The job of managing AIDS policy also requires the heavy use of symbols to convey messages that have political and educational content.[29] Officials who exploit symbols utilize one of the few resources that are available to influence individual behavior. When a chef in a prestigious Sacramento restaurant died of AIDS, California Health Director Ken Kizer took the opportunity to eat a much-publicized meal there. ''The Bon Appetit thing was a good example where I think we did more in a couple of hours to dispel some myths, to help some education, than you could have probably done with hundreds of hours of lectures. It was a symbolic thing, but if their business is any reflection, I think it turned a lot of people around.''[30]

Perhaps there is no better example of the power and utility of symbols and political leadership than Dr. C. Everett Koop, the highest public health officer in the nation. Koop was an unlikely candidate for implementing an aggressive national AIDS prevention campaign. He was brought into the administration in part for his strong pro-life views and was believed to be primarily a champion of its conservative social agenda. Instead, Surgeon General Koop fashioned a frank and controversial personal campaign that pushed his standing and support in the administration to the limit. Most important for the purposes of this study, Koop maximized his use of symbols in the personal performance of his job. Whenever he testified as surgeon general, he wore the striking military garb of his office and used the language of a general going to war. Partly as a result of this orchestrated effort to win the hearts and minds of people at risk, C. Everett Koop has become a household name. He inculcated an esprit de corps in his service that was very impressive.

Certainly at the state and municipal level the opportunities for public exposure and influence are less dramatic than those available to the surgeon general. Nonetheless, the opportunities for a public presence in this issue must be exploited. The proper imagery is probably less that of a general launching a war than of a guerrilla fighter seeking to make small inroads into the difficult and persistent problems of behaviors not in the individual's or society's interest.

3) The ossification of public health "technology" means that there is also room for the creation of new approaches by the exercise of intellectual effort, in order to chip away at groups and problems that public health has historically had little success in reaching.

Much of the debate about AIDS policy has been dictated by old and questionable public health approaches. Although new methods will be difficult to develop, market, and implement, this task should occupy a large share of the executive's effort. Techniques of using the mass media offer the best prospects for public health innovation.[31] In New York an ambitious and frank campaign has been mounted through a collaborative effort of public health officials and advertising agencies working *pro bono*. As Dr. Joseph suggests, the aggressive use of the media asserts the tradition of vigorous public health intervention without the downside of highly coercive, liberty-depriving measures. "I hope when the controversy erupts, that our purpose is not to assault taste. . . . But the Department of Health is not the guardian of public morality. We are the guardian of public health."[32] In Washington, D.C., Commissioner of Health Reed Tuckson has recruited rock musicians to develop an unusual media strategy for AIDS prevention.

4) The creation of an appropriate legal framework for public health means that AIDS policymaking is an inherently political undertaking.

Political leadership requires careful navigation around the shoals of executive authority, the will of the legislature, the sometimes ferocious pressures of special-interest groups, and the tolerances of public opinion.[33] The engineering of a workable legislative and legal context requires the acknowledgment that AIDS is first and foremost a political problem; it then requires careful attention to the applied problems of agenda formation that accompany this issue.[34] Public health executives who most energetically respond to the epidemic perceive the importance of political management. It has been said that Mervyn Silverman believed that "all public health policy was basically political; as someone who relished public approbation, he was a good politician. It was his strength as a public official."[35] Stephen Joseph also observed that "politicization is a good thing, because it brings all that leverage and attention to the issue."

5) Public health officials should see the struggle to control the spread of HIV infection as an opportunity to reassert the traditional mission and authority of public health.

Simply defining AIDS as a political problem and managing it as such does little to limit the impossibility of the task. For Silverman, conceiving the management of the epidemic as a problem of brokering political interests in San Francisco overshadowed the traditional public health concern of fighting contagion. Without a narrow focus on the demands of public health, the public health executive could become paralyzed by the ambiguity of the task. AIDS carries too many civil-libertarian, ethical, special-interest, cultural, and political implications for the public health executive to be attentive to all concerns. Those who have been personally most successful in waging war against the epidemic—with Koop standing as the most visible example—have dared to confront political resistance, instead of searching for accommodation and consensus.

Further, approaching the management of AIDS as essentially a political problem will be foreign and antithetical to the skills and personalities of many who have selected this profession. As Martin Rein has pointed out, there are fundamental differences in the games of science and politics.

The games of science seek to establish patterns of experience that all may share. They are value neutral in the sense that they are deliberately designed to filter out the values of the participants so as to arrive at unbiased "truth.". . . . The proper posture for a gamesman of science must be one of restraint, dispassion, conservatism, the willingness to suspend belief pending more evidence. The games of politics are quite different. They are designed to find one purpose or course of action acceptable to individuals who have begun the play by espousing diverse purposes, values, and actions. . . . The proper posture for a gamesman of politics is one of boldness, persistence, opportunism; the good gamesman is able to mobilize and sustain belief and commitment.[36]

The conflicts between these two games have been most apparent in Bernard Turnock's confrontations with the state legislature in Illinois. As Senator DeAngelis observed of Turnock's approach to AIDS and the legislature: "Health officials want to be clinically correct. The General Assembly wants to be a bit more reactive. I think that sometimes it's extremely difficult for a professional in a field to adjust to the political world as well . . . because they tend to be purists."[37] Despite the demands for scientific integrity in the various aspects of public health work, including the surveillance and reporting of AIDS, the importance of political acumen to this policy area cannot be understated.[38]

CONCLUSION

With the emergence of AIDS in the early 1980s, the job of many state and municipal public health officials shifted from one that was largely "possible" to the stewardship of controlling an epidemic. The major source of impossibility that AIDS introduces into the job is the intractability of sexual and drug-taking behavior that underlies transmission of HIV infection. This transmission has basic properties of collective behavior that make prevention and risk reduction an especially problematic public health undertaking in the early years of the epidemic. Moreover, the logic of collective action suggests that the political dynamics will be stacked against executives who seek an expedited response. Groups centrally concerned with the prevention of HIV infection have been relatively slow to emerge and highly fractured; they have confronted highly articulated special interests who engaged AIDS policies as a by-product of their primary agenda. To make matters more difficult, AIDS presents problems of uncertainty, law, public health strategy, and public opinion that severely constrain the possibilities for control. Although managing this epidemic calls for both political and technical competence, neither of these skills is sufficient by itself. Mervyn Silverman of San Francisco received heavy criticism for being too "political" in his approach to the regulation of bathhouses. Bernard Turnock of Illinois was criticized for being too much of a public health "purist" who did not thrive in the rough-and-tumble world of Illinois politics. The public health management of the AIDS epidemic necessarily brings the conflict between these "games of politics" and "games of science" into sharp relief.

Because the prevalence of HIV infection is largely invisible and its progression—conversion to symptoms, sickness, and death—occurs sometime in the future, the efforts of public health executives to affect the transmission of infection will go virtually unrewarded. Indeed, as the steady, inevitable progression of AIDS mortality and morbidity is broadcast monthly, the thesis that public health officials "failed" in their management and control of the AIDS epidemic will be continually reinforced.

NOTES

1. David Hume, *A Treatise of Human Nature* (London: J. M. Dent, 1952), p. 239.

2. This critique is presented in Lewis H. Kuller and Lawrence A. Kingsley, "The Epidemic of AIDS: A Failure of the Public Health Policy," *Millbank Quarterly* 64, 1 (Supplement) (1986): 56–78; Dennis Altman, *AIDS in the Mind of America* (Garden City, N.Y.: Anchor Press, 1987); and Randy Shilts, *And the Band Played On* (New York: St. Martin's Press, 1987). A more sympathetic account of the public health response is contained in Sandra Panem, *The AIDS Bureaucracy* (Cambridge, Mass.: Harvard University Press, 1988).

3. This example is discussed in Daniel M. Fox, "AIDS and the American Health Policy: A Comparative Perspective," *Millbank Quarterly* 64 (Supplement) (1986): 10.

4. See W. H. McNeill, *Plagues and Peoples* (Garden City, N.Y.: Anchor, 1976), and

Johan Goudsblom, *Sociology in the Balance: A Critical Essay* (New York: Columbia University Press, 1977).

5. See Ann Elder and Ira Cohen, "Major Cities and Disease Crises: A Comparative Perspective" (Paper delivered at the Midwest Political Science Association, 1988), and John Duffy, *A History of Public Health in New York City, 1866–1966* (New York: Russell Sage, 1974).

6. Fox, "AIDS and the American Health Policy," pp. 7–8.

7. Ronald Bayer, "AIDS, Power and Reason," *Millbank Quarterly* 64 (Supplement) (1986): 171.

8. The analysis is a mirror image of that which accompanies the provision of collective goods. In technical terms, it is effectively impossible to restrain people from engaging in behaviors that will put them at some risk of infection, and external benefits will accrue to society if the collective bad is reduced. See Russell Hardin, *Collective Action* (Baltimore: Johns Hopkins University Press for Resources for the Future, 1982), pp. 61–65.

9. See Mancur Olson, *The Logic of Collective Action* (Cambridge, Mass.: Harvard University Press, 1965). A simple formal model of the collective response to the epidemic sees individual behavior as a function of the value of group risk reduction and the "costs" of engaging in safe behaviors. The advantage (Ai) to individuals in joining a collective movement for safe behavior will reflect their own assessment of the value (Vi) of this collective good and its costs (C) such that $Ai = Vi - C$. The value of the gain from protection would be $Vg - (SgP)$, where Sg is the size of the group and P is the rate of protection that will occur from group behavior. The fraction of the benefit from a collective response will be $Fi = Vi/Vg$ and the gain to any individual will be $Vi = (FiPSg)$. The individual will respond in the collective interest only if $Fi > C/Vg$ or, in other words, if $Vi > C$. Even in this simplest case, during the early period of the epidemic all the calculus is working against the mobilization of a group response. The sizes (Sg) of the relevant risk groups are by any standard large, the rate of protective gain (P) small, and the fraction of benefit accruing to any individual will be small.

10. For the IV drug-using population, the application of this theory is obviously problematic. The assumption of rational behavior presents numerous complications in this case. Many practitioners in the substance abuse field, however, argue that addicts may be completely rational with respect to the risks of AIDS even though they are risk-takers in their other activities.

11. This problem is by no means unique to the control of AIDS. See Thomas Schelling, *Micromotives and Macrobehavior* (New York: W. W. Norton, 1984).

12. Allan M. Brandt has made the most direct historical demonstration of the limits of public intervention with respect to venereal disease. See his *No Magic Bullet: A Social History of Venereal Disease in the United States since 1880* (New York: Oxford University Press, 1987), and "AIDS in Historical Perspective: Four Lessons from the History of Sexually Transmitted Diseases," *American Journal of Public Health* 78, 4 (April 1988): 367–71.

13. Bayer, "AIDS, Power and Reason," p. 170.

14. James Allen and James Curran, "Prevention of AIDS and HIV Infection: Needs and Priorities for Epidemiological Research," *American Journal of Public Health* 78, 4 (April 1988): 381–86.

15. Ronald Bayer, *Private Acts, Social Consequences* (New York: Free Press, 1989), pp. 1–19.

16. Larry Gostin, "The Future of Communicable Disease Control: Toward a New Concept of Public Health Law," *Millbank Quarterly* 64 (Supplement) (1986): 81–82.

17. Larry Gostin and William J. Curran, "Legal Control Measures for AIDS: Reporting Requirements, Surveillance, Quarantine, and the Regulation of Public Meeting Places," *American Journal of Public Health* (February 1987): 214–18.

18. For a full description of the Colorado program and its rationale, see Franklyn N. Judson and Thomas M. Vernon, Jr., "The Impact of AIDS on State and Local Health Departments: Issues and a Few Answers," *American Journal of Public Health* 78, 4 (April 1988): 387–93.

19. For an extended discussion of the problems of quarantine as a strategy see David S. Musto, "Quarantine and the Problem of AIDS," *Millbank Quarterly* 64 (Supplement) (1986): 97–117.

20. See Paula A. Treichler, "AIDS, Gender, and Biomedical Discourse: Current Contests for Meaning," in *The Burdens of History,* ed. Elizabeth Fee and Daniel M. Fox (Berkeley: University of California Press, 1988), pp. 190–265; and Susan Sontag, *AIDS and Its Metaphors* (New York: Farrar, Straus, Giroux, 1989).

21. Mona J. Rowe and Caitlin C. Ryan, "Comparing State-only Expenditures for AIDS," *American Journal of Public Health* 78, 4 (April 1988): 424–29.

22. See Tom Boasberg, "New York Must Spend More on AIDS Education," *New York Times,* 11 July 1987, p. 19.

23. For a description of the San Francisco program see Mervyn F. Silverman, "San Francisco: Coordinated Community Response," in *AIDS: Public Policy Dimensions,* ed. John Griggs (New York: United Hospital Fund, 1986), pp. 170–81.

24. See, for example, Johan Goudsblom, "Public Health and the Civilizing Process," *Millbank Quarterly* 64, 2 (1986): 161–87.

25. Silverman's position is described more fully in Mervyn F. Silverman, "Public Health Policy in the Age of Politics," *AIDS and Public Policy Journal* 1, 1 (July 1986): 4–5.

26. Panem, *AIDS Bureaucracy,* p. 19.

27. June E. Osborn, "AIDS: Politics and Science," *New England Journal of Medicine* 318, 7 (February 18, 1988): 446.

28. Interview with Dr. Bernard Turnock in 1987.

29. See, for example, Murray Edelman, *Politics as Symbolic Action* (Chicago, Ill.: Markham, 1971).

30. Greg Lucas, "Ken Kizer: The State's High Profile Health Chief," *California Journal* (June 1987): 293.

31. See, for example, Kenneth Warner, "Television and Health Education: Stay Tuned," *American Journal of Public Health* (February 1987): 87–89.

32. Jane Gross, "Officials Fear Major Debate over New York AIDS Ads," *New York Times,* 11 May 1987).

33. For an extended discussion of the elements of political leadership in the context of managing a public agency, see Laurence E. Lynn, Jr., *Managing Public Policy* (Boston: Little, Brown, 1986), pp. 103–28.

34. See John Kingdon, *Agendas, Alternatives and Public Policy* (Boston: Little, Brown, 1984).

35. Shilts, *And the Band Played On,* p. 21.

36. Martin Rein, "Policy Research: Belief and Doubt," in *From Policy to Practice,* ed. Martin Rein (Armonk, N.Y.: Sharpe, 1983), p. 216.

37. Quoted in Michael D. Kiemens, "Bernard Turnock: Defamer of Illinois Chickens but Defender of Illinois Health," *Illinois Issues* (November 1988): 13.

38. For an introduction to the unique politics of AIDS policymaking see Ronald Bayer, "Five Dimensions to the Politics of AIDS," in *AIDS: Public Policy Dimensions,* pp. 23–33.

9

Consensus Prison Reform:
A Possible Dream

Fritz Byers

For the last thirty years the operation of prisons has been dominated by federal court orders. For decades before this era of judicial intrusion, prisons and jails enjoyed nearly total autonomy, the result of a judicially declared hands-off policy. This principle of restraint fit conveniently with the prevailing societal view of prisons as a world apart. Prison walls served a critical dual function: They locked prisoners in, and they kept them out of sight. In this earlier view, an escape from prison had overtones of an interstellar penetration (a perception that no longer seems to attach to escapes). In any case prisons ran at considerable remove from the rest of the civil world.

Peace was not the norm, of course, in that separate world. Decades of indifference have left only a haphazard and partial record of what prison life was like in the first half of this century. The available evidence does reveal that mostly prisons were dark and cold and violent. Thus, it may indeed be debatable whether judicial intervention in that world is practical or theoretically defensible. But since it is unremarkable to claim that a government should be accountable for the conditions of its civic institutions, it seems particularly hard-hearted to mourn the passing of the era of prison autonomy.

In any event, the long night of ignorance in which the world of corrections labored has ended. In the past twenty-five years virtually no state, and few cities of any size, have been free from the disruption, upheaval, and progress almost invariably associated with litigation in federal court over conditions of confinement at prisons and jails.[1]

My discussion does not focus on the role of litigation in the operation of a correctional institution, or on the impossibility of administering a prison (which Chapter 4 addresses). It is sufficient to observe here that litigation has played a central and apparently indispensable role in the reform of American prisons. Litigation, however, has never been a total solution, and even in the best cases, its adversarial model has largely failed to create meaningful change. The typical history of prison litigation involves interminable cycles of court orders being entered, contested, ignored, and sporadically enforced with uneven results.

This jagged history has led judges and litigants to resort to a juridical instrument of ancient lineage: the special master. This remedial device was embraced in an effort to deal with the emerging perception that prison reform through federal court orders is a particularly complex and unwieldy enterprise. Prison litigation usually produces lengthy, detailed mandatory injunctions, which require vigilant monitoring and enforcement. That hard work takes place in an institution that is remote from the recognized norms of society and accustomed to its nearly gothic isolation. Given these complexities, the process of reform did not work well when cabined in the formal operations of federal court adjudication. Judges and litigators found, over time, that resolution in the courtroom did not tend to translate into actual substantive change. As this knowledge evolved, the law, in its internal organic genius, searched out from among its traditions a solution at once age-old and modern: the use of a court-appointed special master.

THE JOB OF THE SPECIAL MASTER

Simply stated, a special master is an agent of the court, usually appointed under Rule 53 of the Federal Rules of Civil Procedure.[2] Under orders of reference, federal judges can delegate to special masters specific quasi-judicial functions, provided the judge retains the ultimate judicial authority of adjudication.[3]

In a prison case, a special master typically is appointed after the judge has made a preliminary determination that the conditions at the prison are unconstitutional and that some relief must be ordered to secure the constitutional rights of the inmates. At this juncture the master's role can vary greatly, depending on the judge's perception of the magnitude of the problem and the difficulty of the solution. Among the common duties assigned to special masters are the accumulation of facts, the investigation of conditions, the evaluation of compliance with the court's order, and the formal reporting of these findings to the parties. In some cases the master's job has been limited to monitoring and fact finding. In others it has included drafting compliance plans and providing direction and guidance to compliance efforts. Some special masters are ceded authority to actually order certain measures and to punish misconduct. Masterships have been limited to single issues in a single prison or jail, where special expertise and monitoring skills are needed. At the other extreme, masters have been used in cases in which the court order governs virtually every condition and practice inside the prison.

Broadly defined, the master's assignment is to successfully implement the court's decree and thereby terminate the case. A more limited formulation of the job would be simply that the special master is a fact-finding agent assisting the parties and the court in obtaining an accurate portrait of the state of affairs behind prison walls.[4] Notwithstanding this simple characterization, the special master's job is complex.

The process of implementing change in any complex institution is difficult, and the multilayered role of the special master adds to that complexity. In addition to observing, monitoring, and reporting—the obvious duties of a master—the master soon learns that the translation of a remedial decree into operational terms and standards approved by the court, understood by the defendants, acceptable to the plaintiffs, feasible to implement, and susceptible to reasonably objective monitoring is a forbidding task. The hindrances to its achievement are the primary subject of this chapter. First, however, the specific job of a special master needs to be defined. What follows is a reasonably orthodox statement of the special master's duties as set out by an order of reference.

Fact Gathering

The order directs the special master to discover the facts relating to the defendants' compliance with the court's decree. This process is a substitute for the formal fact-finding procedure that occurs in courtrooms through the taking of evidence and the weighing by the fact-finder (judge or jury) of the credibility of that evidence. It ultimately produces the facts upon which the court determines whether the defendants have complied with its order. The special master cannot make legal conclusions, at least not with any authority.[5]

The method by which the special master goes about his or her fact-finding duties is established by the order of reference. Ordinarily, the special master is empowered to obtain access to documents maintained at the prison, to conduct confidential interviews with inmates and staff, and, in some instances, to compel staff at the prison to gather information and respond to questions. This process is extraordinary. It replaces the essence of the Anglo-American judicial procedure —adversarial fact finding, including the opportunity to confront and cross-examine witnesses.

Reporting

The special master is directed to record his or her findings in a report that is distributed to the parties. In some manner the parties must be permitted to review the master's findings and make relevant objections. Such a review theoretically applies the adversary process to the findings, at least to a muted degree. The master's findings are then filed with the court, reviewed by the judge (in light of the objections of the parties), and adopted or rejected as appropriate. At the conclusion of this process, there are ''final'' findings of fact, final in the sense that they are binding between the parties in that litigation.

Promoting Compliance

The special master may be charged, formally in the order of reference or informally by inference, with facilitating the implementation of the court's order.

Where the order is somewhat vague, the special master may assist the defendants in developing policies and procedures that will comply with the order. Where the institutional administration founders in the execution of the order through inexperience or lack of resources, the special master may provide technical expertise and may, in extraordinary circumstances, attempt to discover resources that can be used by the administration to overcome fiscal restraints. For example, if the staff-training program for officers employed at the state's prisons is deficient, a master may arrange for monetary grants and the provision of technical expertise from agencies such as the National Institute of Corrections, in order to alleviate short-term financial problems and to create a program within the state that can, in the future, furnish adequate training.

Other Tasks

Masters may be asked to mediate disputes between the parties, particularly when problems arise regarding the status of compliance with the court's order. Sometimes this role of mediator is decreed in the order, but it may also arise informally. Masters may have to develop a system for reporting and recommending disciplinary measures against staff responsible for noncompliance, as an additional means of promoting obedience to the court's orders. In some cases masters have been given the power to enter orders against the prison administrators, compelling them to take certain actions to conform with the original decree.[6]

Even if the job description is the same, the actual operation of the mastership varies greatly from case to case. The nature of the prison, the personal qualities of the administrators, the composition of the inmate population, the predilections of the judge, and the personality of the master all shape the mastership, and these forces never merge in exactly the same way.

The success of prison masterships has been uneven, but generally judges and litigators have become confident that the use of a master promotes and expedites compliance with the order and termination of the litigation. The phenomenon of mastering does not fit easily within the traditional notions of the judicial function in institutional litigation. Partly because it deviates from tradition and partly because prison reform itself is often intractable, the master's role is profoundly difficult. Competing objectives—even among the constituencies whom the master serves—and the inability to control circumstances that bear directly on his or her success consign the master, on many occasions, to complicated problems. These contrarities may be at the heart of what is meant by "impossible jobs."

IMPOSSIBILITY INHERES IN THE GOALS OF PRISON REFORM AND IN THE STRUCTURE OF THE MASTERSHIP

The special master's job and objectives in institutional reform litigation can be simply stated. Ultimately, however, the mission is more enigmatic and the role more complex than any declaration might suggest, and the nature of the appointment is itself problematic. The illusion of simplicity, and the way that illusion dissolves, will be scrutinized in this section.

The Initial Certainty: Role and Objective

The special master's job may seem more definite than that of other public administrators. He or she is appointed by a judge for the purpose of implementing a judicial decree. Thus, at the outset the objectives have been defined; they are in writing, they have the effect of a judicial mandate, and as a matter of law, they must be sufficiently specific to permit comprehension and accomplishment.[7] Some provisions in the decree may be more specific than others, but generally the judge's order, whether fashioned through consent of the parties or following litigation, must mandate or prohibit behavior in reasonably definite terms. Because the special master's charge is governed directly by the terms of the court's ruling, the mission he or she undertakes at first may appear to be no more complex than reading a court order and figuring out how to execute it. Such an external articulation of aims is a luxury rarely afforded to officers with visible public duties. For example, public health commissioners have only the most general mandate to pursue when they assume the responsibilities of their office.

The impression that the job of the special master is concrete and comprehensible is enhanced at the outset by the circumstances of the appointment and the nature of the task. The special master is cloaked with quasi-judicial authority; at least in the world in which he or she traffics, that endowment is of no little moment. The appointment itself is a judicial act that partakes of the sonority and force of judicial power. Moreover, the judge has actually ceded to the master certain rudiments of judicial power, so the position shares in the legitimacy of the judiciary. Indeed, in certain important particulars, the authority of the special master goes beyond that routinely granted to judicial officers. For example, in most circumstances the constraints of the courtroom and the formal rules of evidence are loosened to permit the special master broad access to documents and personnel as a means of collecting information.[8]

A final aspect of the initial myth of the job flows from the legacy of federal court intervention as a primary agent of social change in the latter half of the twentieth century. Presumably, most high-ranking state officials or lawyers involved in institutional reform litigation are aware of the pertinent institutional histories—schools, mental health hospitals, systems of voter registration—and the manner in which change in these areas has been driven by federal litigation.[9]

An enduring image of the nation's struggle with the imposition of the rule of law in a heated and complex social milieu is the presence of armed troops in the streets of Little Rock, charged with assuring the success of school integration. Equally potent, however, is the image of courageous and indefatigable federal judges, adhering to their oaths to support and defend the Constitution.[10] Such history has had at least a symbolic effect on correctional administrators, who find their prisons under essentially foreign siege as a result of federal litigation.[11]

Certainty Subsides: The Indeterminacy of the Order

The special master may begin his or her job with the comfort of a judicial appointment and a mandate to implement a seemingly discrete set of goals. This serene portrait is short-lived. The court's order, however specific, cannot account for the raw variety of conditions and practices at play in a prison, nor can it compass the lives and responses of confined human beings. Further, even if it speaks with some precision to the infinite diversity of life behind bars, the order is not immutable, for legal and practical reasons.

The Living, Changing Constitution: Substantive Rights. Constitutional litigation is swayed by unavoidable tension created by the indeterminacy of some of the document's most critical provisions, and the particular sources of prisoners' constitutional rights are among the more open-ended. The Eighth Amendment's prohibition against cruel and unusual punishment is the basis of a now-famous and still controversial notion of "evolving standards of decency."[12] The other primary source of prisoners' rights is the Fourteenth Amendment guarantee of due process of law before the government can deprive anyone of life, liberty, or property. Yet the text itself asks the inevitable next question—what process is due?—so instead of one question, there are two: Does the government's action really implicate an interest in life, liberty, or property? If so, what process does the government have to provide before it can deprive someone of that interest? Unfortunately, multiplying the questions does not make the answer any easier to find.[13]

In part because of the indeterminacy of the constitutional sources, judicially created rights are subject to modification and even suspension.[14] Thus, administrators charged with running prisons must meet a shifting standard of conduct; prisoners and their lawyers must change their expectations over time; and to a critical extent, the master's job must be subject to these same pulses.

This problem could be illuminated by a case study of the fate, over the past twenty years, of the putative constitutional right of inmates to contact visitation—that is, personal visits, including physical contact, with people from the outside world. Although such a study is beyond the scope of this chapter, a brief review can establish the familiar dialectic. At the start of federal court intervention in prison affairs, few would have expected that an inmate's right to contact visitation would be resolved on the basis of constitutional doctrine. Yet as litigation swelled, and with it the body of recognized rights, the nature and scope of prison visits were subject to judicial scrutiny. Federal judges were asked to evaluate procedures surrounding visits. Should inmates and their visitors be strip-searched? How long should visits be? Under what circumstances can an inmate's right (or privilege) to visits be suspended? Eventually, perhaps inevitably, inmates claimed that they had a constitutional right to contact visitation. The issue ultimately was resolved by the Supreme Court, which held that there was no such constitutional right.[15]

Perhaps in the end it is best that the court order under which the special master operates does not attempt to address specifically every aspect of prison life. Such an effort would almost certainly fail, and in any case such a comprehensive order would jeopardize the aura of legitimacy that is so crucial to the work of a federal court, because it would violate essential principles of federalism and separation of powers. In any event, the order typically states in general terms the conduct that is prohibited or prescribed. For example, the order may require "staffing and staff surveillance sufficient to ensure that inmates are not subjected to unreasonable risk of harm from other inmates." Such a provision is common, and it declares fairly what courts have determined the Eighth Amendment to guarantee to inmates by way of preventing cruel and unusual punishment. This broad statement of a right may or may not be a proper way to resolve the tensions of applying a vague constitutional stipulation to a concrete civic setting. Of import here is that such a provision, which the master must evaluate and implement, is hardly self-defining. To summarize, then, the master may have in hand a written set of duties, but that does not mean it will be easy to know when they have been discharged.

The Living, Changing Constitution: Federalism. The pressure on the special master is further complicated by tensions regarding the legitimacy of federal court intervention in the affairs of states and localities, an issue that is subject to the flow of fashionable precepts within constitutional thought. In a fundamental sense the special master, working as a federal agent in a state institution, is at the center of this conflict. As a matter of constitutional legitimacy, federal courts are restrained in their ability to impose orders on state prison officials. The public debate on this topic during the confirmation hearings on the nomination of Judge Robert Bork to the Supreme Court provided a fascinating glimpse of how deep and troubled is the question of federal court legitimacy, both as a matter of arcane scholarship and as part of the ongoing life of the federal judiciary.

The master is a quasi-judicial officer. He or she feels concurrently the restraints of that role and the obligation to effect the changes required by the court's order. In doing so, the master must measure the reality of prison life against the articulation of constitutional standards contained in the decree. At this point he or she is directly exposed to the strain of giving normative content to open-ended constitutional provisions. That pressure is augmented by an awareness of the constitutional and political ideal of limited federal court intervention in the affairs of the states. In sum, the abstract pressures of a federalist system inhere in the work of the special master.

These tensions are palpable to a special master and are actually, acutely, and regularly felt. Inmates whose constitutional rights are protected by the order have a legitimate right to know what will be done to enforce that order, and to them, the order and its constitutional platitudes are concrete. Thus, inmates will demand to know how the special master will insulate them from the enormous risks of physical and psychological harm they experience in the prison. Yet assume that the court has decreed that the defendants must have sufficient staff and surveillance to provide internal security for prisoners. Although inmates value their safety, they will probably not perceive an immediate benefit from a staffing order. Indeed, many of the most onerous features of prison life may be heightened by the presence of more staff. Inmates may sense at once the paradox that their victory in court has permitted the prison adminstrators to tighten the clamps on certain aspects of inmate life, such as freedom of movement, intra-institutional mail, and nonmandatory group activities.[16]

The Order Can Change. The evolutionary process of prisoners' rights has an important corollary. The law acknowledges the right of parties to seek changes in injunctions under certain circumstances.[17] To complicate this matter, the condition under which parties may be entitled to modification or a vacation of decrees is itself a doctrinal area that is currently vulnerable to considerable internal pressure.[18]

Thus, one factor that makes the special master's job particularly difficult is that the goals of the job are subject to change, subtle or dramatic, over time. This volatility of goals profoundly influences the ability of the special master to be effective. Whether or not one subscribes to the notion, increasingly fashionable among certain legal academics, of the "radical indeterminacy" of law,[19] it is clear that achieving constitutional conditions in a prison is not a matter of mathematical precison. The words of the order will prevail, and they are hedged in by constraints of federalism and comity, vagueness in the original text, the organic nature of prisons, and the changing state of the law as it relates to and reflects the norms of this society.

Nontextual Objectives

The mutability of the court's order, which guides the master's work, is compounded by the existence of additional, fluctuating goals that the master will also be expected to accomplish. Moreover, even acknowledging the presence of these extrinsic pressures adds an unwieldy dimension to trying to define what the master's job really is.

The prisoners sue to bring about constitutional conditions at the prison. Almost inevitably, however, this objective becomes a colloquialism for "prison reform" in the minds of the inmates and the free citizens interested in the result.[20] Once that change in terminology takes hold, a wide array of expectations arises, and the objectives of the suit become confused with other objectives that do not have a constitutional basis and that instead are matters of public policy.[21]

This proliferation of nonspecific goals has obvious consequences. Public expectations about civic institutions are notoriously fragile, and in the area of prisons, they are remarkably contradictory. As a simple illustration, the prevalence of the concept of law and order has produced a fevered rush toward ill-considered, punitive criminal justice policies—such as determinate sentencing (which fix terms without parole), revocation of prison good-time statutes (which allow sentence reduction for good behavior), retreat from community corrections, and related catastrophes of public policy. This recklessness dissipates somewhat when the public's information is more balanced and is more carefully considered. After the infamous New Mexico prison riot in February 1980, broad political support for prison reform developed, which led in turn to a massive building project, a consensual settlement of a federal court case, and a pronounced dedication toward improving conditions in the state's prisons. That story, although heightened because of the peculiar dynamics of the New Mexico situation, is not unique.[22]

When roving grand juries commission themselves to investigate prison affairs, their formal reports, which are powerful evidence of the values of a community, almost uniformly condemn conditions and practices inside the institutions.[23] Nonetheless, public opinion on this issue, as on virtually any other, will tilt and waver. These vacillations are not capricious; they are the substance of democracy, and it is not irresponsible for politicians to heed them. The point here is that the special master is affected by these tides, and in the end, as the political process lurches toward resolution, he or she may in turn affect that resolution. With or without that participation, however, the political process will have an impact, ultimately and mediately, on the objectives that the special master is expected to achieve.

The Constituencies

Perhaps the most important reason that the special master's objectives are indeterminate is the variation in constituencies which he or she is obligated to serve or at least be accountable to. Strictly viewed, none of these constituencies is relevant, because the master's function is to implement the order, not address particular interests at the expense of others. That view is unrealistic, for several reasons.

First, because the language of the order is to some degree vague, its meaning must be derived largely from the expectations of the parties and the manner in which they implement and enforce it. Moreover, in traditional doctrine, enforcement of the court's order is the responsibility of the plaintiffs. If the plaintiffs, through counsel, wish to barter some rights for others, one would be hard-pressed to find a theory of adjudication that makes such a trade illegitimate. Nor is it easy to see why the master should be disabled from assisting in, or even encouraging, such exchanges.

Even here, however, a problem arises. The term "the plaintiffs" assumes a unity of interest that may or may not be present. "The plaintiffs" are the inmates, who have prevailed in the litigation; their counsel are lawyers committed to represent the interests of the inmates. Yet this is not an easy task. Imagine a prison with five hundred inmates in varying categories. The lawyer represents the class of inmates, but not all of the five hundred inmates share the same concerns. Within the prison there may be a group of inmates who, for whatever reason, are prone to receive misconduct reports for violence against staff and other inmates. The prison administration may want to isolate these inmates for long periods of time and may urge that isolation should be accomplished with a minimum of due process protection and on the basis of broadly inclusive substantive criteria. In this situation it should be apparent that within the class of inmate plaintiffs, there will be diverse responses, generated by self-interest, to the proposed actions of the administration. In the nature of things, it is predictable that the court and the master will turn to plaintiffs' counsel for conscientious representation of the class's interests; but in this representation, the lawyer has to make some hard choices between interests. Those decisions may or may not be responsible.

In all events the master has an essential role in dealing with the inmates' lawyer on a long-term basis. This relationship is crucial, because the lawyer can provide stability in the litigation by distilling the potentially compelling interests within the class and by shaping the class's expectations of the order. At the same time, of course, the inmates' lawyer determines how the case is litigated. A lawyer representing a large and sometimes unwieldy class inevitably makes certain decisions personally, on behalf of the client. Thus the lawyer, in a critical sense, becomes a separate party interested in the process of the mastership.[24]

The inmates themselves are a key constituency for the special master, who will have a direct relationship with them. The broad access to inmates that special masters traditionally are granted creates a personal connection between inmates and the master that is deeper and more immediate than what the inmates have with their lawyers.[25] As a source of direct information, this access is invaluable to the master's attempt to evaluate conditions and practices in the facility and to measure compliance with the court's order. Yet it would be highly unusual if inmates, under the pressures of confinement, isolation, and idleness, were able, in their exchanges with masters, to limit their comments to the scope of the court's order and desist from extraneous complaints. First, the task of defining precisely what is and is not covered by the order often befuddles lawyers in conditions cases, so inmates cannot be expected to be more concise in their thinking. Second, under some circumstances, facially irrelevant conditions may in fact be caused by elemental noncompliance.[26]

The relationship between the special master and prisoners is one that demands careful attention and sensitivity, for it can be transformed by both parties into something quite different from what was contemplated by the order of reference—and one potentially hazardous to the process of compliance. Institutional litigation tends to be long, and the passage of time in a prison certainly has a different feel than it does in the free world. A special master's perspective of progress is not the same as the prisoner's, particularly as the case reaches its final phases. From the special master's viewpoint, inmate complaints about abhorrent conditions and deviant, although hidden, practices can create frustration and irritation, especially when the special master's focus is on the advances that have been made. The master's sense of the progressive history of the prison can appear shockingly detached to inmates who are more present-minded and who see what appears to be a trouble inattention to the intimate particulars of prison life.

Certain aspects of incarceration are unpleasant, painful, psychologically threatening, and dispiriting. The litigation, no matter how successful, will not change that fact. When the special master has concluded that the prison substantially complies with the court's order, the grievances of inmates will only be reminders of how much is, and must remain, unfinished. This realization can be profoundly disheartening.

Inmates are a constituency for the special master, and their expectations are critical because they are parties in the lawsuit, they have obtained relief, and they are entitled to implementation of the order. It is arrogant and insupportable for a special master to ignore that fact. At the same time, the master must be mindful that the court's order defines the inmates' rights and that inmates may not be in the best position to evaluate whether those rights have been secured. Nonetheless, the special master will and must depend on inmates as invaluable sources of information. The tension between this dependency and its hazards is a significant complication in the job of a special master.

Thus, when the special master looks to the inmates' side of the case, he or she sees neither a block of unified interests nor a common spokesperson. The portrait is no clearer on the other side of the case. The term "defendants" fails to convey the range of people and interests who are obligated to provide constitutional conditions. In fact, the "defendants" are likely to be located at widely different positions respecting the terms of the court's order.

First, the defendants are probably represented by a lawyer who must synthesize a set of interests that are not entirely congruent.[27] To illustrate the breadth of the real interests that are lumped under the rubric "defendants," consider a hypothetical case of litigation over the conditions of confinement at a jail. The inmates sue the board of county commissioners, the sheriff, and the chief jailer as named defendants, claiming that the conditions and practices at the jail are unconstitutional. The initial court order is entered by consent. After some period of difficulty in the implementation of the order, a special master is appointed. The master's powers are those set forth generally in orders of reference. An unwritten but critical part of the mandate is to mediate and resolve disputes before they are submitted to the judge.

In such a situation, the master must take into account an exhaustive variety of interests in attempting to solve problems. First, the named defendants have markedly divergent interests. The county commissioners are elected officials, and almost inevitably, they represent a range of political objectives and perspectives. The board's function is to merge those objectives into county policy, but that is no easy accomplishment, particularly in a highly contentious area such as criminal justice policy. The individual constituencies of the commissioner, and their perhaps overlapping political ambitions, complicate the process of even identifying the objectives of the board.

The sheriff, also a named defendant, is an elected official and is a separate constitutional officer in the jurisdiction. The sheriff's constituency may be different from any one group represented on the board, and his or her political aspirations may be such that it would be advantageous to take public positions at odds with the policies chosen by the majority faction on the board. Although the chief jailer typically is a subordinate of the sheriff and serves at his or her pleasure, the goals of these two persons may be quite distinct. If the chief jailer has risen through the ranks at the jail to achieve that position, he or she may feel deep attachment to the facility and its staff. In cases where the sheriff is a politician rather than a professional jailer, the potential conflicts are readily apparent.

The maintenance of adequate constitutional conditions at a jail is a costly endeavor. The sheriff, as an elected official, may be more concerned about the costs and benefits of certain policies at the jail than the chief jailer may be. One can anticipate, then, that there might be significant disputes between the sheriff and the chief jailer over the priority to be given to certain measures that the chief jailer advocates.[28]

In addition to the difficulties of achieving consensus among actors with very different objectives, a special master is also required to fashion agreement among actors who are not formally part of the process but whose views and decisions are critical to the operation of a local community criminal-justice system. For example, in a jail plagued with overcrowding, the discretion of prosecuting attorneys—about whom they should prosecute and for what crimes, the structuring of plea bargaining, and the imposition of sentences—has a dramatic effect on the jail population. These fundamental policy decisions are far beyond the charter of the special master, but they directly affect his or her ability to deal with the jail and its problems.[29] If the solution is to be negotiated, these actors, and the processes by which they make their decisions, must be accounted for. Yet only by overreaching the original mandate can the special master bring them into the process. In the background also are the state court judges, who are not accustomed to the rough barter of negotiation; they pronounce sentences with the legitimate expectation that they will be served under the terms established by them and by statutory law.

Even if the master ignores the complexity of the interests that actually compose ''the defendants,'' he or she can be overwhelmed by simply identifying the direct constituencies that must be served. The master's primary relationship at the prison is with the administration. Administrators and line staff have broad discretion in the day-to-day operation of the institution. The decisions these people make have a profound impact on whether or not the court's order is implemented. Moreover, the quality of life in the prison is formed by the infinite, minute daily decisions of staff in their relations with inmates, and the inmates' perceptions of progress are molded by these decisions. The court's order can be effectively sabotaged by line staff in a thousand ways, many of which will escape detection.

Consequently, the special master's relationship with line staff is critical. From the start, however, this relationship is victimized by ideology and mutually held caricatures. The special master may see line staff as the avatars of an unconstitutional system; conversely, line staff may view the master as an embodiment of an ignorant but judgmental federal court. Until these stereotypes dissolve, the master's job will be impossible.

Certainly the special master must work from the assumption that something is wrong at the prison. Otherwise, the existence of the court's order would be

CONSENSUS PRISON REFORM 189

inexplicable. In fact, in most cases the master's appointment is the result not only of unconstitutional conditions but also of prolonged noncompliance. This failure may be the product of intransigence, incompetence, or more complex forces. The problem is the master's to solve, and so he or she enters the prison as the interloper, a natural adversary of the besieged administrator.

The tension between them is layered with stereotypes. Virtually anyone familiar with prisons and their lore recognizes the classic image of the hard-nosed corrections professionals, who stake their future on obdurate defiance of lawful court orders. This depiction may have been valid sometime in the past, but it is now mostly obsolete. For at least a decade, those within the field of corrections have devoted considerable time to the development of professional standards and a self-policing mechanism of accreditation.[30]

Special masters struggle through stereotypes of their own, of course. Within corrections there is an enduring dichotomy between the line officer and the theoretician, which is felt with particular force by people who have risen through the ranks to positions in the administration. One cannot gainsay the actual difficulties involved in the job of supervising a correctional institution. Those who bear the responsibilities acutely, day to day, cannot be blamed for believing that a federal judge is not particularly well acquainted with those difficulties and is probably poorly positioned to correct them. The special master necessarily labors in the pejorative fallout of that belief. This distrust is further sharpened by the administrator's natural defensiveness against being second-guessed, particularly when the intruder can also condemn and reform.

These feelings are thick in the air when the special master starts his or her job. Unless the experience is extraordinary, emotions will intensify during the initial stages of the mastership. Typically, the master's first official act is to prepare findings that describe to the court and to the parties the extent of noncompliance. This task fulfills the worst fears of the administration and almost inevitably leaves line-staff administrators believing they are censured and misunderstood. Any trust the master has developed with administrators and staff is replaced by feelings of condemnation and personal betrayal. Running a prison is intensely personal work, and there is very little distance between the views of the administrator and their reification in the practices inside the facility. The reports of noncompliance, then, become highly personal.

In any full accounting of the constituencies with which the special master must deal, a word must be included about those actors who have been called the "hidden defendants." For reasons of federal constitutional law, neither the state legislatures nor their members can be made defendants in a federal lawsuit seeking to enforce constitutional standards. Thus, the named defendants will not include the speaker of the house, the chair of the state senate's legislative finance committee, or any of the prominent leaders of state legislatures. Nonetheless, because reform is a costly and highly visible process, achieving compliance with the court's order will cause an enormous drain on the state treasury. It is not uncommon for the budgets of state corrections departments to expand many times over as a result of litigation.[31] This huge cost can lead to significant dislocations in the state's budget as well as a severe backlash among legislators. Some of their rhetoric will reflect sincere concern over the allocation of scarce resources; some will be more opportunistic.

The structure of the case creates a vast gap between the special master and the hidden defendants, which widens as long as political posturing prevails. The special master contributes to this breach to the extent that he or she interprets mastership as narrowly defined within the framework of litigation, thereby necessarily excluding the legislature.[32] At this point, and at many others, the intrinsic tensions of the special master's job are salient and sobering.

A great deal of scholarly thought has gone into the problem of enforcing federal court orders that affect state treasuries without offending the constraints of sovereign immunity. Ultimately, if the order is framed with care, those constraints do not operate. In that sense, then, the remoteness of the state legislature from the active agents of the case has little consequence. On the other hand, this circumlocution is not merely artificial; it has real import for the success of reform. To the extent the state legislature does not participate in the process of reform and sees only its consequences in budget deficits and the need to increase tax revenues, reform will be a political catastrophe. This potential disaster cannot safely be ignored, for the end reforms that are enforced unwillingly and undemocratically are always vulnerable to compelling political critiques. The line between the judiciary and the legislature is real, and one need not be a constitutional theoretician to observe and worry about its obfuscation.

Thus, the world the master enters is not so simple as one might surmise, and its contours are always changing. Among occupations in the public eye, only baseball managers enjoy a less stable tenure than prison administrators. Similarly, counsel who represent the defendants often change in response to political whims, and they may come and go with governors. Nor do the prisoners remain the same, as some depart under the pressures of crowding, parole, and early release.

Changing an institution as complex as a prison is not easy. Doing so when you are the only constant, and all else is flux, may be another sense of what is meant by impossibility.

COAL AND DIAMONDS— THE METALLURGY OF REFORM

The Graduated Implementation of Reform

How does one achieve compliance with the court's order despite all these perceived impossibilities? Perhaps the first and most essential act involves analysis of all the objectives to be accomplished, followed by the development of a coherent and sensible schedule for enactment. If, for example, the order requires the implementation of specific measures in the areas of safety, sanitation, surveillance, discipline, and medical care, but without a graduated time line, such schedules must be developed. The time lines may be sharply contested, because the inmates have probably waited some time to prevail in their lawsuit, and they will not be inclined to wait longer. It is predictable, therefore, that lawyers for the inmates will argue that the unconstitutional conditions have endured long enough and that whatever patience is warranted has been exhausted. That argument cannot be disclaimed, but to embrace it is to consign oneself to profound frustration.

Spreading fundamental reforms over time is essential. Prisons are organic places, with entire cultures of their own.[33] The exploration of this anthropology is beyond the scope of this chapter. However, it is essential to recognize that a change in one aspect of prison life will carom through others in ways that cannot be predicted. As a simplistic example, an increase in surveillance in a prison, caused by increased staffing and more conscientious and consistent posting of staff, could lead to a significant increase in the number of misconduct reports that are issued to inmates. This increase in turn taxes the inmate discipline system. Officers responsible for that system may struggle at first under the drastically increased workload. Simultaneously, the court's order may have imposed new procedures for discipline. If both these changes happen at once, the entire system may threaten to collapse, as large numbers of misconduct reports are dismissed for failure to adhere to the unfamiliar procedures. At this point the master can expect a backlash of formidable proportions.

Is any part of this scenario merely contrived? Certainly correctional administrators are capable of subverting the court's order by implementing a chaotic reform and then blaming the court for the resulting disorder. Nonetheless, the underlying problem is real, and it arises from actual dislocations in the operation of the institution. It is impossible to conceive of a definition of success in correctional reform that would embrace the deliberate destruction of institutional order. As long as the prison exists in its current form, order is preferable to chaos. Chaos is dangerous, and in a prison there is enough danger without the complications of dissolving norms of conduct. It is thus imperative for the special master to advocate, and obtain the parties' consent to, graduated and sensible implementation of reform according to defensible prioritization.

Fostering Consent

Positing the possibility of consent raises perhaps the central coping strategy of the special master. The essential role of compromise in the work of the master is a result of positive and negative pressures that operate on the job: First, there are negative pressures that limit what the special master can accomplish by way of reform in the absence of agreement; and second, there is the positive insight that ultimately the implementation of change through agreement is a key feature of meaningful and enduring reform.[34]

Litigation over prison conditions is almost by definition intractable. The intricacies of an entire living institution cannot readily be portrayed through the fact-finding process that is the core of the Anglo-American judicial system. Even if an accurate picture of conditions and practices at a prison were to emerge from trial, the real constraints on federal judicial power in this area create certain problems in enforcing constitutional norms behind prison walls. Moreover, the definition of compliance with an order, when measured in terms of countless human actions and reactions, is inherently problematic. This confluence of difficulties, as much as anything, explains the extraordinary measure of a special master's appointment.

The quasi-judicial authority of the master does not make the task any easier. The master does not have the power to order that conduct conform to certain constitutional standards, nor can he or she punish disobedience. This is not to degrade or downplay the nature of the master's role; it merely acknowledges the critical constitutional limitations that form the ultimate distinction between the judge and the special master. In this sense, then, the master formally functions, as noted earlier, as an expeditious fact-finder, a role that is complex but potentially valuable. The role is defensible because prison conditions are not easily suscepti-ble to determination through an ordinary process of adversary fact finding. If, however, the litigation remains intensely adversarial, this short-circuiting ma-neuver is not likely to work.[35]

Thus, the special master may be most effective in attempting to propose resolution of contested issues. Whenever possible, the law strongly favors the amicable settlement of disputes, and certainly that maxim applies forcefully to the area of prison reform. In the absence of consensual reform, prison lawsuits are almost fated to last decades (and entire careers).

One can easily enumerate the benefits of consensual reform.[36] The parties have plenary control over what they agree between themselves to do with the problems they face within the litigation. They, unlike federal courts, are not constrained by the doctrines of comity, federalism, nonintrusiveness, and related concerns. Without these constraints, a particular problem that may have a constitutional dimension can be solved through the detailed explication of standards and guidelines—more detailed than a federal court legitimately can include in an injunction. For example, faced with the problem of security staffing, parties can engage in a comprehensive statement of security staffing, posting, surveillance, and staff training. Ultimately, specificity of this kind may fall within the federal court's authority, but the exercise of that authority is certainly doubtful. Moreover, in the absence of proof that a less intrusive order—preserving administrative discretion—has failed, there is a significant question as to whether such a detailed order would be valid. Thus, the process of conciliation itself is a means of solving one of the major ingredients of impossibility in the task of a special master—the indeterminacy of objectives.

At the next phase of the case, conciliation is also of great benefit. In attempting to achieve compliance, unforeseen difficulties will arise. If the goals of reform have been defined by consent, the possibility that problems in the pursuit of those goals can be resolved amicably is surely increased. No doubt disputes will arise, but it is reasonable to expect that if consent has been injected into litigation, the habit of conciliation will take hold.

The Definition of Success

In an earlier section of this chapter, I observed the prevalence of the view that there is little, if any, substantive content to constitutional standards, at least as they relate to due process. This retreat from substance and the elevation of process are rooted deep in a constitutional theory. Interestingly, there is a corollary in a primary strategy for the master in fulfilling this difficult job. The approach of monitoring compliance through the review of documents becomes the primary focus of the master's work.

As the special master's work progresses, he or she must develop a method for monitoring compliance with the court's order. Over the past several decades, prisons have become laden with paperwork. Usually, however, the particular documentation the prison has developed for its own needs does not correspond to the requirements of the special master. For example, it is routine for a prison to maintain a logbook that records all "incidents" in the prison. These incidents are of concern to the special master, but the master's view of them, and his or her need to monitor and report on them to the parties and the court, demands recording a very different set of facts than is routinely taken down. For example, an incident in which a prison guard uses force against an inmate presents different concerns for the special master than it does for the prison administrators, and the normal record of the incident may not serve the master's needs.

The way a prison event is reflected in documents becomes critical. The master ultimately must depend on those documents to describe life at the prison, and he or she develops expectations of what the documents should look like and what should be learned from them. Those expectations eventually define the monitoring task. In simple terms, the documentary record replaces the event.

I do not mean to imply here that the documents are falsified; in my experience such falsification is rare. Yet when the special master's directions to staff identify specific factors that must be recorded concerning an incident, the specification itself redefines the nature of a "use of force incident" along preconceived lines. By virtue of this direction, the documents may not be wholly accurate. The document, however, exsits as a concrete source of information for the special master, and to a certain extent it will become more important to the special master than the reports he or she receives from inmates.

The phenomenon of how documents come to define reality at the prison is worth some reflection. The task of monitoring conditions in the prison is itself fundamentally impossible. The special master does not live at the prison, and in the final analysis, only someone who does live there can understand how it operates and what it feels like to be confined there. How can the special master, even with the broadest form of access, really understand what life is like inside the prison? Yet that is the very essence of the master's task: The order addresses conditions of confinement, and if the special master is to monitor successfully the conditions of confinement, he or she must exhibit a comprehension of the dimensions of that life. Yet, I repeat, that is impossible. Inevitably, an oblique view of the institution must be developed, and it is developed primarily through records. The substitution may or may not be legitimate, but it appears to be unavoidable.

Charges of fabrication aside, a meaningful critique can be lodged against this monitoring process. Consider, for example, the issue of cellblock rounds. A federal court order commonly requires a staff member assigned to a cellblock to tour that cellblock once every half hour. Let us assume that on a particular cellblock the staff member in fact conducts this round. Moreover, the special master has requested that the administration maintain a logbook in each cellblock in which the touring staff member is required to record the time of the round. The logbook then is turned over the the special master, and it reveals that for the most part—say, 95 percent of the time—the rounds are conducted. That logbook is substantive evidence of compliance with the court's directive. How does it evaluate, however, the nature of the round that is conducted? Can a special master ever know, for example, the degree of attentiveness of the staff members as they conducted these rounds? This example merely suggests that the underlying qualitative aspect of the order is generally lost in certain compromises that the special master must make in order to avoid the essential impossibility of the job; that is, monitoring the quality of prison life.[37]

A compromise in this area has to be made, but this compulsion does not spare the criticism that in the end the special master's report on compliance reflects only in an imperfect and perhaps fundamentally inaccurate way the true state of affairs inside the prison. In the often fractious milieu of prison reform, this imperfection generates charges and countercharges that are dismaying and inescapable. Subterfuge, forgery, capitulation—such is the language that surrounds the process of defining reform in terms of procedures for monitoring compliance. These charges are not surprising. The point to be observed here is that the combination of indeterminate constitutional standards, limitations on the ability of an outsider ever to apprehend the true nature of life inside a prison, and the various constraints on normative judgments by the special master compel an accommodation by the master, in which the parties to the lawsuit must participate. The essence of the accommodation involves a redefinition of compliance that eradicates or diminishes the impossibility that inheres in the job of the special master.

I am not sure that this accommodation even makes the actual job any easier. I am confident, however, that it provides a perspective for achieving the objectives of the job that the special master is at least able to live with. And over time, as he or she works within these new definitions of mastership and success, the other participants in the process may come to adopt them as well. This approach is the essence of coping with impossibility.

AFTER THE FALLOUT:
THE LANDSCAPE AFTER REFORM

Thinking about the impossible aspects of being a special master, and the ways in which a master can face them, leaves one wondering what a prison that goes through this process looks like afterward and how the master survives the chore. These are not easy questions to answer. Apart from the incidental issues raised, the larger questions about the political environment in which the work is undertaken and how it responds to the potentially undemocratic forces of litigation require evaluation.

The record of masterships is uneven but, on balance, positive. When measured in terms of the related values of (a) implementing constitutional mandates, (b) without undue delay, (c) with a minimum of human suffering, (d) without exhausting the increasingly strained judicial resources, and (e) with accommodation of political considerations, I believe a fair comparison between prison-conditions cases with masters and without masters would demonstrate a historical advantage for the former.[38] How is this so, in view of the myriad problems identified above?

Briefly stated, the impossibility of the job can be successfully compromised if the master succeeds in redefining the nature of the problem and then solving it on shared terms. The litigiousness of American society is often remarked on, but there has been little substantive demonstration that litigation is in fact a poor way to solve problems. Especially in the context of prison reform, the process of litigation simply cannot accomplish the real objectives. Procedural constraints make the judicial fact-finding process singularly unproductive; similarly, in the absence of consent, a court order mandating reform is not likely to be effective, and the resulting complications yield a skepticism about judicial power that serves no one.

Particularly where ideological precepts abound, as in the field of prison reform, the posturing of parties in litigation creates an aura of trench warfare that is not conducive to achieving anything more than retrenchment. In fact, as with most other disputes, there is much more common ground between prisoners and prison administrators than is generally recognized. It is, I believe, precisely the nature of litigation that prevents the parties from seeing how little is genuinely in contention. A special master is uniquely positioned to produce the best possible agreement between parties and to help them define the specific grounds of dispute, without escalation.

This is all by way of saying that if the problem is removed from the context of litigation and redefined as a matter of identifying the scope of agreement on specific principles, the impossibility of prison reform is transmuted into a less forbidding enterprise of essentially political compromise.[39] In this revised arena, fiscal constraints will operate, but they can be rationally analyzed and compared with the cost of alternative policy decisions—such as determinate sentencing, endless expansion and renovation of existing facilities, recurrent capital allocation for new buildings, and the expense of litigation.

For example, if the parties no longer have to defend their separate positions for the purpose of the case, they can express their shared concerns for safety. One of the striking results of negotiations between the real parties in interest over matters such as internal prison operations is how frequently the caricature of intrusive outsiders is replaced by the realization that no one actually aspires to take over the daily operation of a prison. Once the prison administrator is assured that he or she will run the prison after all, the administrator is much more interested in using the process to solve the problems that really are beyond his or her ken. For instance, the administrator may already have fought and lost battles in the legislature for funding programs that are desired but not currently affordable. When that issue arises during a cooperative discussion rather than during litigation, the parties to the case may forge a common cause that would otherwise have been unthinkable.[40]

In brief, litigation and its artifices are in many ways counterproductive to successful resolution of disputes. That may be by design, for there is some substance to the opinion that courts exist only as punishment for people who are unable to resolve their own disputes. The application of this wry formulation to civil rights litigation is probably hard-hearted, but its underlying verity should not be ignored. Certainly the relative values given to political and judicial solutions to broad societal problems has shifted dramatically in the last thirty-five years—and continues to shift. In any event, a final homily suggests the way a special master can at once deal with the impossible aspects of the job and yet accomplish something substantive.

It must be remembered that when special masters are done with their work; have filed every compliance report that will be filed; have constructed every system for recordkeeping and internal accountability; and have framed every procedure needed to operate the facility—after they have done all these things and departed, the prisons will still be standing; the administrators will be operating them; and the prisoners will still be incarcerated. This simple, pragmatic thought is sufficient in itself to suggest that in the end the master's job, however difficult it may seem, is framed to succeed. Although this realization can be pejoratively described as cooption and capitulation, that is an inappropriate judgment for what is essentially a decision to involve the principals in solving their own problems. Whether their solutions have merit is open to debate, and it is a political question. The point here is that special masters do their job best when they help transform litigation into a means of letting that interactive process work.

CONCLUSION

Necessarily this chapter leaves much unexplored. The argument advanced here leaves off precisely at the point where another study might undertake to assess whether masterships designed to produce consensus are more or less successful than prison litigation. My argument involves principle and pragmatism. In principle, I am concerned about the antidemocratic nature of judicially imposed reform and about the manner in which such reform and its complications undermine exactly the most essential aspects of the Anglo-American tradition. Practically, I worry about whether any meaningful change can ever be imposed in a hostile climate and about the effect on the morale of real people who have to live in the fragile and menacing world of a prison.

It is by now a truism of pop psychology that people change their values to justify their behavior. That facile formula may apply to the argument made here. It may be that compromise becomes attractive only because the special master cannot, for several reasons, accomplish what he or she has been appointed to do; but I don't think so. I am sure at least that the impossibilities I have identified above are real, and they can be formidable impediments in the effort to reform a prison. There may be other ways to overcome those impossibilities than the ones I propose here; some of them may even work. At the point where legal formalism, political accountability, and practical concerns merge, however, one would be hard-pressed to defend any solution that does not involve the people who have to live with the consequences of any master's acts.

NOTES

1. See generally, Fritz Byers, "Special Masters and Prison Reform: Real and Imagined Obstacles," *Ohio State Journal on Dispute Resolution* 3, 2 (1988): 361.

2. Since the rules of civil procedure for federal courts were codified, a large number of states have modeled their rules of civil procedure after the federal rules. Accordingly, most states have an equivalent to Federal Rule of Civil Procedure 53. Professor Nathan has argued that courts have the inherent authority to appoint persons unconnected to itself to assist in the accomplishment of basic court objectives. Vincent M. Nathan, "The Use of Masters in Institutional Reform Litigation," 10 *Toledo Law Review* 419 (1979): 423–433. The concept of inherent authority is problematic.

3. A judge can appoint a special master in any kind of case. Historically, a master was often used in property disputes, in which a judge sought the advice of a realty expert as to property boundaries, riparian rights, and related matters requiring a degree of expertise not commonly associated with the judiciary. In this section, I will describe the duties typically assigned to special masters appointed in cases involving prisons or jails. Unless the context makes clear a different usage, the term *prison* means a prison or jail. This forced synonymity does not imply that a special master's job is the same in either institution, because in critical respects, some of which are discussed below, the jobs are crucially distinct.

4. There is a significant question as to whether a court has an independent interest in the enforcement of its order. Historically, a court's order inured to the benefit of one of the parties, and if that party was unable to secure enforcement of the order, the court was unconcerned. At the same time, the law of criminal contempt developed, which has as its primary tenet that the court's authority must be vindicated any time its orders are disobeyed. These concepts, both of which have strong roots in Anglo-American jurisprudence, are at considerable tension with each other. They are frequently placed in dramatic contrast during prison litigation.

5. Rule 53 provides that the special master may make conclusions of law, and if they are not objected to, the court may accept them. If the parties object to the master's conclusions of law, however, those conclusions are entitled to no weight or deference, and the judge is required to come at the legal issues anew. In contrast, the findings of fact are to be accepted by the court unless those findings are clearly erroneous.

6. It is not incontrovertible whether such a delegation to the special master is constitutional.

7. For example, Rule 65(d) of the Federal Rules of Civil Procedure requires that every order granting an injunction be specific in terms and describe in reasonable detail the act or acts sought to be restrained.

8. The deeply problematic nature of this authority, respecting its distortion of fundamental principles of Anglo-American jurisprudence, is beyond the scope of this chapter. For a basic doctrinal statement of what due process protections are minimally required to ensure that the mastership does not deprive parties of their constitutional rights and does not abrogate the fundamental imperatives of Article III of the United States Constitution, see *Ruiz v. Estelle* 679 F.2d 1115 (5th Cir. 1982).

9. A brilliant account of the social, political, and legal struggle concerning segregation is contained in Richard Kluger, *Simple Justice: The History of Brown v. Board of Education and Black America's Struggle for Equality* (New York: Knopf, 1976).

10. See generally, Jack Bass, *Unlikely Heroes* (New York: Simon & Schuster, 1981).

11. Of course, as was true in the area of school desegregation, institutional reform litigation involving change imposed by federal judges has produced a rhetoric of defiant opposition. Over time, this rhetoric affects the movement toward reform, so that, as in all things, change becomes more in the nature of a dialectic. That dialectic can be traced by the major appellate decisions in institutional reform over the past twenty-five years. For a striking expression of the current political posturing in response to federal litigation, see the proposed resolution of the Western State Governors' Association, "Support for a Revised Federal Policy on Consent Decrees Affecting the States," July 7, 1987.

12. See *Trop v. Dulles,* 356 U.S. 86 (1958).

13. On this and related points regarding the due process clause (particularly the unwieldy questions required by contemporary doctrine), see John Ely, *Democracy and Distrust: A Theory of Judicial Review* (Cambridge, Mass.: Harvard University Press, 1981). Also, see Laurence H. Tribe, *Constitutional Choices* (Cambridge, Mass.: Harvard University Press, 1985).

14. The notion that a judge makes the law carries the necessary corollary that a judge can change the law. This positivism is antithetical to the idea of common-law reasoning, although certain critics have attempted to equate the two methodologies by caricaturing the common-law model. See F. Cohen, "Transcendental Nonsense and the Functional Approach," 35 *Columbia Law Review* 809 (1935). The shocking instability of announced rules of law during the last fifty years of American history is the result of the substitution of positivist fiat for common-law reasoning.

15. The process described in the text is related to a schematic that is commonly applied in doctrinal studies by members of a currently fashionable academic clique, self-styled Critical Legal Studies. This schematic, briefly stated, traces the identification of a new substantive right, its expansion, its promise, and the ultimate truncation of that promise regrettably short of where the particular "crit" (as they wryly call themselves) hoped the law would lead. See, for example, Fran Olsen, "The Politics of Family Law," *Law and Inequality* 2 (February 1984): 1–19. The larger point that is served by this analysis remains, in the work of most crits, somewhat obscure. See J. Singer, "The Player and the Cards," 94 *Yale Law Journal* 1.

16. There is a paradox here that may or may not emerge as the special master works through these problems, with the aid and advocacy of counsel for the parties. The paradox

is illustrated by the following situation, which occurred during negotiations assisted by the author. The issue of security staffing was under discussion, and the lawyers for the inmates proposed a particularly stringent and highly intrusive security system that would have subjected inmates to a wide range of body searches and movement restrictions. The prison administration was strongly opposed to plaintiffs' proposal, arguing instead that inmates should be permitted to move about unhindered by such searches.

Of course, beyond these facial positions, other interests were at stake. It was, for example, clear that the additional responsibility of staffing security posts and ensuring that body searches were done thoroughly but with an appropriate respect for the inmate's personal privacy was of great concern to the administration. In contrast, plaintiffs' counsel was focused on the exigency of keeping inmates alive in a particularly tense, racially divided institution. To accomplish that worthy goal, minor sacrifices of convenience and freedom properly were made.

17. See Rule 60, Federal Rules of Civil Procedure. This rule, which sets forth standards for modification or vacation of court orders, is essentially a codification of preexisting common law relating to the ongoing jurisdiction of courts of equity. Thus, even though a court order has been fixed, and the special master may take from that order a certain definitive charter, the parties in the litigation may from time to time seek to change that order through formal pleadings asking the court's exercise of equitable discretion.

18. See *New York State Association v. Carey*, 706 F.2d 956; *Duran v. Elrod*, 713 F.2d 292 (7th Cir. 1983); and *Newman v. Graddick*, 740 F.2d 1513 (11th Cir. 1984).

19. See, for example, Singer "The Player and the Cards."

20. It is not uncommon for public interest groups to form and develop in the areas of the country with highy visible prison-conditions litigation. These groups play an important role in public education, but part of that educational process tends to obscure the distinction between prison reform and the accomplishment of constitutional prisons. Indeed, even within the corrections profession, the standards the professionals have developed for themselves in many cases exceed what federal courts have been willing to impose as a matter of federal constitutional law. See, e.g., American Correctional Association, *Standards for Adult Correctional Institutions*, 2d ed. (College Park, Md., 1981).

21. For example, in many circles, a prison industries program, designed to inculcate usable skills that will aid inmates after release, is considered a good idea. Inmates probably do not have a constitutional entitlement to such a program, however. In criticizing the operations of a prison, it is easy to confuse the problems of constitutional magnitude (e.g., violence) with a probable cause (idleness) and decide that the remedy is constitutionally mandated.

22. [Editor's Note: The author currently serves as the special master in the federal court litigation involving conditions at the New Mexico prisons. Accordingly, he is unable to discuss the details of that litigation.]

23. Grand Jury Report, January–April 1983 Term, Santa Fe County, N. Mex.

24. Certainly the plaintiff inmates form the real party in interest in the litigation. Nonetheless, that class counsel for inmates play an extraordinarily important role in shaping the litigation can hardly be gainsaid, nor does this role represent an improper arrogation of responsibility by counsel.

25. Typically, plaintiffs' counsel obtain access to their clients through the traditional procedures of attorney visitation that are in place at all detention and correctional facilities. For legitimate and illegitimate reasons, these procedures can be extremely cumbersome and do not always promote full, accurate, and candid exchange of information and views. By virtue of the order of reference, these procedures do not encumber the special master's access to inmates.

26. For example, cancellation of evening meetings of prison social groups (such as a prison Christian fellowship council) might not directly reflect noncompliance but might be

the product of insufficient staffing that hamstrings the ability of the administration to move inmates safely during nonpeak hours. A special master must be attuned to these kind of complaints, for what they may reveal about actual noncompliance. There is an instrumentalist purpose here, in that the special master ignores the immediate concerns of inmates and transforms the expression of those concerns into a very different focus. That transformation is appropriate when viewed in light of the special master's responsibility to the court, but it demonstrates the potential hazards of direct contact with inmates.

27. This job may be impossible.

28. By choosing the example of a jail, the public scrutiny of these decisions has been maximized. It is a truism in the area of governmental studies that the severity of politics increases as the political entity becomes more localized. This applies precisely to the world of prisons. At a superficial yet telling level, the share of a county budget consumed by jail operations is considerably greater than the share of a state's budget consumed by correctional operations—and vastly greater than the share of the federal budget that is allocated to the Federal Bureau of Prisons.

For this reason, an intriguing if implausible means of coping with the current crisis in corrections would be to federalize the entire endeavor. If the budgets for all local, state, and federal detention and incarceration facilities were consolidated into one budget item in the federal budget, the intense fiscal constraints felt by many local governments wrestling with antiquated jails would be considerably diminished. The repercussions of this reform on the ideal of federalism, of course, are dramatic and perhaps untenable.

29. For instance, a master's efforts to manage a crowded jail can be entirely unraveled if, for reasons extraneous to the case, the prosecuting attorney decides to change positions on the enforcement of so-called victimless crimes (e.g., prostitution).

30. There are serious reservations about this trend, and the accreditation process is particularly subject to critique. Those reservations, however, do not detract from the point in the text, which is that corrections professionals as a group are busy presenting themselves, to one another and to onlookers, as concerned about standards and quality.

31. For example, the portion of the annual budget of the Texas Department of Corrections allocable to the provision of care for mentally ill and mentally retarded prisoners has grown from $7 million to $82 million as a result of the *Ruiz v. Estelle* litigation.

32. In characterizing this view as narrow, I do not mean to imply that it is unacceptable. A strong case can be made that the limitations on federal jurisdiction, and on the federal judiciary, also should constrain the special master in his or her dealings. To the extent it does not, one must wonder about the nature of the role and its constitutional legitimacy.

33. See, for example, the pioneering work by Erving Goffman on the concept of total institutions; also, for frequently brilliant analysis of the internal cultures of prisons, see Ben H. Bagdikian, *Caged* (New York, Harper & Row, 1976).

34. At a deeper level there is a significant question whether *any* court-imposed change will become finally effective in the absence of conciliation. In the end, prison administrators will run the prison, and it will be their attitudes that shape the quality of institutional life. In a democratic society, perhaps, that ultimate resolution is appropriate. (The antidemocratic nature of judicial activism has long been noted, and that case can be made from any of a variety of political perspectives.) Sociological analysis of school districts subject to court-ordered desegregation, and the responses, immediately and over time, by local school boards, would make a fascinating case study of the nature of judicial power and persuasion.

35. As noted previously, facts found by a special master ultimately must go through the sieve of a formal Article III adversarial proceeding before they can become final. If the litigation remains intensely adversarial, then the special master is unlikely to develop a factual record that will not be subject to vociferous attack from one party or the other. In this case, the special master's work is merely a predicate for further complicated litigation before the federal judge, and nothing has been achieved by way of saving time or the tedium

of courtroom proceedings. Indeed, a layer of complexity has been added to that proceeding, because the nature of the fact-finding process, the evidentiary basis for the finding, the parties' objections thereto, and the court's review of them will become a complex machination, from which it is predictable that little good will come.

36. For a superb discussion of the role of consent in the structure of Anglo-American jurisprudence, see Alexander M. Bickel, *The Morality of Consent* (New Haven, Conn.: Yale University Press, 1975).

37. The discussion in the text suggests certain fundamental philosophical, or jurisprudential, implications that are far beyond the scope of this chapter. Briefly stated, the dilemma observed in the text, and the ultimate compromise that it occasions, are part of the powerful traditional argument against judicial intrusiveness. The concept of safety in a correctional institution (as it relates to the constitutional prohibition of cruel and unusual punishment) and the idea of comity are topics on which the competing views in the fundamental philosophical debate could almost paradigmatically set out their arguments. That discussion is for another time.

38. A work of this kind would be fascinating, although its intricacies are staggering. The academic dispute over masters has not yet engaged in any form of empirical research, a task that itself might be impossible. There are strong criticisms of masterships in print, including John J. DiIulio, *Governing Prisons: A Comparative Study of Correctional Management* (New York: Free Press, 1987). That criticism, however, is intensely value-laden and is largely without empirical merit.

39. Daniel Moynihan has discussed the concept of "maximum feasible disagreement." The application of this concept in the area of prison reform has particularly strong appeal.

40. For example, why should inmates and prison administrators have divergent interests on the issue of funding for a comprehensive program for vocational training for inmates?

The Contributors

FRITZ BYERS is an attorney in Toledo, Ohio, who specializes in special masters work. He was a law clerk for United States District Judge William Wayne Justice of the Eastern District of Texas, the presiding judge in *Ruiz v. Estelle*, one of the leading cases involving the use of special masters to implement judicial decrees in a state-wide prison system. He currently serves as special master in *Duran v. Anaya* in New Mexico and as monitor in *Fambro v. Fulton County* in Georgia and he also served as court monitor in *Morales Feliciano v. Barcela Romero* in Puerto Rico—all cases involving the use of special masters to implement judicial decrees in relation to conditions and practices in correctional institutions. He has published articles on civil rights and on special masters and prison reform.

JOHN J. DIIULIO, JR., is an associate professor of politics and public affairs at Princeton University and chair of the Woodrow Wilson School's domestic and urban policy graduate program. His doctoral dissertation received the American Political Science Association's Leonard D. White Award for the best dissertation in public administration in 1986. He is the author of *Governing Prisons: A Comparative Study of Correctional Management* (1987) and of *No Escape: The Future of American Corrections* and *Barbed Wire Bureaucracy* (both forthcoming). He has done consulting work for the National Institute of Justice, the National Institute of Corrections, the New York City Board of Corrections, and other agencies.

JOHN C. GLIDEWELL is professor of psychology and human development at Vanderbilt University. He has also taught at Washington University in St. Louis and at the University of Chicago. He is a diplomate of the American Board of Professional Psychology in industrial and organizational psychology. He has published five monographs and some seventy articles in scientific journals and has been a consultant on organizational problems to major corporations and nonprofit organizations. His research has dealt with the relationships between individuals and organizations, the exercise of authority, decisions under stress, and the development and change of social norms. He is currently writing a book about the chief executive officers of corporations.

ERWIN C. HARGROVE is professor of political science and of public policy at Vanderbilt University. From 1976 to 1985 he was director of the Vanderbilt Institute for Public Policy Studies. He has also served on the faculty at Brown University and as senior fellow at the Urban Institute. His research work has focused on political and administrative leadership from the White House to the grass roots. His book *Jimmy Carter as President: Leadership and the Politics of the Public Good* received the Neustadt Award of the Presidency Research Group of the American Political Science Association in 1989 for the best book on the presidency published in 1988. Another recent book, edited with Jameson Doig, *Leadership and Innovation: Entrepreneurs in Government*, is a study of creative public managers.

IRA ISCOE is the Ashbel Smith Professor of psychology and the director of the Institute of Human Development and Family Studies at the University of Texas at Austin. He has been Distinguished Visiting Scientist at the National Institute of Mental Health and has served as president of the American Psychological Association's Division of Community Psychology and president of the Southwestern Psychological Association. He is the author of a number of scholarly articles on community psychology and mental health.

EDWARD F. LAWLOR is an associate professor at the School of Social Service Administration and a member of the faculty of the Center for Health Administration Studies at the University of Chicago. He has written widely on issues of health administration and policy, AIDS policymaking, and access to health services for the aged and poor. He is a member of the Chicago Board of Health and chairs the medical assistance policy committee for the Illinois Health Care Summit.

LAURENCE E. LYNN, JR., is a professor in the School of Social Service Administration and the Graduate School of Public Policy at the University of Chicago. He was recently dean of the School of Social Service Administration. He has taught at Harvard and Stanford universities and has been a senior fellow at the Brookings Institution. He has also held senior positions with the federal government, including director of program analysis at the National Security Council; assistant secretary for planning and evaluation, Department of Health, Education and Welfare; and assistant secretary for program development and budget, Department of the Interior. His publications include *The State and Human Services, Designing Public Policy, Managing Public Policy, The President as Policy Maker,* (coauthor), and *Knowledge and Policy: The Uncertain Connection* (editor). He is past president of the Association for Public Policy Analysis and Management.

GARY E. MILLER, M.D., was commissioner of the Texas Department of Mental Health and Mental Retardation from 1982 to 1988. He is currently clinical professor of psychiatry at the University of Texas Medical School in Houston and director of professional services at HCA Gulf Pines Hospital in Houston. He has directed the state mental health agencies in Georgia (1972–74) and New Hampshire (1976–82) and was assistant commissioner for the New York State Department of Mental Hygiene (1970–72). He has written over twenty-five published articles and book chapters on various aspects of the delivery of mental health, mental retardation, and substance abuse services. Dr. Miller is board certified in psychiatry and in administrative psychiatry.

MARK H. MOORE is the Guggenheim Professor of criminal justice policy and management at the Kennedy School of Government, Harvard University, and the faculty chairman of the school's Program in Criminal Justice Policy and Management. He has published a number of articles and monographs on institutional analysis and public management. He is coauthor of *Inspectors-General: Junkyard Dogs or Man's Best Friend?* (1986) and contributed "What Sort of Ideas Become Public Ideas?" to *The Power of Public Ideas* (1988).

Index